IFIP Advances in Information and Communication Technology 744

IFIP Advances in Information and Communication Technology

The IFIP AICT series publishes state-of-the-art results in the sciences and technologies of information and communication. The scope of the series includes: foundations of computer science; software theory and practice; education; computer applications in technology; communication systems; systems modeling and optimization; information systems; ICT and society; computer systems technology; security and protection in information processing systems; artificial intelligence; and human-computer interaction.

Edited volumes and proceedings of refereed international conferences in computer science and interdisciplinary fields are featured. These results often precede journal publication and represent the most current research.

The principal aim of the IFIP AICT series is to encourage education and the dissemination and exchange of information about all aspects of computing.

More information about this series at https://link.springer.com/bookseries/6102

Elena-Ioana Vatajelu
Editor

VLSI-SoC: Technology Advancement on SoC Design

32nd IFIP/IEEE International Conference on Very Large Scale Integration - System on a Chip, VLSI-SoC 2024
Tangier, Morocco, October 6–9, 2024
Revised Selected Papers

Springer

Editor
Elena-Ioana Vatajelu
CNRS – TIMA Laboratory
Grenoble, France

ISSN 1868-4238 ISSN 1868-422X (electronic)
IFIP Advances in Information and Communication Technology
ISBN 978-3-032-09574-9 ISBN 978-3-032-09575-6 (eBook)
https://doi.org/10.1007/978-3-032-09575-6

This Springer imprint is published by the registered company Springer Nature Switzerland AG
The registered company address is: Gewerbestrasse 11, 6330 Cham, Switzerland

Preface

The VLSI-SoC Conference, the premier international forum in the field of Very Large Scale Integration Systems-on-Chip, was proud to present its 2024 edition in the vibrant city of Tangier, Morocco. Over the years, VLSI-SoC has established itself as a pivotal platform that brings together leading researchers, innovators, and practitioners to share groundbreaking advances, explore emerging trends, and shape the future of VLSI and SoC technology.

Organized jointly by Delft University of Technology (Netherlands) and Abdelmalek Saadi University (Morocco), and co-sponsored by IFIP, IEEE, the Council on Electronic Design Automation (CEDA), and the IEEE Circuits and Systems Society (CAS), this edition offered a comprehensive program. The conference featured a dedicated tutorial day, a three-day technical program with plenary keynote addresses, oral and poster presentations, embedded tutorials, and two plenary panel sessions, complemented by an engaging social agenda. Beyond the technical sessions, the conference provided a vibrant environment for the exchange of knowledge, collaboration, and inspiration.

The strength of this event lay in the collective effort of many contributors: the authors, whose technical insights advanced the field; the reviewers, who dedicated time and expertise to ensure a rigorous and constructive evaluation process; the local organizing committee, which provided warm hospitality and seamless logistics; and the session chairs, who fostered meaningful discussions during the presentations. We extend our deepest gratitude to all of them.

For the 2024 edition, the conference received 112 submissions, of which 65 were submitted as regular papers. A single-blind peer review process was employed, with each paper evaluated by four to five independent reviewers. Following this rigorous process, 25 papers were selected for oral presentation in the technical program. Among these, the 8 highest-ranked papers were invited to submit extended versions for inclusion in this volume. These invited papers underwent a second single-blind review process, in which each manuscript was evaluated by three reviewers to ensure the highest academic and editorial standards.

This book is the result of that multi-stage process. It reflects the state of the art in research and development and captures the richness and diversity of topics addressed at VLSI-SoC 2024. We trust that this volume will serve as a valuable reference for researchers, practitioners, and students alike, and that it will inspire further innovation in this dynamic field.

This volume gathers extended and peer-reviewed contributions from VLSI-SoC 2024, reflecting some of the most recent advances and open challenges in Very Large Scale Integration and Systems-on-Chip research. The chapters have been organized thematically to highlight the central scientific and engineering problems that drive innovation in the field: efficiency, data and memory management, and reliability in the face of growing complexity and security demands.

The first part is dedicated to the pursuit of efficiency and performance, a timeless but ever-evolving challenge in VLSI. Contributions in this section demonstrate how new circuit architectures, arithmetic techniques, and hardware–software optimizations can significantly reduce power, area, and computational depth while sustaining or even enhancing system throughput. The second part turns to memory and data-centric architectures, reflecting the fact that modern SoCs are often constrained not by raw computational power but by the ability to handle data movement and storage efficiently. This section presents advances in non-volatile memory integration, application-aware memory management for heterogeneous platforms, and novel data formats that enable more efficient training of machine learning workloads. Together, these contributions highlight the important role of memory hierarchies and data handling strategies in shaping system-level performance. The third part addresses the theme of reliability and trustworthiness. As hardware becomes both more pervasive and more exposed, resilience against faults and adversarial manipulation has become as essential as performance. The contributions in this section cover topics ranging from scalable verification methodologies for arithmetic circuits to FPGA-based fault attack resilience and novel frameworks for logic locking. These works demonstrate the community's growing recognition that trust in hardware is a first-order design objective. By structuring the volume around these challenges, this book provides readers with more than a snapshot of individual research results. It offers a curated perspective on the priorities and trajectories that are shaping the future of VLSI and SoC design. We hope that this collection will serve both as a reference for specialists and as a source of inspiration for researchers and practitioners seeking to tackle the next generation of challenges in efficient, data-driven, and trustworthy computing systems.

Elena Ioana Vatajelu

Organization

Organizing Committee

General Chairs

Said Hamdioui	Delft University of Technology, The Netherlands
Anass El Haddadi	ENSA, Morocco

Program Chairs

Hussam Amrouch	Technical University of Munich, Germany
Ioana Vatejelu	TIMA Grenoble, France

Industrial Liaison Chairs

Ibrahim Elfadel	Khalifa University, UAE
Victor Grimblatt	Synopsys Chile Innovation Center, Chile

Tutorial Chairs

Leticia M. B. Pöhls	RWTH Aachen University, Germany
Yuanquing Cheng	Beihang University, China

Special Session Chairs

Baker Mohammad	Khalifa University, UAE
Saraju Mohanty	University of North Texas, USA

Panel Chairs

Hassen Aziza	Aix-Marseille Université, France
Annachiara Ruospo	Politecnico di Torino, Italy

Awards Chairs

Fatih Ugurdag	Özyeğin University, Turkey
Tiziana Margaria	University of Limerick, Ireland

PhD Forum Chairs

Florenc Demrozi	University of Stavanger, Norway
Nahla El-Araby	Technische Universität Wien, Austria

Publication Chairs

Moritz Fieback	Delft University of Technology, The Netherlands
Anteneh Gebregiorgis	Delft University of Technology, The Netherlands

Finance Chairs

Motta Taouil	Delft University of Technology, The Netherlands
Carlo Galuzzi	Delft University of Technology, The Netherlands

Web Chairs

Heba Abunahla	Delft University of Technology, The Netherlands
Mark van Beusekom	Delft University of Technology, The Netherlands

Sponsorship Chair

Mohamed Bouhorma	Abdelmalek Essaâdi University, UAE

Local Arrangements Chairs

Nabila Harboul	Future Professionals Academy, The Netherlands
Jaber El Bouhdidi	ENSA, Morocco
Asmae El Arrassi	Delft University of Technology, The Netherlands

Steering Committee

Chi-Ying Tsui	Hong Kong University of Science and Technology, China
Fatih Uğurdağ	Özyeğin University, Turkey
Graziano Pravadelli (Chair)	University of Verona, Italy
Ian O'Connor	École Centrale de Lyon, France
Ibrahim Elfadel	Khalifa University, UAE

Luis Miguel Silveira	INESC ID, Portugal
Manfred Glesner	TU Darmstadt, Germany
Masahiro Fujita	University of Tokyo, Japan
Matthew Guthaus	University of California Santa Cruz, USA
Ricardo Reis	Universidade Federal do Rio Grande do Sul, Brazil
Salvador Mir	CNRS, France

Program Committee

Program Chairs

Hussam Amrouch	Technical University of Munich, Germany
Ioana Vatejelu	TIMA Grenoble, France

Topic Chairs

T1 — Analog Design: Co-chairs

Salvador Mir	TIMA Laboratory, France
Martin Andraud	UC Louvain, Belgium

Topics: Modelling, Simulation, Verification, and Prototyping of Analog, Mixed-Signal, RF, Sensors, and IoT Circuits

T2 — Digital Design: Co-chairs

Joachim Rodrigues	Lund University, Sweden
Dimitrios Soudris	National Technical University of Athens, Greece

Topics: Modelling, Simulation, Verification, and Prototyping of Circuits and Systems, SoC, NoC, Reconfigurable, IoT, and Low-Power Architectures

T3 — Design for AI Hardware and Emerging Applications: Co-chairs

Ian O'Connor	École Centrale de Lyon, France
Panagiotis Dimitrakis	NCSR "Demokritos", Greece

Topics: Unconventional Computing, Brain Inspired Computing, Computation-in-Memory, Photonics, Quantum, etc.

T4 — EDA Tools and Methodologies for IC Design: Co-chairs

Katell Morin-Allory	TIMA Grenoble, France
Tara Ghasempouri	TalTech, Estonia

T5 — Hardware Dependability: Co-chairs

Ibrahim Elfadel	Khalifa University, UAE
Paolo Bernardi	Politecnico di Torino, Italy

Topics: Design for Testability, Reliability, Fault Tolerance, Security, Safety, and Variability

Program Committee Members

Hasan Al-Nashash	American University of Sharjah, UAE
Lutfi Albasha	American University of Sharjah, UAE
Mohamed Atef	United Arab Emirates University, UAE
Bevan Baas	University of California, Davis, USA
Alberto Bosio	Lyon Institute of Nanotechnology, France
Anupam Chattopadhyay	Nanyang Technological University, Singapore
Luc Claesen	University of Hasselt, Belgium
Nahla El-Araby	TU Wien, Vienna, Austria and Canadian International College, Cairo, Egypt
Moritz Fieback	Delft University of Technology, The Netherlands
Carlo Galuzzi	TU Delft, The Netherlands

Anteneh Gebregiorgis	Delft University of Technology, The Netherlands
Victor Grimblatt	Synopsys, Chile
Xinfei Guo	Shanghai Jiao Tong University, China
Matthew Guthaus	University of California Santa Cruz, USA
Ilker Hamzaoglu	Özyegin University, Turkey
Michael Hübner	Brandenburg University of Technology Cottbus, Germany
Maksim Jenihhin	Tallinn University of Technology, Estonia
Srinivas Katkoori	University of South Florida, USA
Johann Knechtel	New York University, USA
Victor Kravets	IBM, USA
Martin Kumm	University of Applied Sciences, Fulda, Germany
Sohaib Majzoub	University of Sharjah, UAE
Piero Malcovati	University of Pavia, Italy
Tiziana Margaria	University of Limerick, Ireland
Ricardo Martins	Instituto de Telecomunicações/Instituto Superior Técnico — University of Lisbon, Portugal
Farhad Merchant	University of Groningen, The Netherlands
Mahmoud Meribout	Khalifa University of Science & Technology, USA
Jose Miranda	EPFL, Switzerland
Saraju Mohanty	University of North Texas, USA
Jose Monteiro	INESC-ID, IST ULisboa, Portugal
Kashif Nawaz	Technology Innovation Institute, UAE
Letícia Bolzani Poehls	Catholic University of Rio Grande do Sul, Brazil
Graziano Pravadelli	University of Verona, Italy
Mahmoud Rasras	New York University Abu Dhabi, UAE
Annachiara Ruospo	Politecnico di Torino, Italy
Mihai Sanduleanu	Khalifa University of Science and Technology, UAE
Wala Saadeh	Western Washington University, USA
Mazen Saghir	American University of Beirut, Lebanon
Muhammad Shafique	New York University Abu Dhabi, UAE
Kaveh Shamsi	University of Texas at Dallas, USA
Carlos Silva-Cardenas	Pontificia Universidad Católica del Perú, Peru
Kostas Siozios	Aristotle University of Thessaloniki, Greece
Mottaqiallah Taouil	Delft University of Technology, The Netherlands
Theocharis Theocharides	University of Cyprus, Cyprus
Chun-Jen Tsai	National Yang Ming Chiao Tung University, Taiwan
H. F. Uğurdağ	Özyeğin University, Turkey
Jaime Viegas	Khalifa University, UAE
Arnaud Virazel	LIRMM, France

Amer Zakaria	American University of Sharjah, UAE
Matthew Ziegler	IBM, USA

Contents

Efficiency and Performance

A Wide-Range Low-Power Phase Interpolation-Based Delay Line with a Linearity Improvement Technique

Mohammadreza Esmaeilpour(✉), Jan Lappas, Chrisitan Weis, and Norbert Wehn

University of Kaiserslautern-Landau (RPTU), Kaiserslautern, Germany
{m.esmaeilpour,jan.lappas,christian.weis,norbert.wehn}@rptu.de
http://ems.eit.uni-kl.de

Abstract. This paper presents a novel low-power and wide-range phase interpolation-based delay line implemented in 12 nm FinFET technology. The proposed architecture to the best of our knowledge is the most efficient delay line in terms of power consumption, area and linearity in advanced technology nodes due to low complexity and complete controllability over delay range, resolution and operating frequency. The analysis in this paper shows that the input slew rate significantly affects the linearity of the delay line. Consequently, a linearity improvement technique is proposed to control the slew rate, which significantly improves the linearity of the delay line over a wide frequency range. To evaluate the performance of the proposed phase interpolation-based delay line, two common fine delay line architectures including RC delay using binary-weighted capacitors and variable driving strength buffer were designed and simulated in 12 nm FinFET technology to compare with this work. The simulation results demonstrate that the proposed delay line achieves a 30% decrease in power consumption and a 25% reduction in area compared to the RC delay line. In addition, the differential nonlinearity (DNL) values for the variable driving strength buffers range from −1.52 LSB to 3.56 LSB while this work shows significant improvement in terms of linearity with DNL variations of only −0.22 LSB to 0.17 LSB. The proposed delay line consumes 0.56 mW at 5 GHz operating frequency and 0.8 V supply voltage, surpassing other previous studies.

Keywords: Digitally controlled delay line (DCDL) · Phase interpolator · Fine tuning · Delay element · Delay-locked loop (DLL)

1 Introduction

Variable delay lines are widely utilized in different VLSI applications like clock generators [1], delay locked loops (DLLs) [2–4], ring oscillators and time-todigital converters (TDCs) [5]. Furthermore, the growing demand for high performance and low power DRAM interfaces requires power efficient and high resolution delay lines to maximize the timing margin by accurate phase shift during read training operation [6]. Wide frequency range and high linearity are further important design metrics for delay lines which should be considered in the mentioned applications.

Published by Springer Nature Switzerland AG 2026
E. -I. Vatajelu (Ed.): VLSI-SoC 2024, IFIP AICT 744, pp. 3–16, 2026.
https://doi.org/10.1007/978-3-032-09575-6_1

Several delay line approaches have been proposed to address different design requirements. Binary-weighted capacitors delay line is the most common approach, which is implemented via using a cascade of two inverters and digitally controlled capacitors connected to the output of the first inverter [7]. Due to the large area and hardware complexity, metal-oxide-metal (MOM) capacitors are replaced with an array of MOSCAPs to provide tunable delay [4, 8, 9]. However, to achieve the desired resolution and wide delay range in advanced technology nodes, where the parasitic capacitors are small, the MOSCAPs should be large enough to provide the required capacitance [10]. In addition, the first stage inverter needs to be sized appropriately to charge the large capacitors at the target operating frequency. Due to the mentioned design constraints, this approach dissipates considerable power and silicon area. Another common implementation is the current-starved inverter (CSI) [3], in which NMOS and PMOS arrays are employed to control the current and change the delay accordingly. Despite high resolution and good jitter performance, the CSI topology suffers from limited delay range, poor linearity and high sensitivity to process variations [8]. Thyristor-based delay element [11] is another conventional topology that is controlled by current sources. Although the thyristor-based delay element benefits from high power supply rejection ratio (PSRR), complex biasing circuits and static power consumption make this topology an unreliable option for low-power applications.

Phase Interpolator (PI) is a viable approach to be utilized as a high-linear and power-efficient delay line. The phase interpolation is performed through integrating two input clocks with different phases and forming an output with an in-between phase [12]. The main advantages of using phase interpolators include wide frequency range and constant resolution. The conventional phase interpolator design is based on injecting two weighted currents triggered by different phase clocks into a shared load [13]. However, this approach suffers from high power consumption and severe nonlinearity due to the process, voltage and temperature (PVT) variations. Literature [14] proposed an all-digital phase interpolator consisting of a group of connected output multiplexers. Our analysis shows that the uncontrolled slew rate of the input signals causes high fluctuations in differential nonlinearity (DNL) and integral nonlinearity (INL) of the delay line.

In this paper, a novel wide-range, high-linear and low-power phase interpolation based delay line in 12 nm FinFET technology is presented. The proposed architecture can be used in high speed memory interfaces and all digital delaylocked loop (ADDLL) for fine tuning due to the wide frequency range and high linearity in advanced technology nodes. Compared to other topologies, the proposed delay line exhibits noticeable improvement in power consumption due to the reduced hardware complexity. Since the slew rate of the input signals plays a major role in the linearity of the delay line, a pair of identical resistors was added to the inputs of the phase interpolator block. This technique noticeably improves the linearity of the delay line over a wide frequency range. Due to the significant effect of the number of control bits, input slew rate and delay difference between the input signals on the linearity of the delay line, detailed design considerations and trade-offs will be discussed in the following sections. Furthermore, two commonly used fine delay lines including binary-weighted capacitors and variable driving strength buffers were implemented in 12 nm FinFET technology and compared with this work. The simulation results indicate that the proposed delay line exhibits the best overall performance in power consumption, area and linearity compared to previous studies. The remainder of this paper is organized as follows. Section 2 introduces the circuit diagram of the proposed delay line. Post-layout simulation results, design constraints and comparison with prior studies are discussed in Sect. 3. Finally, Sect. 4 concludes this work.

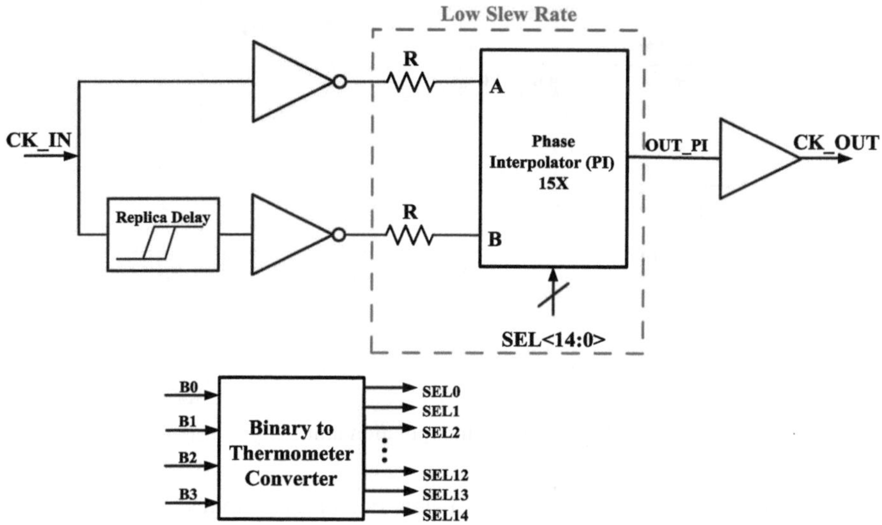

Fig. 1. Architecture of the proposed phase interpolation-based delay line.

2 Circuit Description

Figure 1 depicts the overall architecture of the proposed phase interpolation-based delay line, which consists of 15 units of PI cell, a replica delay cell to produce desired time difference between the input signals and a 4-bit binary to thermometer converter (BTC). Additionally, two identical resistors are added to the input of the PI block to improve the linearity over a wide frequency range. These resistors decrease the slew rate of the input signals, providing enough time for the phase interpolator block to merge the input signals. The BTC is employed to generate control bit stream for the PI units to perform the interpolation process.

The selection of an appropriate PI unit is essential for maintaining low slew rate in the interpolation block, which is a necessary requirement to achieve high linearity over a wide frequency range. The PI unit consists of an array of 2:1 multiplexers which are controlled by 15 thermometer codes as shown in Fig. 2. By increasing the control bit, the phase of CK_OUT shifts from A to B and generates delay steps for different control codes. The interpolation is performed at the output of the multiplexers, which guarantees the lowest possible value for the slew rate of OUT_PI to ensure high linearity while adjusting the control bits.

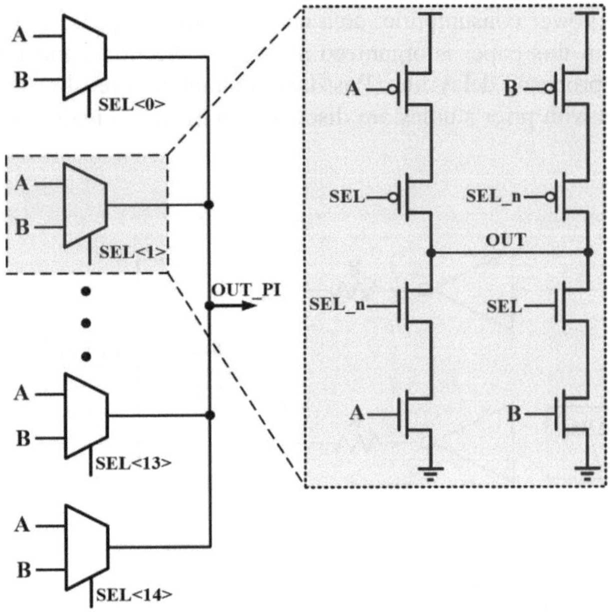

Fig. 2. Phase interpolation unit.

Another solution to achieve a decreased slew rate at the output node is to use pass transistor logic (PTL)-based multiplexers. However, our analysis indicates that due to the direct coupling between the input and output of the pass transistor logic, the input can be affected during the interpolation process. Consequently, the linearity of the delay line worsens because of constant variations in input and output.

3 Post-Layout Simulation Results and Discussions

3.1 Slew Rate

As previously mentioned, the linearity of the phase interpolation-based delay line is mainly affected by the slew rate of the input signals. Figure 3 depicts the effect of the slew rate on DNL values at 2.5 GHz and 5 GHz input frequency. It can be seen that decreasing the slew rate can effectively improve the linearity of the phase interpolator regardless of the frequency. Thus, a pair of resistors is added to the input of the phase interpolator unit. The value of the resistors should be properly chosen based on the target frequency and the number of PI units to ensure a rail-to-rail signal at the output of the phase interpolation block.

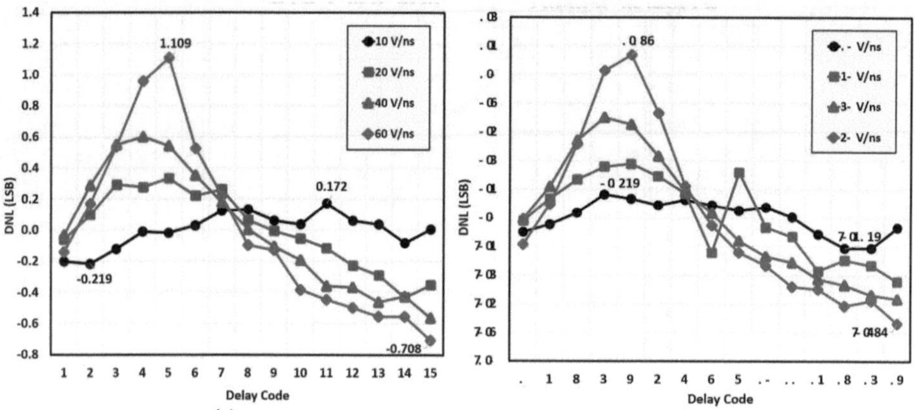

(a) (b)

Fig. 3. Effect of input slew rate on DNL at, (a) 2.5 GHz, (b) 5 GHz.

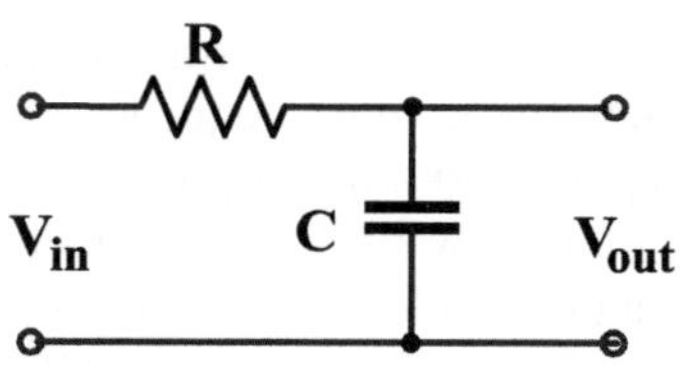

Fig. 4. Equivalent RC circuit of the phase interpolation unit.

In order to validate the mentioned concept, the phase interpolation unit in Fig. 1 can be simplified as an RC network shown in Fig. 4, in which the input signal is an ideal voltage step of height V_0. The output voltage V_{out} can be defined as [15]

$$V_{out} = V_0\left[1 - exp(-t/\tau)\right] \tag{1}$$

where $\tau = R \times C$ and C is the equivalent parasitic capacitance of the multiplexers. From Eq. 1, the slew rate can be derived as [15]

$$SR = \frac{dV_{out}}{dt} = \frac{V_0}{\tau} exp\left(-\frac{t}{\tau}\right) \tag{2}$$

As shown in Eq. 2, the slew rate is related to the height of the input voltage step V_0 and $1/\tau$. Considering fixed values for V_0 and C, the slew rate can be controlled by changing the input resistor to achieve the best performance of the phase interpolation unit.

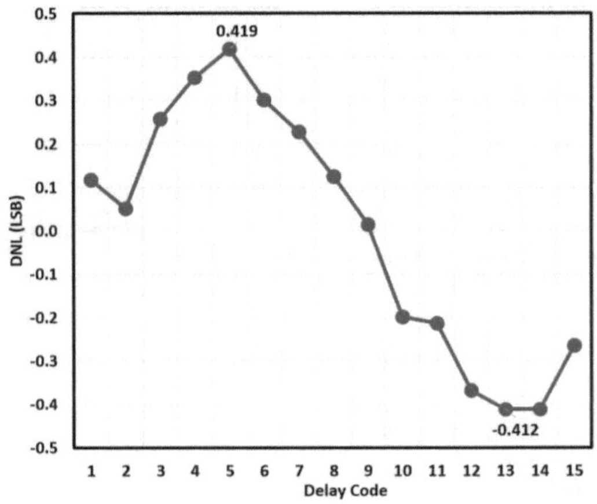

Fig. 5. DNL variations at 10 GHz.

On the other hand, increasing the input frequency along with decreasing the slew rate may cause duty cycle distortion at the output node since the output signal cannot reach a full rail-to-rail swing. The simulation results show that an input slew rate within a range of 10 V/ns is the optimum value for an input frequency range of 2.5 GHz to 5 GHz to achieve good linearity and maintain 50% duty cycle at the output node. However, it is recommended to increase the input slew rate of the PI block to achieve a proper function in terms of linearity and output duty cycle for higher frequencies. As an example, Fig. 5 depicts the DNL values of the proposed delay line at 10 GHz. In this case, the input slew rate was set to 20 V/ns to achieve an acceptable linearity and output duty cycle.

3.2 Delay Difference

Another design metric that significantly affects the linearity of the PI-based delay line is the delay difference between the input signals. This delay is supposed to be quantized by the PI units and generate delay steps. Figure 6 shows the effect of input delay difference on DNL values at 2.5 GHz and 5 GHz input frequencies. Our analysis shows that increasing the input delay difference with the same number of control bits causes larger delay resolution, decreasing the linearity of the proposed delay line. As shown in Fig. 6, maintaining a resolution in the range of 1 ps to 2 ps results in lower fluctuations in DNL values. Thus, the proposed delay line in this work is recommended to be employed for fine tuning.

To achieve the mentioned delay resolution range while increasing the input delay difference, the number of control bits is required to increase proportionally. However, increasing the number of bits leads to significant growth in hardware complexity and power consumption. Consequently, an appropriate choice between the number of control bits and replica delay can effectively improve the linearity and power consumption.

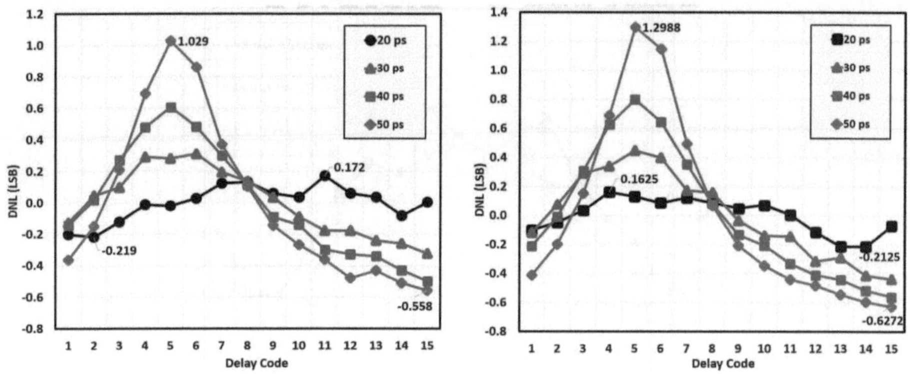

(a) (b)

Fig. 6. Effect of input delay difference on DNL at, (a) 2.5 GHz, (b) 5 GHz.

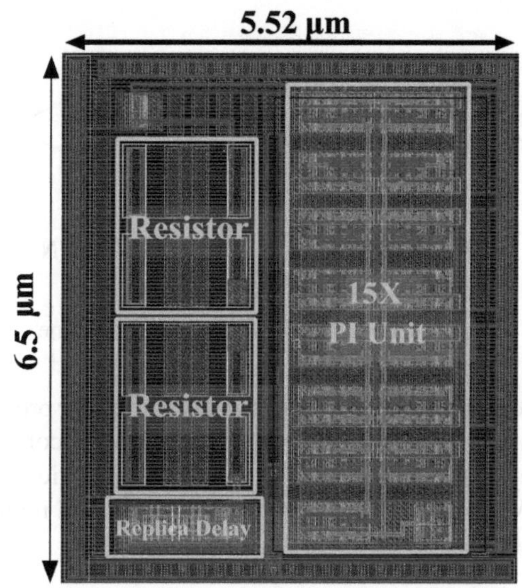

Fig. 7. Layout view of the proposed delay line.

3.3 Power, Area and Corner Analysis

The proposed phase interpolation-based delay line was designed and symmetrically laid out in 12 nm FinFET technology. The 4-bit structure with a replica delay of 20 ps dissipates 0.56 mW at 5 GHz input frequency and a 0.8 V supply voltage.

Due to the importance of good matching in the linearity of the delay lines, the proposed topology with an input slew rate of 10 V/ns and a replica delay of 20 ps was laid out as shown in Fig. 7. It occupies 5.52 μm × 6.5 μm of area.

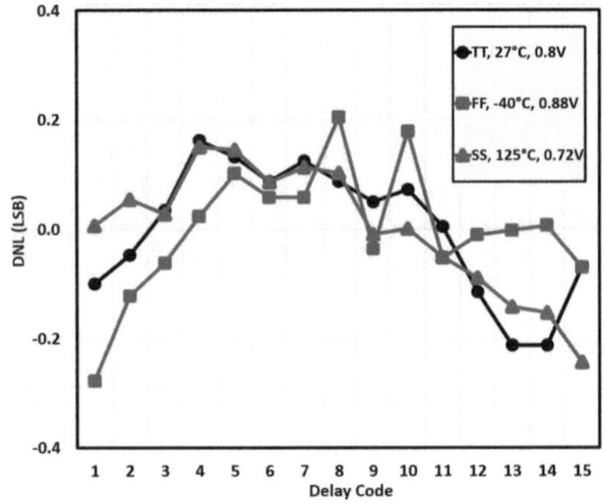

Fig. 8. DNL variations at PVT corners.

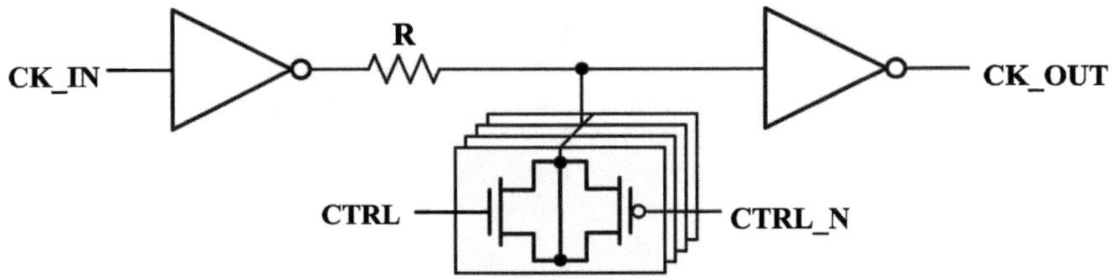

Fig. 9. Circuit diagram of the RC delay line.

To assess the performance of the proposed delay line under process, voltage and temperature (PVT) variations, the DNL values for three different corners were calculated at 5 GHz input frequency as shown in Fig. 8. The DNL values varies between –0.3 LSB and 0.2 LSB across all PVT corners indicating good linearity and monotonic characteristic of the proposed delay line.

3.4 Comparison with Prior Studies

In order to compare the proposed phase interpolation delay line with prior studies, two commonly used fine delay lines including RC delay with binary-weighted capacitors and variable driving strength buffer were designed and laid out in 12 nm FinFET technology. Figure 9 illustrates the RC delay line, in which the capacitor is constituted by a network of binary-weighted MOSCAPs. To minimize output duty cycle distortion, both PMOS and NMOS transistors are used to build the MOSCAPS [8, 9]. By adjusting the control bits, the load of the input inverter can be varied, resulting in changing rise and fall times of the inverted input signal. The second inverter then generates a non-inverting delayed output signal.

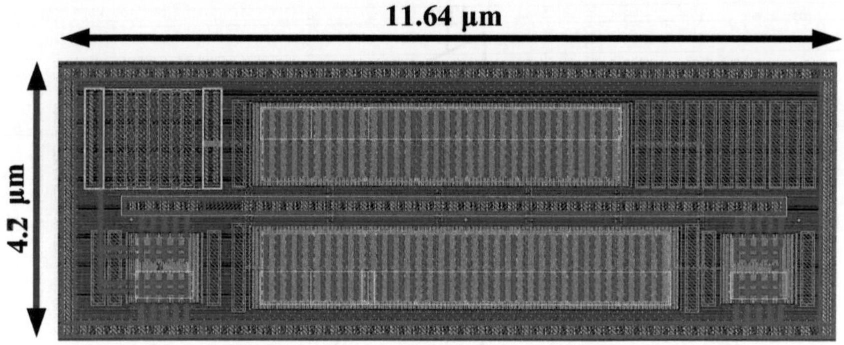

Fig. 10. Layout view of the RC delay line.

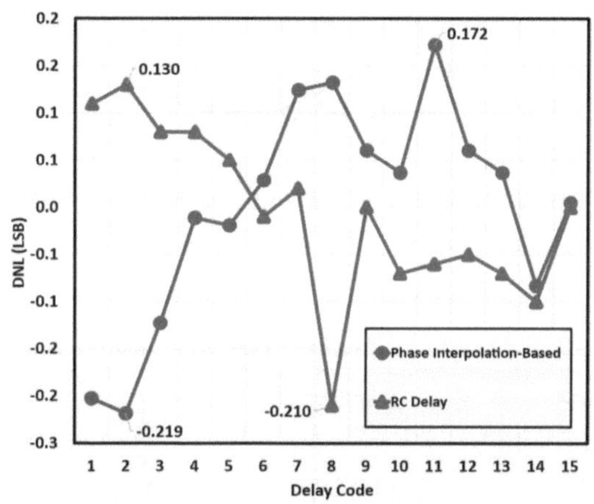

Fig. 11. DNL comparison between RC delay line and PI-based delay line

As mentioned earlier, the binary-weighted capacitor-based delay lines mainly suffer from high silicon area and power consumption due to the large MOSCAPs. To fairly compare this topology with the proposed PI-based delay line, a 4-bit RC delay line was designed and laid out in 12 nm FinFET technology as shown in Fig. 10. In terms of area, the RC delay line occupies 48.89 μm^2 while in this work the area is decreased by 25% to only 35.88 μm^2. In addition, the power consumption of both architectures was calculated at 2.5 GHz input frequency and 0.8 V supply voltage. Due to reduced hardware complexity, the proposed delay line dissipates only 300 μW, demonstrating a 30% reduction in power consumption in comparison with the RC delay line, which consumes 420 μW.

Since linearity is a critical metric in the design of delay lines, the DNL values of the RC delay line were calculated and compared with those of this work as shown in Fig. 11. It can be seen that linearity is equally good in both topologies while this work demonstrates better performance in terms of power consumption and area.

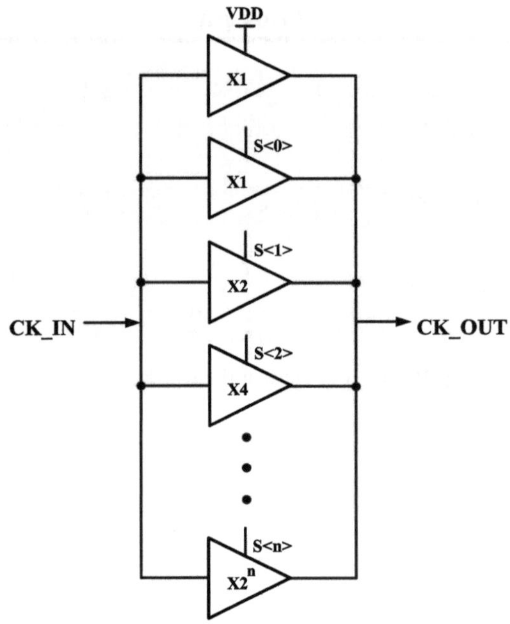

Fig. 12. Architecture of the variable driving strength buffer delay line.

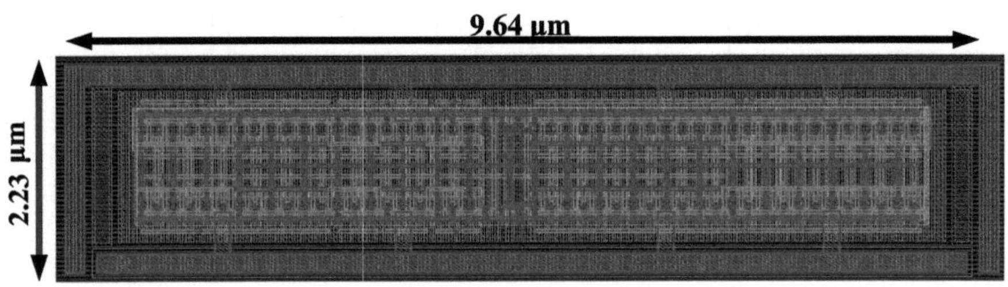

Fig. 13. Layout view of the variable driving strength buffer delay line.

A buffer with variable driving strength is another common approach for implementing a delay line [16]. Figure 12 depicts the circuit diagram of an n-bit variable driving strength buffer delay line, which consists of an array of tri-state buffers with binary-weighted sizing. When the control bits are zero, the input signal propagates through only one buffer, providing the highest delay value. By increasing the control bits, the driving strength of the buffer network increases and provides delay steps for different bit streams. To evaluate the performance of the buffer with variable driving strength approach and compare it with the proposed approach, a 4-bit structure was designed and laid out in 12 nm FinFET technology as shown in Fig. 13. It occupies 21.5 μm^2 of area and dissipates 120 μW at 2.5 GHz input frequency and 0.8 V supply voltage.

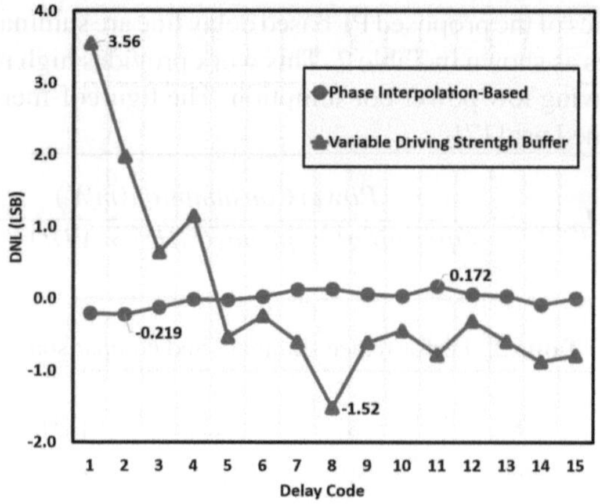

Fig. 14. DNL comparison between variable driving strength buffer and PI-based delay line.

Despite having low power consumption and silicon area, the variable driving strength buffer suffers from severe nonlinearity. Figure 14 depicts the comparison between the proposed PI-based delay line and variable driving strength buffer in terms of DNL variations. The DNL values of the variable driving strength buffer vary between −1.52 LSB and 3.56 LSB, showing severe nonlinearity and multiple missing codes. On the other hand, the DNL values in this work range from −0.22 LSB to 0.17 LSB, which indicates high linearity and fully monotonic behavior. Table 1 summarizes the characteristics of the proposed PI-based delay line and the aforementioned topologies.

Table 1. Comparison of delay line architectures in 12 nm FinFET.

Parameter	RC delay line	Variable driving strength buffer	This Work
Resolution (ps)	1	1.35	1.25
$DNL_{max}(LSB)$	0.13	3.56	0.17
$DNL_{min}(LSB)$	−0.21	−1.52	−0.22
Power (μW)	420	120	300
Area (μm^2)	48.89	21.5	35.88

The significant advantage of the proposed PI-based delay line compared to previous topologies is the full controllability of the resolution and slew rate, which effectively enhances the linearity while the tunability of prior schemes can only be achieved through selecting the number of cells [11]. In addition, reduced hardware complexity and low power consumption make this work a practical topology for low-power applications.

The characteristics of the proposed PI-based delay line are summarized and compared with previous studies as shown in Table 2. This work provides high resolution and linear delay steps while having low power consumption. The figureof-merit (FOM) for power consumption is defined as: [17]

$$FOM_{power} = \frac{PowerConsumption(mW)}{OperatingFrequency(GHz) \times VDD^2(V^2)} \tag{3}$$

Table 2. Performance summary and comparison.

Parameter	[8]	[18]	[12]	[13]	This Work
Technology (nm)	65	130	28	65	12 FinFET
Supply Voltage (V)	1.2	1.2	0.9	1.2	0.8
Frequency (GHz)	2.5	1.2	6	8	5.0
Resolution (ps)	0.82	1.95	–	–	1.25
Power (mW)	1.25	11.25	2.2	13	0.56
FOM*power*	0.347	6.5	0.452	1.16	0.175

4 Conclusion

In this paper a novel wide-range and low-power phase interpolation-based delay line is presented. The proposed topology is a practical option for fine tuning in high-performance and low-power applications due to the reduced hardware complexity and full controllability over delay range, resolution and operating frequency. The analysis in this paper shows that the input slew rate and the delay difference are the most important metrics for the linearity of the phase interpolation-based delay line. To control the input slew rate, a pair of identical resistors is added to the input of the phase interpolation unit, which noticeably improves the linearity of the delay line. For a fair comparison of the performance of the proposed delay line with previous studies, two commonly used fine delay lines including the RC delay line and the variable driving strength buffer were implemented and laid out in 12 nm FinFET technology. The comparison results indicate that the proposed delay line exhibits the best overall performance in terms of power dissipation, area and linearity compared to mentioned topologies. The proposed PI-based delay line consumes 0.56 mW at 5 GHz operating frequency and 0.8 V supply voltage.

Acknowledgments. This work was supported partly by the German Federal Ministry of Education and Research (BMBF) within the project DGen4Test under contract no. 16ME0904K and by EuroHPC-JU funding under grant no. 101034126.

References

1. Cheong, H.H., Kim, S.: A power-efficient and fast-locking digital quadrature clock generator with ping-pong phase detection. In: 2021 IEEE International Symposium on Circuits and Systems (ISCAS), pp. 1–4 (2021). https://doi.org/10.1109/ISCAS51556.2021.9401383
2. Park, H., Sim, J., Choi, Y., Choi, J., Kwon, Y., Kim, C.: A 2.4–8 ghz phaserotator delay-locked loop using cascading structure for direct input–output phase detection. IEEE Trans. Circ. Syst. II: Express Briefs **69**(3), 794–798 (2022). https://doi.org/10.1109/TCSII.2021.3113926
3. Yang, R.J., Liu, S.I.: A 2.5 ghz all-digital delay-locked loop in 0.13 μm cmos technology. IEEE J. Solid-State Circ. **42**(11), 2338–2347 (2007). https://doi.org/10.1109/JSSC.2007.906183
4. Quchani, M.E., Maymandi-Nejad, M.: Design of a low-power linear sar-based all-digital delay-locked loop. In: 2019 27th Iranian Conference on Electrical Engineering (ICEE), pp. 118–124 (2019). https://doi.org/10.1109/IranianCEE.2019.8786365
5. Chen, C.C., Chen, C.L., Fang, W., Chu, Y.C.: All-digital cmos time-todigital converter with temperature-measuring capability. IEEE Trans. Very Large Scale Integrat. (VLSI) Syst. **28**(9), 2079–2083 (2020). https://doi.org/10.1109/TVLSI.2020.3007587
6. Tsai, C.W., Chiu, Y.T., Tu, Y.H., Cheng, K.H.: A wide-range alldigital delay-locked loop for ddr1–ddr5 applications. IEEE Trans. Very Large Scale Integrat. (VLSI) Syst. **29**(10), 1720–1729 (2021). https://doi.org/10.1109/TVLSI.2021.3098171
7. Abdulrazzaq, B., Abdul Halin, I., Kawahito, S., Sidek, R., Shafie, S., Md Yunus,N.: A review on high-resolution cmos delay lines: towards sub-picosecond jitter performance. SpringerPlus 5 (2016). https://doi.org/10.1186/s40064-016-2090z
8. Angeli, N., Hofmann, K.: A low-power and area-efficient digitally controlled shuntcapacitor delay element for high-resolution delay lines. In: 2018 25th IEEE International Conference on Electronics, Circuits and Systems (ICECS), pp. 717–720 (2018). https://doi.org/10.1109/ICECS.2018.8617948
9. Song, J., Choi, W.S.: A highly linear digitally controlled delay line with reduced duty cycle distortion. In: 2022 19th International SoC Design Conference (ISOCC), pp. 398–399 (2022). https://doi.org/10.1109/ISOCC56007.2022.10031551
10. Morales, J.I., Chierchie, F., Mandolesi, P.S., Paolini, E.E.: Design and evaluation of an all-digital programmable delay line in 130-nm cmos. In: 2019 XVIII Workshop on Information Processing and Control (RPIC), pp. 209–213 (2019). https://doi.org/10.1109/RPIC.2019.8882166
11. Esmaeilzadeh, M., Audet, Y., Ali, M., Sawan, M.: A wide-range low-powerthyristor-based delay element with improved temperature sensitivity. IEEE Trans. Circuits Syst. II Express Briefs **70**(7), 2370–2374 (2023). https://doi.org/10.1109/TCSII.2023.3245562
12. AbdelHadi, A., Allam, M., Ibrahim, S.: A high-linearity 6-ghz phase interpolator in 28-nm cmos technology. In: 2017 Japan-Africa Conference on Electronics, Communications and Computers (JAC-ECC), pp. 41–44 (2017). https://doi.org/10.1109/JEC-ECC.2017.8305774
13. Wu, G., et al.: A 1–16 gb/s all-digital clock and data recovery with a wideband high-linearity phase interpolator. IEEE Trans. Very Large Scale Integrat. (VLSI) Syst. **24**(7), 2511–2520 (2016). https://doi.org/10.1109/TVLSI.2015.2508045
14. Sim, J., Park, H., Kwon, Y., Kim, S., Kim, C.: A 1–3.2 ghz 0.6 mw/ghzduty-cycle-corrector using bangbang duty-cyle-detector. In: 2021 IEEE International Symposium on Circuits and Systems (ISCAS). pp. 1–4 (2021). https://doi.org/10.1109/ISCAS51556.2021.9401792
15. Razavi, B.: Design of Analog CMOS Integrated Circuit, 1st edn. McGraw Hill, Boston (2001)
16. Yao, C.Y., Ho, Y.H., Chiu, Y.Y., Yang, R.J.: Designing a sar-based all-digitaldelay-locked loop with constant acquisition cycles using a resettable delay line. IEEE Trans. Very Large Scale Integrat. (VLSI) Syst. **23**(3), 567–574 (2015). https://doi.org/10.1109/TVLSI.2014.2313131

17. Bayram, E., Aref, A.F., Saeed, M., Negra, R.: 1.5–3.3 ghz, 0.0077 mm^2, 7 mwall-digital delay-locked loop with dead-zone free phase detector in 0.13 μm cmos. IEEE Trans. Circ. Syst. I: Regular Papers **65**(1), 39–50 (2018). https://doi.org/10.1109/TCSI.2017.2715899
18. Jung, D.H., Ryu, K., Park, J.H., Jung, S.O.: All-digital process-variation-calibratedtiming generator for ate with 1.95-ps resolution and maximum 1.2-ghz test rate. IEEE Trans. Very Large Scale Integrat. (VLSI) Syst. **26**(6), 1015–1025 (2018). https://doi.org/10.1109/TVLSI.2018.2801030

Quantum Carry-Save Modular Addition with Optimized Depth and Resource Utilization

Siyi Wang[1](✉), Eugene Lim[1], Xiufan Li[2], Jerrie Feng[1], and Anupam Chattopadhyay[1]

[1] Nanyang Technological University, Singapore, Singapore
siyi002@e.ntu.edu.sg

[2] Centre for Quantum Technologies, National University of Singapore, Singapore, Singapore

Abstract. Shor's factorization algorithm, as one of the most significant achievements in quantum computing, exhibits an exponential speedup compared to the corresponding classical algorithm. In Shor's factorization algorithm, modular exponentiation is one of the most computationally intensive components, which relies on the modular addition.

This work aims to explore novel designs for enhancing the efficiency of quantum modular addition. In particular, we introduce a novel quantum modular addition framework based on carry-save architecture, which facilitates the conversion of multiple 2-addend quantum operations within modular addition into a single 3-addend operation, thereby reducing the computational depth. Compared to the most efficient existing quantum modular addition, our design has achieved an impressive result - a reduction in Toffoli Depth by up to 33.33%, while maintaining comparable Toffoli Count and Qubit Count. Additionally, we propose a refined framework that incorporates constant moduli to further enhance performance. This research underscores the potential of carry-save architecture as a promising technique for accelerating quantum modular arithmetic as well as advancing the development of quantum computing in general.

Keywords: Quantum Computing · Quantum Arithmetic · Toffoli-depth Optimization · Carry-save Adder · Modular Addition

1 Introduction

Shor's algorithm [1] has firmly established itself as an approach in quantum algorithms to efficiently factor large integers into their prime factors. By leveraging on its two key operations, modular exponentiation and its component modular addition, Shor's algorithm can work exponentially faster than classical algorithms. Therefore numerous efforts have been made to push the boundaries on modular exponentiation, as it's one of the most computationally intensive components in Shor's algorithm.

Recent works have achieved many improvements in reducing the bottleneck of modular exponentiation by enhancing the design of its main component, modular addition, through efficient implementations of Clifford+T gates. However, it still remains

Published by Springer Nature Switzerland AG 2026
E. -I. Vatajelu (Ed.): VLSI-SoC 2024, IFIP AICT 744, pp. 17–32, 2026.
https://doi.org/10.1007/978-3-032-09575-6_2

challenging to develop modular addition frameworks with a lower gate depth and gate count.

In this work, we propose a novel quantum modular addition framework that utilizes the Clifford+T gate set and classical carry-save adders (CSAs). Additionally, we introduce a refined variant of this framework that incorporates constant moduli to further optimize performance. We consolidate multiple 2-addend quantum operations within modular addition into a single 3-addend operation, greatly reducing the overall depth of the quantum circuit. Our work addresses a hot-in-discussion arithmetic problem: quantum modular addition, expressed as $(a + b) \bmod N$. Here, N represents an n-bit binary number, while a and b represent n-bit binary numbers less than N. This operation usually involves checking if $a + b > N$, and if so, subtracting N to ensure the result is within the range $[0, N - 1]$. In our specific design, we implement the modular addition by involving a three-operand addition $a + b + (-N)$ in the framework. This chapter has the following contributions:

- Highlight the potential of carry-save architecture by enhancing the performance of quantum arithmetic designs.
- Propose a quantum modular addition framework leveraging carry-save architecture, with a refined design that incorporates constant moduli, to optimize quantum resource usage.
- Accelerate Shor's algorithm through improving modular addition efficiency.

2 Background

2.1 Clifford+T-Based Modular Addition Framework

Typical architectures realize modular addition with gates in the Clifford+T set. We denote the elementary adder block and subtractor block by *Add* and *Sub* separately. The circuits input quantum states that correspond to the binary representation of the numbers and output $|S\rangle$ as the result of modular addition. Here we enumerate four types of popularly cited modular addition frameworks in literature.

- *VBE Modular Addition Framework.*

Quantum modular adder based on ripple-carry adders was proposed by Vedral, Barenco, and Ekert in 1996, which we refer to as VBE in this chapter [2]. As shown in Fig. 1, VBE framework contains 5 adders and subtractors with reversible CNOT gates and Toffoli gates. After that, Cucarro et al. [3] proposed an improved modular adder with more efficient full adder blocks. However, this framework only solves the modulo calculation when N is the power of two, causing a lack of extendability to general problems. So we omit the Cucarro modular design in this chapter.

- *Beckman Modular Addition Framework.*

Figure 2 depicts Beckman's quantum modular framework made from adderbased comparators, full adders, and subtractors [4]. To standardize the performance estimation, we transform all adder-based operations, especially the comparators, into quantum adders and subtractors. Inspired by Beckman's work, Takahashi and Kunihiro propose their modular addition framework composed of 2 comparators and 1 adder or subtractor

[5]. But their implementation of comparators is based on Draper's Fourier basis addition [6] which implies a large number of T gates. Haner et, al. [7] utilize recursive adder and Carry gates to build the comparators. The intuition is straightforward such that, by comparing the values of b and $N - a$, we can determine whether to add a or subtract $N - a$ and revert the indicator to the zero state.

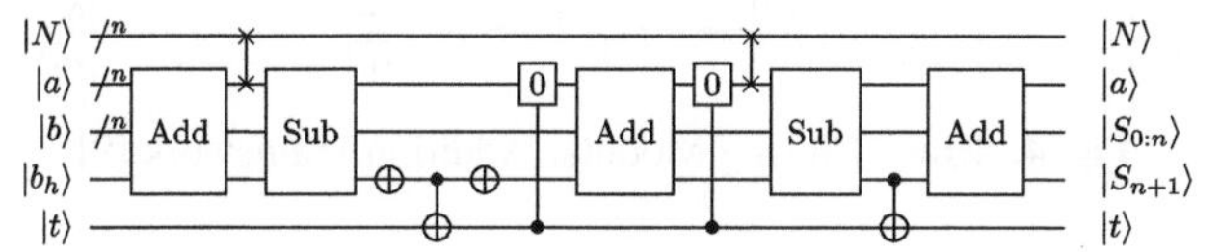

Fig. 1. VBE Modular Addition Framework [2].

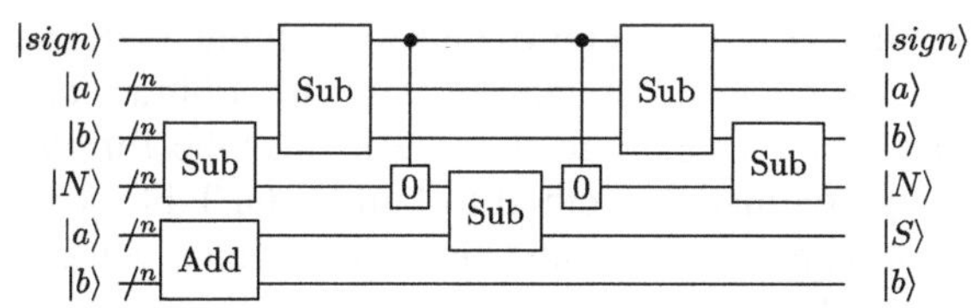

Fig. 2. Beckman Modular Addition Framework [4].

– *Van Meter Modular Addition Framework.*

In 2005, Van Meter and Itoh constructed a more efficient modular addition framework by removing the last 2 adder blocks in VBE that were used to undo the carry overflow [8], as is shown in Fig. 3. Controlled U_a and $U{-a,N}$ represent the data loading oracles that set the register with respect to the value of the control qubit. The limitation of this framework is that it requires multiple calls of data loading oracle which complicates circuit operations.

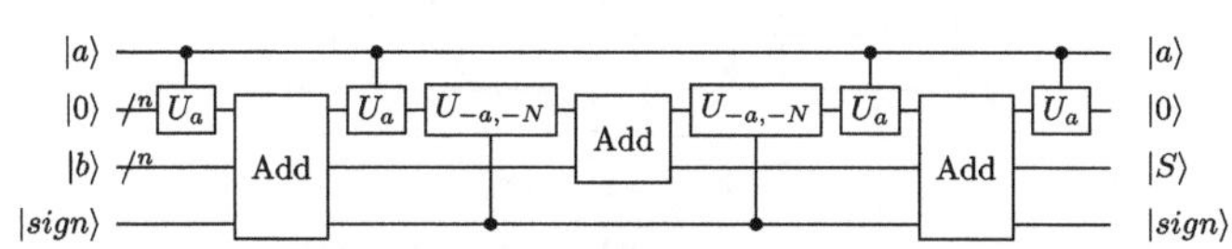

Fig. 3. Van Meter Modular Addition Framework [8].

– *Rines-Chuang Modular Addition Framework.*

In 2018, Rine et al [9] enhanced Beckman's design [4] by splitting each integer adder into forward and reverse sub-sections. The implementation of Rines-Chuang's modular addition framework is depicted in Fig. 4. It is constructed with 1 integer adder and 2 integer subtractors. Every forward and reverse block-pairs are denoted with the subscripts F and R respectively. Intermediate results of the forward block are utilized to control its subsequent reverse block in the second integer adder.

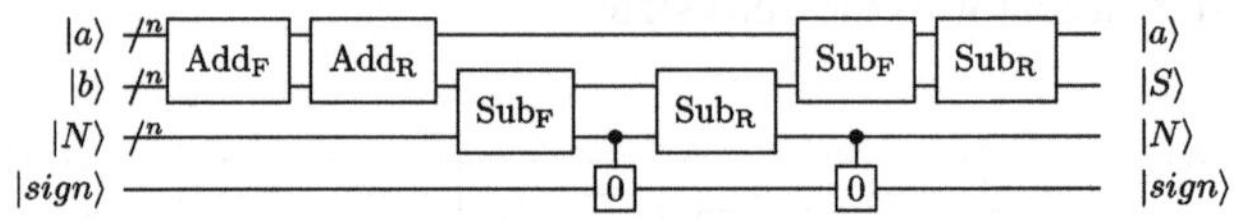

Fig. 4. Rines-Chuang Modular Addition Framework [9].

2.2 QFT-Based Modular Addition Framework

Apart from the circuit designs with Clifford+T gates, modular addition frameworks are also developed in Fourier basis [10–12]. These algorithms utilize quantum Fourier transformation (QFT) and its inverse as subroutines [13, 14]. However, the complexity associated with QFT arithmetic contributes to its limited adoption in experimental studies. Specifically, the controlled rotation gates with arbitrary angles are practically infeasible to operate in the current stage of hardware than the Toffoli gate. Besides, even the state-of-the-art approximation method to build a QFT block requires $O(n\log n)$ T gates, complicating the experimental realizations [15]. Hence, we only focus on quantum designs based on the Clifford+T gate set in this work.

3 Carry-Save Architecture

3.1 Carry-Save Structure

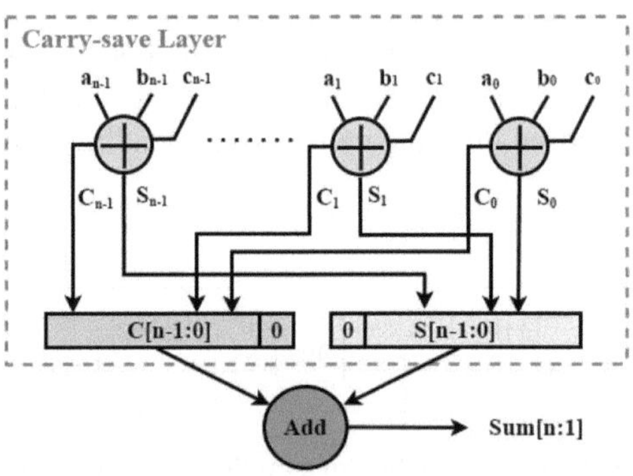

Fig. 5. A depiction of the Carry-Save architecture for multi-operand addition, illustrating the case where the number of operands is 3.

Various types of adders are available in classical arithmetic, such as ripple carry adders, carry-lookahead adders, and etc. Among these designs, the carry-save adder (CSA) [16] emerges as a high-speed, low-cost design with low latency, making it ideal for efficiently calculating multi-operand additions.

The carry-save architecture is summarized in Fig. 5. It achieves the addition of three n-bit inputs by first calculating the partial sum S and shifted carry-out vector C outputs using a Carry-save layer. Subsequently, the partial sum and shifted carry-out vector can be added using any n-bit adder, such as a ripple carry adder or carry look-ahead adder, to produce the sum of the multioperand addition.

3.2 Quantum Implementation

The quantum implementation of carry-save architecture relies on two primary components: the Carry-Save layer comprising a series of full adders operating in parallel, and a quantum full adder. Extensive research has already been done on the quantum full adder design [17–21]. As such, our work will focus on the Carry-Save layer.

$$S = a \oplus b \oplus c \tag{1}$$

$$C = ab \oplus ac \oplus bc \tag{2}$$

We are particularly interested in the shifted carry-out vector C and partial sum S of a 1-bit CSA that can be computed using Formulas 1 and 2. Particularly, it is worth noting that for hardware implementation, the quantum XOR logic is generally cheaper than OR logic. We note that the function of this basic unit aligns with that of a quantum full adder. Thus by leveraging the quantum full adder circuit illustrated in Fig. 6, the quantum Carry-save layer can be constructed.

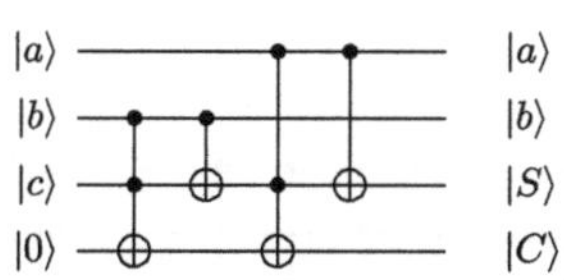

Fig. 6. Quantum Full Adder.

3.3 Advantages in Efficiency

Previous research [2, 4, 8], suggests that quantum implementations of addition involving three numbers using only 2-addend additions will lead to multiple sequential addition operations. The resulting circuit experiences the full propagation delay of both full adders, giving a depth of $O(2 \cdot TD_{Add})$, where TD_{Add} denotes the Toffoli Depth of a specific quantum adder for n-bit addition.

In comparison, our quantum implementation uses a Carry-save layer and one full adder. The quantum CSA layer only has a Toffoli Depth 2. Its resulting CSA-based quantum circuit for 3-addend addition will possess a Toffoli Depth of only $O(2 + TD_{Add})$, which significantly improves the sequential addition implementation.

4 Our Designs

4.1 Evaluation Metrics

To evaluate the importance of different components in our framework, we employ three metrics commonly used in many works [22–25] in quantum computing. These metrics are widely accepted benchmarks for comparison and can be conveniently expressed at the T-gate level:

- **Toffoli Depth(TD)**: By counting the number of computational layers containing Toffoli gates, this metric quantifies the time complexity of the quantum circuit.
- **Toffoli Count(TC)**: This metric is utilized to evaluate the gate complexity and resource consumption of quantum circuits, directly calculating the cumulative number of Toffoli gates.
- **Qubit Count(QC)**: This metric reveals the qubit requirement of the quantum circuit.

For specific quantum circuit, if a comprehensive evaluation at T-gate level are required, various T gate decomposition methods are then necessarily taken into consideration as further optimizations.

4.2 Main Components

The following are the five main components of our design:

- **CSA Module** represents the Carry-save Architecture utilized in our work. As demonstrated in Sect. 3, the CSA module consists of a series of full adders operating in parallel, as depicted in Fig. 7.

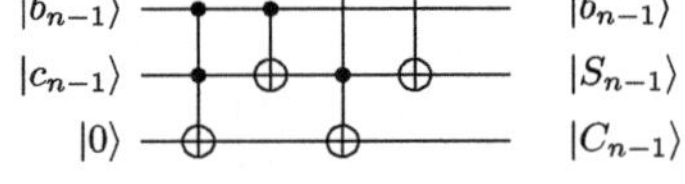

Fig. 7. Quantum Carry-save Architecture.

- **Add Module** represents a quantum adder. In quantum arithmetic, there are various types of adders, such as ripple carry adders [2, 3], carry-lookahead adders [17, 19, 26, 27], etc. In this work, we adopt prominent works detailed in Sect. 5.
- **Sub Module** denotes a quantum subtractor, which is a direct application of the quantum adder.

$$a - b = \left(a' + b\right)' \tag{3}$$

As shown in Eq. 3, the process involves bit-wise complementation of a, followed by its addition to b, yielding $a' + b$. Subsequently, the bits of a and the output qubits are complemented. Given that bit-wise complementation can be achieved using quantum NOT gates, the cost of a quantum subtractor is close to that of the corresponding adder.

- **Set 0 Module** offers same as the VBE Modular framework [2], the set 0 operation can be implemented using a series of CNOT gates.
- **Uncompute S Module** is used to uncompute the partial sum S, which can be achieved through a series of CNOT gates, as detailed in Fig. 8.

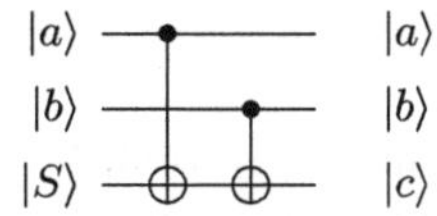

Fig. 8. Quantum Uncompute S Module.

4.3 Initial Design

We present a comprehensive construction for the initial carry save-based quantum modular addition framework in these six step (Fig. 9).

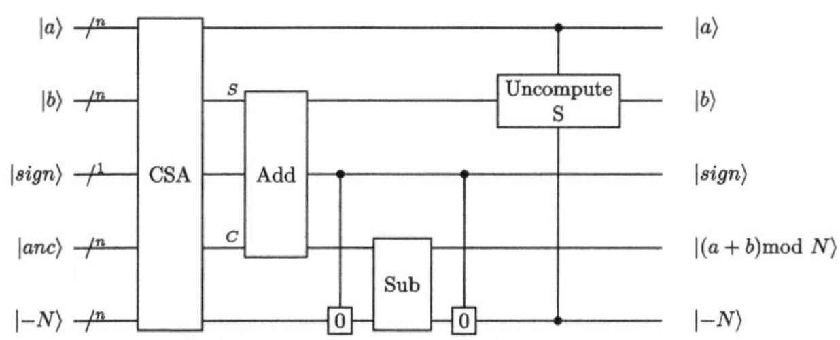

Fig. 9. Initial Modular Addition Framework

- **Step 1**: The carry-save layer is performed to calculate the partial sum, S, and the shifted carry, C. For n-bit modular addition, all inputs and outputs in this step have a length of n qubits. In terms of the detailed costs, the TC is $2n$, the QC is $4n$, and the TD is 2.
- **Step 2**: A signed addition is applied to S and C to calculate the sum of $(a + b - N)$, with the initial sign set to 0. The associated costs include a TC of TC_{Add}, a TD of TD_{Add}, and there's an additional ancilla qubit required, totaling $1 + Anc_{\text{Add}}$.
- **Step 3**: Utilize Set 0 Module, which is constructed only with CNOT gates. The sign qubit serves as the control qubit for this module. If the sign is in the state $|0\rangle$, indicating $(a + b - N) \geq 0$, the Set 0 gate toggles $|-N\rangle$ to the state $|0\rangle$. Otherwise, $|-N\rangle$ passes through the module unchanged. This step incurs no requirement for TC, TD, and additional ancilla.

- **Step 4**: Perform a subtraction if the sign qubit is $|0\rangle$, computing $(a + b - N) - 0$. Otherwise, $(a + b - N) - (-N)$ is calculated to restore the original value of $a + b$. As for the cost, TC is TC_{Add}, TD is TD_{Add}, with no additional ancilla required.
- **Step 5**: The previous Set 0 Module is uncomputed by applying all the CNOT gates in reverse order. For this step, there is no additional TC, TD, or ancilla required.

Step 6: After applying the Uncompute S Module in the final step, all qubits except the final result of $(a+b)$ mod N are uncomputed. Here, no additional TC, TD, or ancilla are required.

4.4 Refined Design

In Shor's algorithm, the fundamental operation, $(a + b)$ mod N, involves a constant modulus N for a given factoring problem. Prior research [28, 29] suggests that incorporating constant moduli into the quantum modular addition framework, rather than treating N as a variable, can reduce overall costs. Therefore, in addition to the initial design, we also introduce a refined framework that exploits constant moduli to enhance overall efficiency.

- **Step 1**: The refined carry-save layer is specifically constructed based on the value of moduli N. If the i-th bit of N is 0, the subcircuit shown in Fig. 10a is used; otherwise, the subcircuit in Fig. 10b is employed. Compared to the initial carry-save layer, this design reduces the resource requirements by n QC and n TC, with the TD decreasing from 2 to 1.

Fig. 10. Quantum Circuit for Refined Step 1.

- **Step 2**: This step follows the same procedure as Step 2 in the initial design. Specifically, a signed addition operation is performed on S and C to calculate the result of $(a + b - N)$, starting with an initial sign of 0.
- **Step 3**: Unlike the initial design, which utilizes a Set 0 module, this refined step employs CNOT gates to construct a Set N module, enabling the subsequent computation of $(a + b)$ mod N. It does not require any extra TC or TD, though it does introduce a requirement for n extra ancillary qubits.
- **Step 4**: This subtraction circuit operates similarly to Step 4 in the initial design. When the sign qubit is in the state $|0\rangle$, the circuit performs the subtraction $(a + b - N) - 0$. Conversely, when the sign qubit is in the state $|1\rangle$, the circuit computes $(a + b - N) - (-N)$, effectively restoring the original value of $a + b$.
- **Step 5**: In this step, the Set N Module from the previous stage is uncomputed by applying the CNOT gates in the opposite order. No additional resource requirements are imposed in terms of TC, TD, or ancillary qubits.

– **Step 6**: In this step, the refined Uncompute S Module is applied, with its structure depending on the specific value of moduli N. If the i-th bit of N is 0, the subcircuit in Fig. 11a is used; otherwise, the subcircuit in Fig. 11b is employed. Upon completion of the Uncompute S Module, all qubits are uncomputed, retaining only the final result of $(a + b) \bmod N$.

Fig. 11. Quantum Circuit for Refined Step 6.

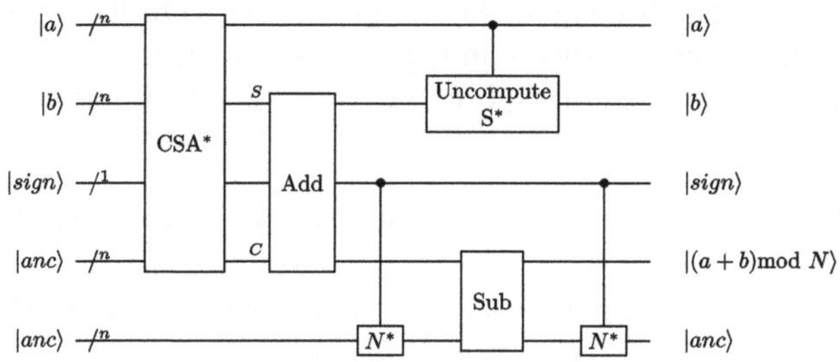

Fig. 12. Refined Framework for Modular Addition with Constant Moduli. All the refined components are marked with an * and are described in detail in this section.

Following the six steps outlined above, a refined quantum carry-save modular addition architecture with constant moduli is constructed, as illustrated by the detailed quantum circuit in Fig. 12. The performance of this refined design will be discussed in Sect. 5.3.

5 Results and Discussion

5.1 Experiment 1: Comparison with Prominent Quantum Modular Addition Frameworks.

After reviewing [27], we choose three adders in Table 1 as our adder blocks since they exhibit optimal TC, TD, QC among all other quantum adders, respectively. Table 2 clearly demonstrates that the effectiveness of a proposed quantum modular addition framework largely relies on the Add module, representing a quantum adder. A performance comparison between our proposed quantum modular addition framework and other relevant prominent works is summarized in Fig. 13, where we note the following:

Table 1. Efficient Quantum adders utilized in Experiment 1.

Adder	TD	TC	QC
Gayathri [30]	n	n	$3n + 1$
Takahashi [31]	$2n - 1$	$2n - 1$	$2n + 1$
Optimal TD [27]	$\log n + 1$	$\frac{n \log n}{2}$	$n + n \log n + \lceil \log n \rceil + 2$

- The framework structure determines the modular adder efficiency. Our structure consistently demonstrates the lowest TD compared to all others, as shown in Fig. 13a. In terms of TC, the Rines-Chuang framework with Gayathri adder block achieve the lowest TC cost, with our design closely following as the second lowest, as depicted in Fig. 13b. However, when using a low TC Add block, the Rines-Chuang framework gains more significant advantages. Our design exhibits a QC that falls slightly below the Beckman framework, as shown in Fig. 13c. When the ancilla of the adder block is high, our design shows similar QC to the Rines-Chuang framework.

Table 2. Performance analysis of different quantum modular addition frameworks.

Modular Addition	Year	Toffoli Depth	Toffoli Count	Qubit Count
VBE [2]	1996	$5 \times TD_{Add}$	$5 \times TC_{Add}$	$3n + 2 + Anc_{Add}$
Beckman [4]	1996	$5 \times TD_{Add}$	$6 \times TC_{Add}$	$5n + 1 + 4 \times Anc_{Add}$
Van Meter [8]	2005	$3 \times TD_{Add}$	$3 \times TC_{Add}$	$3n + 1 + Anc_{Add}$
Rines-Chuang [9]	2018	$3 \times TD_{Add}$	$3 \times TC_{Add}$	$3n + 1 + 2 \times Anc_{Add}$
Our Design	–	$2 + 2 \times TD_{Add}$	$2n + 2 \times TC_{Add}$	$4n + 1 + Anc_{Add}$

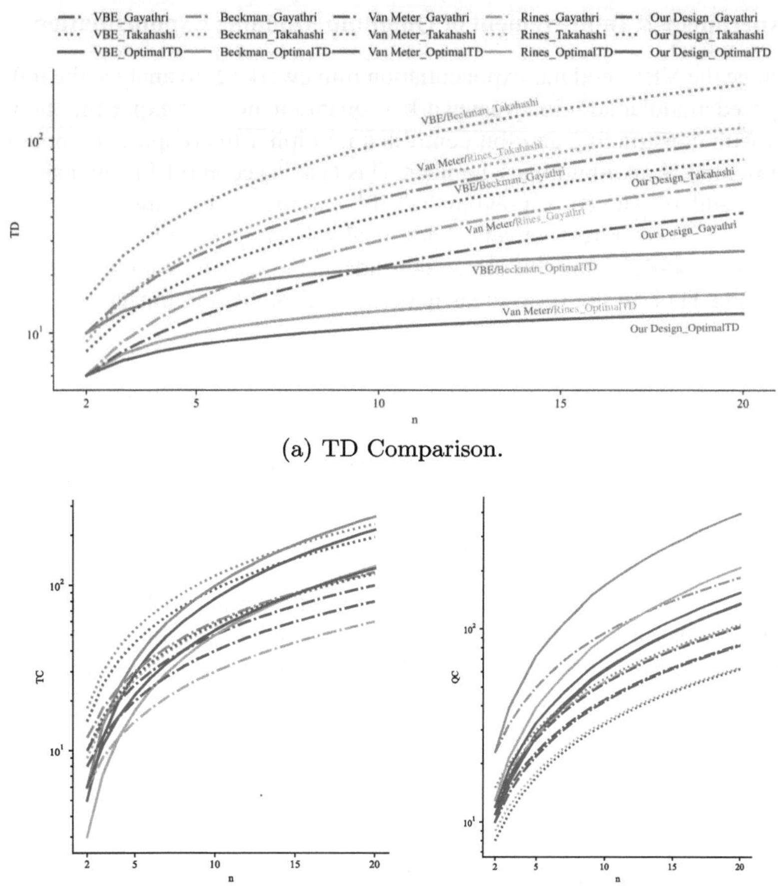

(a) TD Comparison.

(b) TC Comparison.

(c) QC Comparison.

Fig. 13. Comparative Cost Analysis of the Proposed Initial Quantum Modular Adders. Here, n denotes the qubit-width of the modular addition.

- The choice of adder block significantly impacts the overall performance of modular adders. Within the same modular framework, utilizing Gayathri Adder achieves the lowest TC, while employing adder block with Optimal TD results in the lowest TD. Besides, using Takahashi Adder allows for achieving the lowest QC.
- Our adder block with Optimal TD minimizes notable time requirements by achieving the lowest TD. Comparing our Gayathri adder block variation, which scores the second lowest TC and shows its advantage in reducing Toffoli resource usage. On the other hand, our design incorporating the Takahashi adder block achieves the fourth lowest QC.

Our designs exhibit commendable efficiency across various cost metrics in comparison to existing efficient quantum modular addition framework. We achieved up to 33.33% reduction in TD, while keeping TC and QC at comparable levels.

5.2 Experiment 2: Improvement of Quantum Modular Exponentiation

We leverage the VBE modular exponentiation framework [2] to analyze the influence of our proposed modular addition framework on quantum modular exponentiation circuits. We start with constructing an n-bit controlled multiplier to compute $ax \bmod N$, where x is represented as an n-bit binary number. This task is accomplished by using repeated modular N adders. The corresponding TD, TC and QC cost of this circuit are detailed in Formulas 4, 5, and 6 respectively. Additionally, it's important to note that the cost of the Set State Module within this circuit depends on the specific scenario. Under the best case, TC and TD cost are 0, whereas under less favorable circumstances, TC and TD cost are n.

$$TD_{C-MODMul} = 2n \times SETState + n \times TD_{MODAdd} \tag{4}$$

$$TC_{C-MODMul} = 2n \times SETState + n \times TC_{MODAdd} \tag{5}$$

$$QC_{C-MODMul} = 1 + n + QC_{MODAdd} \tag{6}$$

Building upon the n-bit controlled modular multiplier, the VBE modular exponentiation can be constructed to calculate $a^x \bmod N$, where x is an n-bit binary number. The Formulas 7, 8, and 9 illustrate the number of calls to our modular adder block required to perform an n-bit modular exponentiation.

$$\begin{aligned} TD_{MODExp} =& 2n \times TD_{C-MODMul} \\ =& 4n^2 SETState + +2n^2 TD_{MODAdd} \end{aligned} \tag{7}$$

$$\begin{aligned} TC_{MODExp} =& 2n \times TC_{C-MODMul} \\ =& 4n^2 SETState + 2n^2 TC_{MODAdd} \end{aligned} \tag{8}$$

$$\begin{aligned} QC_{MODExp} =& n + QC_{C-MODMul} \\ =& 1 + 2n + QC_{MODAdd} \end{aligned} \tag{9}$$

By employing our proposed structure, a 60% reduction in addition operations in both VBE quantum modular multiplication and VBE quantum modular exponentiation can be achieved.

5.3 Experiment 3: Comparison with Constant-Based Modular Addition Designs

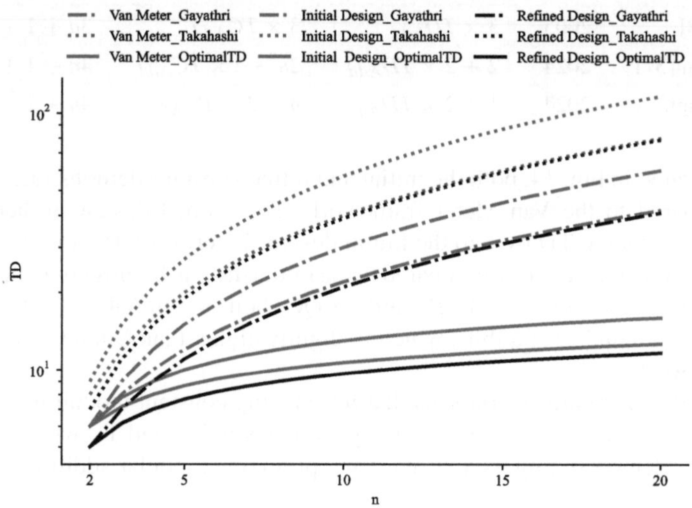

(a) TD Comparison.

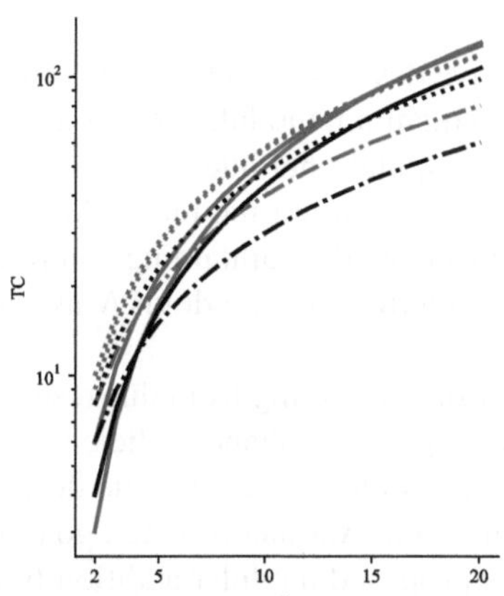

(b) TC Comparison.

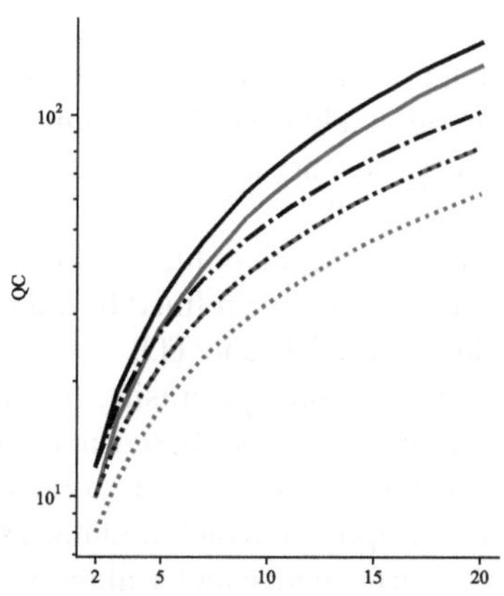

(c) QC Comparison.

Fig.14. Comparative Cost Analysis of Refined Quantum Modular Adders. Here, n denotes the qubit-width of the modular addition. Notably, both the initial and refined designs exhibit the same QC.

In this experiment, we evaluate the performance of the refined design proposed in Sect. 4.4. The detailed resource requirements are summarized in Table 3.

Table 3. Performance analysis of Constant-Based Modular Addition Frameworks.

Modular Addition	Year	Toffoli Depth	Toffoli Count	Qubit Count
Van Meter [8]	2005	$3 \times TD_{Add}$	$3 \times TC_{Add}$	$3n + 1 + Anc_{Add}$
Initial Design [31]	2024	$2 + 2 \times TD_{Add}$	$2n + 2 \times TC_{Add}$	$4n + 1 + Anc_{Add}$
Refined Design	2024	$1 + 2 \times TD_{Add}$	$n + 2 \times TC_{Add}$	$4n + 1 + Anc_{Add}$

As illustrated in Fig. 14, both the initial and refined designs demonstrate a reduction in TD compared to the Van Meter framework. The refined design further improves efficiency by reducing TD by 1 to the initial design. In terms of TC, the refined design achieves a significant reduction compared to the initial design, highlighting the advantage of incorporating constant moduli. Regarding QC, both the initial and refined designs require the same number of qubits, which is slightly higher than Qubit Count of the Van Meter framework.

Overall, this comparison confirms that introducing constant moduli in the quantum modular addition framework can effectively reduce both TD and TC while maintaining the same QC, demonstrating its advantage in optimizing modular addition circuits.

6 Conclusion

In this chapter, we focused on exploring innovative designs to enhance the efficiency of quantum modular addition. We presented a novel quantum modular addition framework based on carry-save architecture, reducing the computational intensity associated with modular addition. When compared against existing quantum modular addition framework, our framework can reduce up to 33.33% in TD while maintaining comparable TC and QC. Furthermore, the refined framework, which treats the modulus N as a constant, further reduces both TC and TD.

We are excited about promising future directions stemming from this research, such as leveraging measurement-based uncomputation [33] to enhance efficiency. There is still a lack of further exploration on related quantum modular arithmetic designs, such as modular multiplication and modular exponentiation. Another research goal of ours is to assess the performance and scalability of this proposed modular addition framework within large-scale quantum algorithms, such as the Shor's algorithm.

Acknowledgement. This research is supported by the National Research Foundation (NRF), Singapore under its Quantum Engineering Programme Initiative. This research is partly supported by MoE Tier 1 grant on Quantum Cryptanalysis.

References

1. Shor, P.W.: Polynomial-time algorithms for prime factorization and discrete logarithms on a quantum computer. SIAM J. Comput. **26**(5), 1484–1509 (1997). https://doi.org/10.1137/S0097539795293172

2. Vedral, V., Barenco, A., Ekert, A.: Quantum networks for elementary arithmetic operations. Phys. Rev. A **54**(1), 147–153 (1996). https://doi.org/10.1103/PhysRevA.54.147
3. Cuccaro, S.A., Draper, T.G., Kutin, S.A., Moulton, D.P.: A new quantum ripple-carry addition circuit (2004). https://arxiv.org/abs/quant-ph/0410184
4. Beckman, D., Chari, A.N., Devabhaktuni, S., Preskill, J.: Efficient networks for quantum factoring. Phys. Rev. A **54**(2), 1034–1063 (1996). https://doi.org/10.1103/PhysRevA.54.1034
5. Takahashi, Y., Kunihiro, N.: A quantum circuit for Shor's factoring algorithm using 2n + 2 qubits. Quant. Info. Comput. **6**(2), 184–192 (2006)
6. Draper, T.G.: Addition on a quantum computer (2000). https://arxiv.org/abs/quant-ph/0008033
7. Ha¨ner, T., Roetteler, M., Svore, K.M.: Factoring using 2n + 2 qubits with toffoli based modular multiplication. Quantum Info. Comput. **17**(7–8), 673–684 (2017)
8. Van Meter, R., Itoh, K.M.: Fast quantum modular exponentiation. Phys. Rev. A **71**(5) (2005). https://doi.org/10.1103/PhysRevA.71.052320
9. R. Rines and I. Chuang, "High performance quantum modular multipliers," 2018. [Online]. Available: https://arxiv.org/abs/1801.01081
10. Beauregard, S.: Circuit for shor's algorithm using 2n+3 qubits (2002). https://arxiv.org/abs/quant-ph/0205095
11. Fowler, A.G., Devitt, S.J., Hollenberg, L.C.L.: Implementation of shor's algorithm on a linear nearest neighbour qubit array (2004). https://arxiv.org/abs/quant-ph/0402196
12. Pavlidis, A., Gizopoulos, D.: Fast quantum modular exponentiation architecture for shor's factorization algorithm (2012). https://arxiv.org/abs/1207.0511
13. Atchade-Adelomou, P., Gonzalez, S.: Efficient quantum modular arithmetics for the isq era (2023). https://arxiv.org/abs/2311.08555
14. Yuan, Y., et al.: An improved qft-based quantum comparator and extended modular arithmetic using one ancilla qubit. New J. Phys. **25**(10), 103011 (2023). https://doi.org/10.1088/1367-2630/acfd52
15. Nam, Y., Su, Y., Maslov, D.: Approximate quantum fourier transform with o(n log(n)) t gates. NPJ Quant. Inform. **6**(1) (2020). https://doi.org/10.1038/s41534-020-0257-5
16. Earle, J.: Latched carry-save adder. IBM Techn. Disclosure Bull. **7**(10), 909–910 (1965)
17. Wang, S., Chattopadhyay, A.: Reducing depth of quantum adder using ling structure. In: 2023 IFIP/IEEE 31st International Conference on Very Large Scale Integration (VLSI-SoC), pp. 1–6. IEEE (2023)
18. Efficient depth optimization in quantum addition and modular arithmetic with ling structure. In: IFIP/IEEE International Conference on Very Large Scale Integration-System on a Chip, pp. 73–89. Springer (2023)
19. Wang, S., Baksi, A., Chattopadhyay, A.: A higher radix architecture for quantum carry-lookahead adder. Sci. Reports **13**(1) (2023). https://doi.org/10.1038/s41598-023-41122-4
20. Wang, S., Lim, E., Chattopadhyay, A.: Boosting the efficiency of quantum divider through effective design space exploration. In: IEEE International Symposium on Circuits and Systems (ISCAS) (2024)
21. Wang, S., Li, X., Lee, W.J.B., Deb, S., Lim, E., Chattopadhyay, A.: A comprehensive study of quantum arithmetic circuits. arXiv preprint arXiv:2406.03867 (2024)
22. Lim, S., et al.: Optimized quantum circuit implementation of payoff function. In: 2023 IFIP/IEEE 31st International Conference on Very Large Scale Integration (VLSI-SoC), pp. 1–6. IEEE (2023)
23. Zi, W., Wang, S., Kim, H., Sun, X., Chattopadhyay, A., Rebentrost, P.: Efficient quantum circuits for machine learning activation functions including constant tdepth relu. arXiv preprint arXiv:2404.06059 (2024)
24. Baksi, A., et al.: Quantum implementation of linear and non-linear layers. In: 2024 IEEE 37th International System-on-Chip Conference (SOCC), pp. 1–6. IEEE (2024)

25. Wang, S., et al.: New results in quantum analysis of led: Featuring one and two oracle attacks. Cryptology ePrint Archive (2024)
26. Draper, T.G., Kutin, S.A., Rains, E.M., Svore, K.M.: A logarithmicdepth quantum carry-lookahead adder. Quant. Info. Comput. **6**(4), 351–369 (2006)
27. Wang, S., Deb, S., Mondal, A., Chattopadhyay, A.: Optimal toffoli-depth quantum adder. in arXiv, 2024. https://arxiv.org/abs/2405.02523
28. Markov, I.L., Saeedi, M.: Constant-optimized quantum circuits for modular multiplication and exponentiation. Quantum Info. Comput. **12**(5–6), 361–394 (2012)
29. Cho, S.-M., Kim, A., Choi, D., Choi, B.-S., Seo, S.-H.: Quantum modular multiplication. IEEE Access **8**, 213244–213252 (2020)
30. Gayathri, S.S., Kumar, R., Samiappan, D., Kaushik, B.K., Haghparast, M.: T-count optimized wallace tree integer multiplier for quantum computing. Int. J. Theoret. Phys. **60**, 1–13 (2021)
31. Takahashi, Y., Tani, S., Kunihiro, N.: Quantum addition circuits and unbounded fan-out. Quant. Inf. Comput. **10**, 10 (2009)
32. Wang, S., Lim, E., Li, X., Feng, J., Chattopadhyay, A.: Minimum depth quantum modular addition through carry-save architecture. In: 2024 IFIP/IEEE 32nd International Conference on Very Large Scale Integration (VLSI-SoC), pp. 1–6. IEEE (2024)
33. Luongo, A., Miti, A.M., Narasimhachar, V., Sireesh, A.: Measurementbased uncomputation of quantum circuits for modular arithmetic. arXiv preprint arXiv:2407.20167 (2024)

Efficient DNN Training Using Vectorized Block-Scaled GeMMs with Adaptive Block Shapes

Nitish Satya Murthy[1,2](✉), Nathan Laubeuf[1], Debjyoti Bhattacharjee[1], Francky Catthoor[3], and Marian Verhelst[1,2]

[1] Imec, Kapeldreef 75, 3001 Leuven, Belgium
nitish.satyamurthy@imec.be
[2] ESAT, KU Leuven, Kasteelpark Arenberg 10, 3001 Leuven, Belgium
[3] MicroLab, NTUA, 15780 Athens, Greece

Abstract. Reduced precision datatypes have become essential to the efficient training and deployment of Deep Neural Networks (DNNs). A recent development in the field has been the emergence of block-scaled datatypes: tensor representation formats derived from floating-point, that share a common exponent across multiple elements. While these formats are being broadly adopted and optimized for by DNN-specific inference accelerators, the potential benefits for training workloads on general-purpose vector processors has yet to be thoroughly explored. This work proposes implementations of block-scaled general matrix multiplications (GeMM) for DNN training at the edge using commercially available vector instruction sets (ARM SVE). Using these implementations, we highlight an accuracy-speed trade-off involving the shape of shared exponent blocks—vectors or squares. We exploit this result to optimize the training of fully connected networks by adapting the shared exponent block shapes during training. We also explore deployments on scalable hardware vector lengths utilizing different degrees of data-level parallelism. We demonstrate more efficient DNN training with our block-scaled datatypes compared to standard IEEE 32-bit floating point (FP32) formats through effective hardware-software cooptimizations.

Keywords: DNN training · Block-scaled datatypes · Vector processors · ARM Scalable Vector Extension (SVE) ISA

1 Introduction

Recent concerns regarding privacy, reliability, and latency have led to a growing interest in techniques to efficiently train DNNs at the edge [1]. This becomes even more essential for tasks that depend on real-time or online learning, for effective functionality. Continuous control robotics tasks encounter such challenges, where the robots are mostly battery-powered and need to operate in dynamic environments [2]. Desirable robotic control in such scenarios demands efficient DNN training through the environmental interactions of the robot in the field [3].

Published by Springer Nature Switzerland AG 2026
E. -I. Vatajelu (Ed.): VLSI-SoC 2024, IFIP AICT 744, pp. 33–47, 2026.
https://doi.org/10.1007/978-3-032-09575-6_3

Some of the most notable efforts towards efficient DNN training at the edge have focused on using reduced precision datatypes to accommodate the limited memory and compute resources typically available to edge processors. Despite the success of these efforts at deploying DNNs in their inference regime using low precision fixed-point integers [4], the training of DNNs under these conditions remains a significant challenge. Faced with more stringent precision and dynamic range constraints, the execution of backpropagation – principal training algorithm of DNNs – has motivated the exploration of more complex data representations [5, 6].

Among such representations, block-scaled datatypes are gathering increasing attention. By associating a common scale to a block of numbers, block-scaled datatypes are able to combine the deployment efficiency of fixed-point datatypes with the dynamic range of floating-point types [7–9]. However, most reported implementations of block-scaled datatypes have so far required specific hardware support [7, 10, 11].

Performing block-scaled quantization requires the selection of which and how many elements share a common exponent or scale. To maximize computational efficiency when using block-scaled DNNs, the block quantization axis should align with the accumulation axis in GeMM, as that enables efficient fixed-point accumulations within each block. DNN training typically involves transpose and quantization operators in the backward pass, in contrast to only forward passes in inference. If these operators are non-commutative, block-scaled DNN training will result in extra block transformation overheads [12, 13], which we analyze later in Sect. 3.1.

To achieve high accuracy within the latency and energy constraints of edge deployment, it is crucial to make the training process adaptable. Adaptive training by dynamically varying quantization parameters based on convergence requirements, has been considered for block-scaled datatypes in the past for custom hardware, by means of varying bit precision [10] and blocksizes [11]. However, these methods cannot be adapted directly for deployment on general-purpose vector processors.

This work is an extension of our previous work [14] to address these research challenges. Our programming model now enables deployment support for scaled hardware vector lengths to utilize more data-level parallelism and provide higher speedups, further increasing the flexibility of our kernels. This is critical for accommodating block sizes that differ from the hardware vector lengths during exponent handling and requantization operations of our block-scaled kernels. We also provide more ablation studies for the adaptive training setup to justify our approach. Our main contributions are as follows:

- We propose square block shapes as opposed to conventional vector shapes for block-scaled datatypes and implement GeMMs using them on ARM vector processors targetting diverse hardware vector lengths.
- We develop an adaptive block-scaled DNN training approach, by initially performing "coarse-commutative" training followed by "fine-adaptation" to allow accuracy-training time trade-off.
- Our proposed method can enable increased speedups and reduced memory footprint requirements for fully-connected NN (FCNN) using adaptive training over baseline FP32 models while reaching similar training performances.

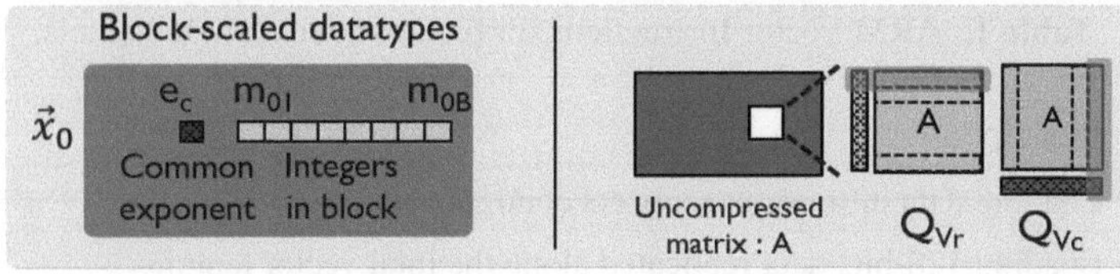

Fig. 1. Block-scaled datatypes with vector (row/column) are demonstrated.

The rest of the paper is organized as follows: Sect. 2 discusses the background and related works. Section 3 explains our methods. Sections 4 and 5 describe our experimental setup and results respectively. Lastly, we conclude in Sect. 6.

2 Background and Related Work

2.1 Block-Scaled Datatypes for DNN Training

Block-scaled datatypes: Extensive research has been done on number representations for efficient DNN executions [15]. Most popular datatypes are floating point (FP) and fixed-point/integer (FXP) types. FP numbers generally have good dynamic range over FXP, however require more complex HW computation units. Block-scaled formats combine the 2 datatypes, by sharing a common exponent among multiple FXP numbers in a block as depicted in Fig. 1. Block-scaled datatypes are recently gaining traction due to their deployment ease and desirable HW-SW trade-offs [7, 9, 12]. Block-scaled dot-product computation with operands $\vec{x}_0$, $\vec{x}_1$ with block size B, common scales e_0,e_1, integers $m_{0,i}$,$m_{1,i}$ for $i = (0,1,...,B-1)$ is as shown in Eqs. (1)–(2). The equations also showcase efficient FXP computation within a block, and enhanced dynamic range through common exponents.

$$\vec{x}_j = 2^{e_j}\left[m_{j,0}, m_{j,1}, ..., m_{j,B-1}\right] \text{ for } j = (0, 1) \tag{1}$$

$$\vec{x}_0 \cdot \vec{x}_1 = 2^{e_0+e_1} \sum_{i=0}^{B-1} (m_{0,i} * m_{1,i}) \tag{2}$$

There are multiple variants of block-scaled quantizations depending on the number representation of each block element being sub-byte [7], minifloat [12, 16]; multi-level scaling [9]; static requantizations [17], etc. Most of the previous approaches involved custom HW implementations. Few works targeted general-purpose vector processors, but only evaluated tensor-level exponents [18, 19]. In contrast, we focus on optimizing block-scaled GeMM kernels for DNN training through flexible block shapes and sizes utilizing only the available vector processor instructions (described in Sect. 2.2) in commercial ISAs [20].

Quantized DNN training: Considering a DNN with layer L involving forward propagation of uncompressed activations $A^{[L]}$ and weights $W^{[L]}$, the following equations represent the computations involved during block-scaled training.

$$A^{[L+1]} = Q_{Vr}\left(A^{[L]}\right) \times Q_{Vc}\left(W^{[L]}\right) \tag{3}$$

Table 1. ARM Vector Instructions for block-scaled GeMM kernels.

Instruction	Description
svld1	Loading data into vector registers contiguously
svld1rq	Loading 128-bits data replicated along the total vector length
svld1ub	Extended 32-bit element load to vector registers
svdup	Duplication of a scalar value along total vector length
svst1b	Storing truncated 8-bit values into memory
svdot_lane	Indexed 4-way int8 dot product in int32 outputs, with index specifying which 8-bit integer group in the first vector operand is reused
svasr/svlsl	Shift lanes of vector register by the values in another vector operand
svmaxv	Return maximum value of the vector register

$$G^{[L]} = Q_{Vr}\left(Tr\left(A^{[L]}\right)\right) \times Q_{Vc}\left(E^{[L+1]}\right) \tag{4}$$

$$E^{[L]} = Q_{Vr}\left(E^{[L+1]}\right) \times Q_{Vc}\left(Tr\left(W^{[L]}\right)\right) \tag{5}$$

Where, Q_{Vr} and Q_{Vc} are block-scaled quantizers like in Fig. 1 for vectors in the row and column direction respectively (quantization direction along GeMM accumulation axis), Tr is a transpose operator, L is the layer index, $\times$ denotes matrix multiplication operator. Equation (3) is the forward pass which is calculated end-to-end for all indices L, and all intermediate uncompressed $A^{[L]}$ are stored for later usage. Equation (4) calculates the gradients $G^{[L]}$ for their respective weights $W^{[L]}$ using all stored $A^{[L]}$. Equation (5) represents the error propagation computed in the opposite direction of Eq. (3). Note that the quantizer nodes enable the GeMM operations to be computed in efficient block-scaled computations.

2.2 ARM Vector Instructions

Vector extensions (such as SVE and SVE2) offer architectural enhancements designed to improve the performance of compute-intensive applications, such as AI workloads due to their SIMD compute capabilities [21]. These extensions introduce a scalable vector length (ranging from 128 to 2048 bits) that allows flexible and efficient parallel processing. Block-scaled computing formats allow representing wide dynamic ranges with fewer bits and offer the possibility to improve the compute efficiency. The mapping of the block-scaled types using vector instructions presents multiple challenges, since the instruction set extension does not natively support these formats [20]. Furthermore, auto-vectorization of the block-scaled computation kernels cannot be performed by an off the shelf compiler effectively. Careful mapping is required to allow full utilization of the available vector lanes. Some of the instructions used for this mapping are summarily shown in Table 1. The conversion and alignment of data formats also need to be carefully performed to minimize the overheads associated with management of the data movement between the processor and the memory subsystem. The support for integer operands by these extensions can be effectively leveraged while computing in the block-scaled domain, as we demonstrate in the following sections.

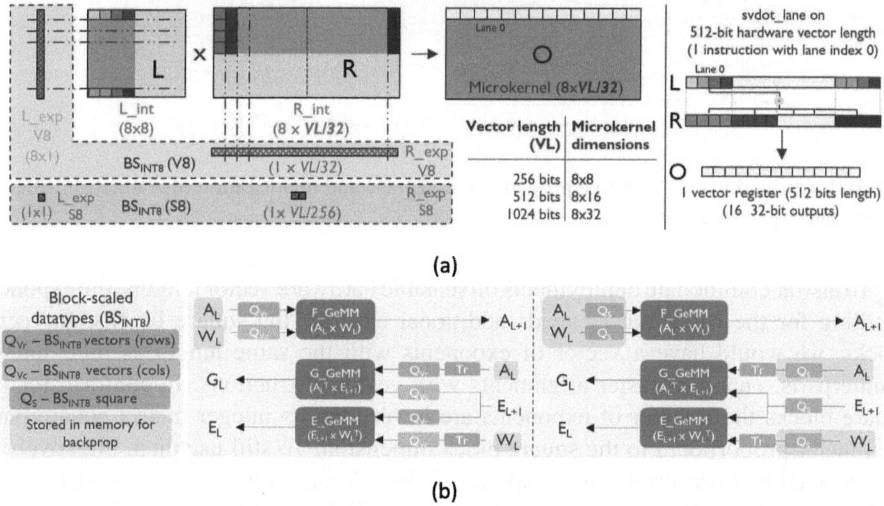

Fig. 2. (a) Illustration of matrix multiplication microkernel with integer parts and exponent parts (V8 and S8 configurations) using scalable vector length instructions. Note that each block element and their common exponent are 8-bit integers. An example of lane-based dot product using ARM SVE 512-bit vector length instruction is also illustrated. (b) The optimizations in DNN training computation graph for square shapes by reversing the orders of quantization and transpose operators in the backward pass.

3 Block-Scaled Integer (BS_{INT8}) GeMMs for DNN Training

3.1 Optimizing Block Shapes for DNN Training

Figure 2a illustrates the microkernel calculation part of a bigger GeMM kernel. With BS_{INT8} quantization, the matrix multiplication involves a series of parallel integer operations on the mantissa's and a single shared exponent operation shown previously in Eq. (2).

The integer matrix-multiplication part is mainly computed using lane-based dot product instructions that output 32-bit integers. With a vector block-scaling approach, based on the alignments of block-quantization and accumulation axes, the left (right) matrix should involve row-wise (column-wise) blocks resulting in a column (row) exponent vector. On the other hand, square blocks will have a single scalar exponent for each 8x8 block tile.

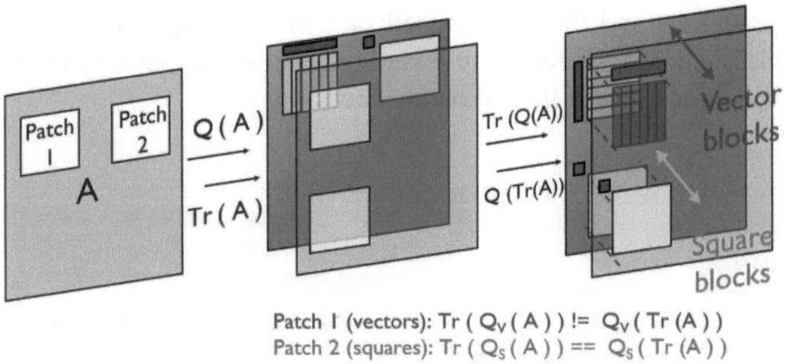

Fig. 3. Investigating commutative property of transpose and quantization operators for different block-scaled quantizations.

To also accommodate deployments on scalable hardware vector lengths, the exponent handling for the right matrix needs additional care for the square blocks. In vector blocks, we would have a vector of exponents with the same length as their integer counterparts, enabling easier alignments with vector instructions. In contrast, for the square blocks the number of exponents are lower than its integer matrix counterparts by a factor proportional to the square block dimension. To still use them effectively in a vectorized manner, each scalar exponent is broadcasted for the corresponding lanes of the vector through predications, which induces slight overheads and redundancy, but ensures good vectorization during deployments and enables storing fewer exponents in memory.

We propose utilizing square blocks instead of conventional vector blocks, due to their advantage of being commutative in quantization-transpose operations as illustrated in Fig. 3. It details how the operation orders of performing transpose and block-scaled quantization leads to different outputs for vector shapes (patch 1), while producing the same outputs for square shapes (patch 2). This allows us to reverse these operation orders for squares in backward passes, leading to optimization opportunities as shown in the training computation graphs in Fig. 2b.

Figure 2b demonstrates that block-scaled activations ($Q_S(A^{[L]})$) and weights ($Q_S(W^{[L]})$) can be stored with their common exponent for later usage in the backward passes for square blocks. This leads to lower memory footprint and data transfer costs. Moreover, this circumvents having to perform extra quantizations before GeMMs by storing already block-quantized values. Vector block-scaled values, on the other hand, would after transpose, lose their common exponent per element of the block, and hence have to be stored in non-compressed formats. Note that the requantization operations on scalable vector length hardware also need to be done iteratively using predication by masking out parts of the vector instructions with the selected block size values.

Notations: In the rest of the paper, we represent our block-scaled datatypes by $BS_{INT8}(V/S)$ for vector/square block shapes respectively. Block size is denoted by a number next to the shape. Ex.: $BS_{INT8}(V8)$ denotes vector blocks sharing an 8-bit exponent among 8 elements of INT8 numbers. $BS_{INT8}(S8)$ forms a square block of 8x8, sharing an exponent among 64 elements.

```
L, R: Left/right integer. Dimensions: L-(MxK), R-(KxN)
B: Block size (B),
Lexp, Rexp: exponent matrices for L and R resp.
                                                                  Instruction
Lp = pack(L)                                                      (count and type)
Rp = pack(R)                                                      Nexp   V8 8x
for (x=0; x<M; x+=8):                                                    S8 1x
  for (y=0; y<N; y+=8):
    Vaccs[0:7] = 0;                                               1- vector load (R)
    Ecur[0:Nexp] = Lexp[0:Nexp] + Rexp[0];                        1- scalar load (L)
    for (b=0; b<K/B; b+=1):                                       1- Compute
      for (z=0; z<B; z+=4):
        Lv1 = svld1rq(Lp[x : x+16, y]);
        Lv2 = svld1rq(Lp[x+16 : x+32, y]);                        3-Load (vector)
        Rv  = svld1(Rp[z : z+4, y : y + 8]);

        Vaccs[0:4] = svdot_lane(Lv1, Rv, index=[0:4]);            8-Computes (vector)
        Vaccs[4:7] = svdot_lane(Lv2, Rv, index=[4:7]);

      Enew[0:Nexp] = Lexp[x*K/B + (b+1)] + Rexp[(b+1)*K/B + y];
                                                                  1- vector load (R)
      Sh = | Enew - Ecur |;               3 - Exponent handling   1- scalar load (L)
      Pred = svcmpge(Enew, Ecur);                                 1- Compute

      svasr/svlsl(Pred, Vaccs[0:7], Sh[0:7]);                     16 compute

    Requantized output store of Vaccs
```

Instr. counts excluding packing/requantization:
(M/8) * (N/8) * ((1+2*N$_{exp}$) + (K/B*B/4*(3+8)) + (K/B-1)*(1+5*N$_{exp}$+16))

V8 (N$_{exp}$=8) : M*N/64*(17+11/4*K+57*(K/B-1))
S8 (N$_{exp}$=1) : M*N/64*(3+11/4*K+22*(K/B-1))

Fig. 4. Pseudo-code for our GeMM kernel on a 256-bit vector length processor using BS_{INT8} formats with square and vector shapes, also highlighting the instruction counts for either scenario.

3.2 Vectorized BS_{INT8} GeMM kernels for efficient computation on vector processors

While the previous subsection justified our square blocks and its impact on the DNN training complexity, there is additional impact on the GeMM computations themselves. Figure 4 shows the pseudo-code of our BS_{INT8} vectorized kernel implementations using ARM SVE vector instructions, along with the difference in instruction counts due to block shapes. Our block-scaled GeMMs involve an integer calculation part, and separate exponent handling computations (highlighted in blue) for aligning exponents of different block partial accumulations.

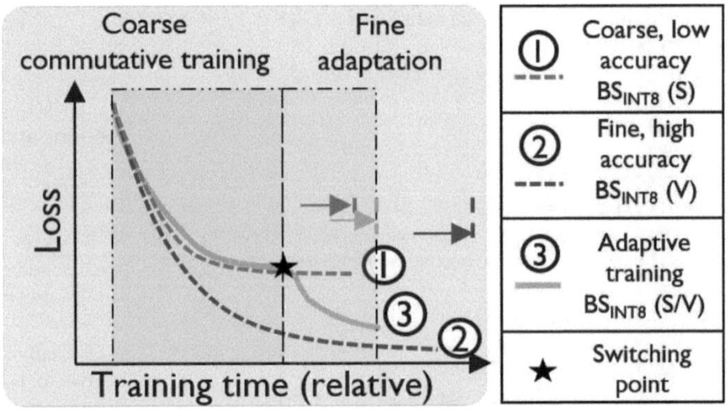

Fig. 5. Adaptive training for accuracy-speed trade-offs.

The reduced GeMM instruction count for square versus vector shapes mainly arises from exponent handling overheads due to their different number of exponents for the same matrix dimensions. The block size along accumulation axis directly relates to the alignment overhead needed for performing block-scaled GeMM kernels. It is important to note that the number of elements sharing a common exponent is not identical among the two shapes, rather, the number of elements in the accumulation direction is kept similar instead. This leads to square shapes having higher compression ratios than vectors, leading to also lower instruction counts, however, at the cost of higher approximation errors as will be seen in Sect. 5.1.

3.3 Adaptive DNN Training Through Vectorized BS_{INT8} GeMMs (vector and square)

We propose an adaptive training approach here to obtain an optimized solution that properly trades off HW and SW metrics as illustrated in Fig. 5. The previous subsections described the differences in HW metrics (instr. counts, memory footprint) due to different block-shaped kernels. However, these block shapes which have different compression ratios would also lead to different training qualities (SW metrics - loss/accuracy) due to different quantization errors.

Algorithm 1 details our adaptive approach to change block shape during the training process. A quantization configuration is set to first perform $BS_{INT8}(S8)$ training and then switch to $BS_{INT8}(V8)$. We define a hyperparameter α that is used to split the total training process amongst these 2 configurations. This follows the principle of performing a coarse training search that is more computationally efficient and later performing fine adaptation which is slower, but more accurate. As shown in Sect. 5.3, performing this multi-stage training helps in reaching co-optimized solutions based on accuracy-speed trade-offs.

Algorithm 1: Adaptive BS_{INT8} DNN training with block shapes

```
    Inputs:
    confs - [BS_INT8(S8), BS_INT8(V8)]
    Max epochs - E_max
    Epoch ratios among confs - E_r = [α, 1-α]
    DNN model (with weights W) - M_W
for id in [0,1] do
    DNN model quant ← confs[id]                    # Block-scaled quantization
    if id = 0 then
        M_W ← random initialization
    else
        M_W[id] ← M_W[id - 1]                      # Model weight transfer
    end
    for t = 1 to E_r[id] · E_max do
        Train DNNs iteratively updating M_W        # Supervised training
        Monitor average loss, L = []
    end
    Save model weights, M_W[id]
end
```

4 Experimental Setup

Workload: We analyze FCNN models which are used to predict the system dynamics of continuous control robotics tasks for benchmarking our training approach. As mentioned in Sect. 1, these tasks require real-time or online learning based on the robot interactions with the environment at the edge. Hence, efficient embedded runtime training techniques would aid in optimizing task performance with limited resource constraints.

These robotics tasks involve FCNNs with state-action pair inputs – current robot state values and actions that control the robot. It outputs a probability distribution (mean and standard deviation) for the next state values, capturing the uncertainty in its predictions, which is utilized for effectively controlling the robot based on user specifications [3]. This work focuses on analyzing different training performances by simulating our BS_{INT8} quantization configurations in PyTorch using quantization libraries [22]. The cartpole models use 3 layered FCNN with 500 hidden neurons (balance a pole in upright position). The pusher and reacher models use 3 layers with 200 neurons (push an object and reach a goal using a robotic arm respectively). The halfcheetah model uses 4 layers and 200 neurons (should move/run fast). ReLU activations, an Adam optimizer with initial learning rate of 0.001 and a Gaussian loss function are used in all scenarios. While this task is used for mainly demonstrating our training approach, the same techniques are applicable to any generic DNN training task which involve GeMM operations.

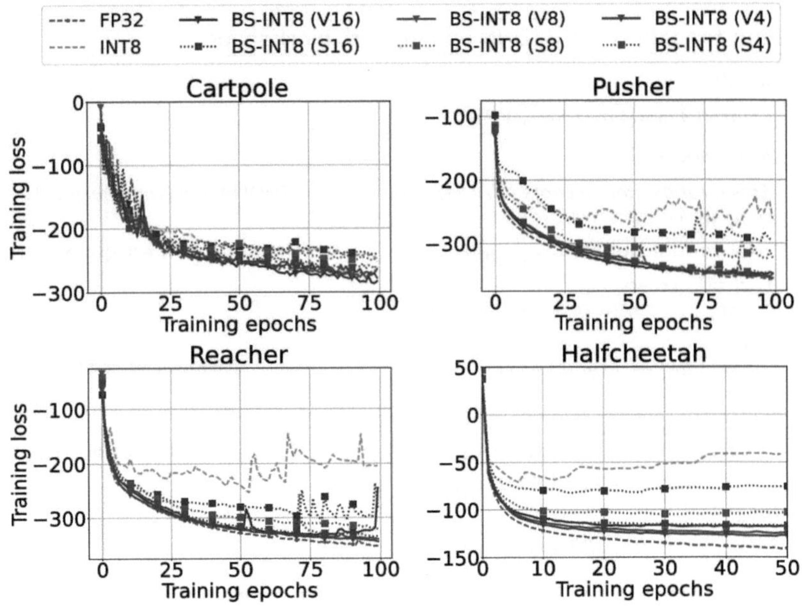

Fig. 6. Impacts of block-scaled datatypes (shape/sizes) on DNN training quality (Baseline models – FP32 and INT8).

Target HW details: We target general-purpose vector processors, in particular ARM v8.4a+ architectures with SVE extension because of its wide-spread usage in the edge and mobile community. Our experiments are run with different hardware vector lengths of 256, 512 and 1024 bits. We benchmark our kernel runs through instruction/cycle counts on a gem5 [23] MinorCPU model with 64kB L1 cache and 1MB L2 cache memories.

Kernel code configurations: All matrices of GeMM operands are assumed to be stored in row-major formats. Furthermore, in BS_{INT8} configurations, the exponent and integer matrices are stored separately. The code implementation is written in C using vector intrinsic functions from ARM C Language Extensions (ACLE) for high efficiency deployments. ARM GCC cross-compiler 12.3 was used on x86–64 host platforms targeting aarch64 platforms.

5 Results and Analysis

5.1 DNN training curves due to block-scaled datatypes (vector and square)

We analyze here the impacts of block shapes (S/V) and sizes (4/8/16) on the training quality for different datatypes. As observed from Fig. 6, the quality is worse for square configurations due to larger number of block elements that share a common exponent. The quality also reduces for increasing block sizes (highest for INT8 with tensor-level scales), which is more prominent in the relatively more complex task - halfcheetah. Hence, although the square blocks are more suited for training computationally, it is still prone to degradation in training quality. This provides us with crucial design parameter choices that can be selected based on the desired user requirements.

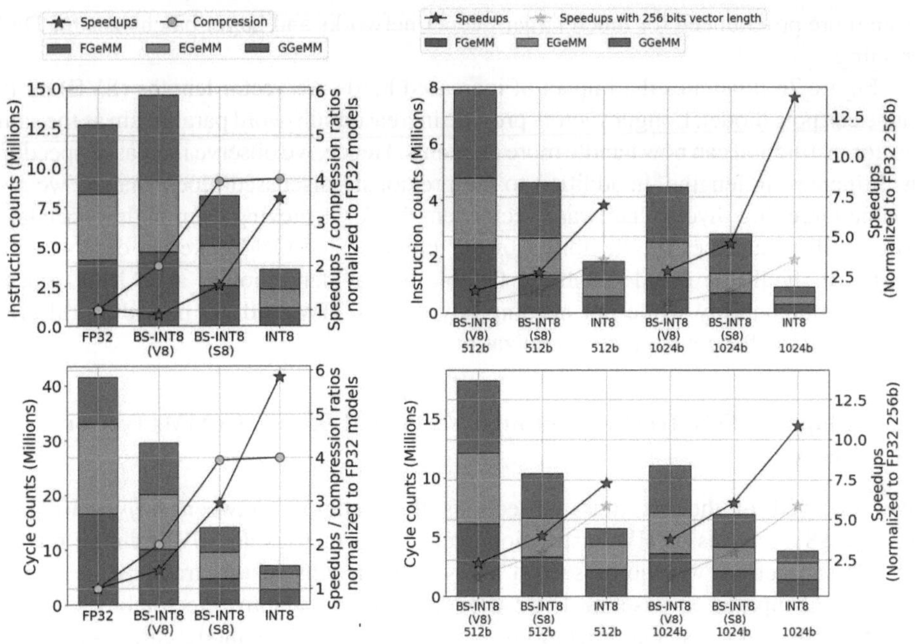

(a) 256 bits vector length (b) Increased vector lengths (512/1024-bits)

Fig. 7. Vectorized GeMM kernels execution profiling for cartpole FCNN model with different datatypes depicting instruction/cycle counts, speedup and memory compression ratios. Cycle counts are a better system-level metric and would hence be used hereafter for relative speedup comparisons.

5.2 Benchmarking BS_{INT8} Vector and Square GeMM Kernels

While previously, we looked at the training quality impacts with $BS_{INT8}(S/V)$ formats, the GeMM kernel deployment was not analyzed. We analyze the instruction/cycle counts for performing GeMMs in the different phases of backpropagation and compare them with different baseline datatypes (FP32 and INT8). In Fig. 7a, we can firstly observe the split-up of instruction and cycle counts for the cartpole model, compared across different datatypes with 256-bit vector length instructions. Each operation phase (FGeMM for FWD, GGeMM and EGeMM for BWD gradient and error computations as in Eqs. (3), (4) and (5) respectively) require similar counts as they involve GeMMs of similar dimensions. Additionally, we observe increasing speedups as we go from FP32, BS_{INT8} (V8), BS_{INT8} (S8) to non-blocked INT8, while also correspondingly exhibiting increased quantization errors. This speedup increase from V8 to S8 is mainly due to the reduced overheads of exponent handling as seen earlier in the pseudo-code in Fig. 4. The figure also shows the compression ratios leading to reduced memory footprints and data transfer costs, while handling intermediate activations during backpropagation. Note that BS_{INT8} (V8) has only 2× compression, as we need to store exponents for each element as seen in earlier sections. For the cartpole task, the activation memory requirement per iteration can be reduced from 193 kB for FP32 to 49 kB for BS_{INT8} (S8). This benefit would be even more pronounced for much larger/deeper networks and larger batchsizes for DNN training.

Figure 7b illustrates the impact of increased hardware vector lengths (SVE) on the same cartpole model. Longer vectors provide increased sub-word parallelism as the same vector instruction can now handle more elements. Hence, we observe increased speedups with increasing lengths. In addition to the previously discussed block shapes, we also enable targetting diverse hardware vector lengths for achieving even higher speedups. This further enhances the flexibility of our block-scaled GeMM kernel deployments. Lastly, it should be noted that these flexible deployment choices arise from processor programmability while not needing any custom HW, and yet providing different configurations for potential co-optimizations.

5.3 Adaptive DNN Training Through Vectorized BS_{INT8} GeMMs (vector and square)

We observed in the previous subsections the trade-off between $BS_{INT8}(V8)$ and $BS_{INT8}(S8)$ in terms of HW instruction/cycle count metrics and SW training quality. In this subsection, we showcase and analyze the results of this trade-off as seen in Fig. 8a. Compared to baseline FP32 models, our non-adaptive vector block models achieve $0.9-1.4\times$ faster computations, while the square block models are $2-3\times$ faster across different tasks for deployments on a 256-bit vector length hardware.

At the extreme end of block granularity lies the baseline INT8 models with tensor-level exponents, which are fast but suffer significantly in quality as also previously observed in the convergence noise of loss curves in Fig. 6. In order to enable fast training computations while not incurring degradation in training quality, we utilize our adaptive training approach as was described in Algorithm 1. It involves the use of a tunable hyperparameter α that decides the ratio of training epochs performed first using $BS_{INT8}(S)$ and the rest using $BS_{INT8}(V)$ GeMMs. Figure 8a shows the results of this approach with different ratios, achieving more co-optimized solutions than non-adaptive block-scaled datatypes and other baseline datatypes. For $\alpha = 0.95$, we observe very close speedups to $BS_{INT8}(S)$, while ensuring no significant accuracy loss for most tasks. We can reach even higher speedups with longer hardware vector lengths as depicted in Fig. 8a, demonstrating its impacts on our adaptive and non-adaptive block-scaled GeMM kernel deployments.

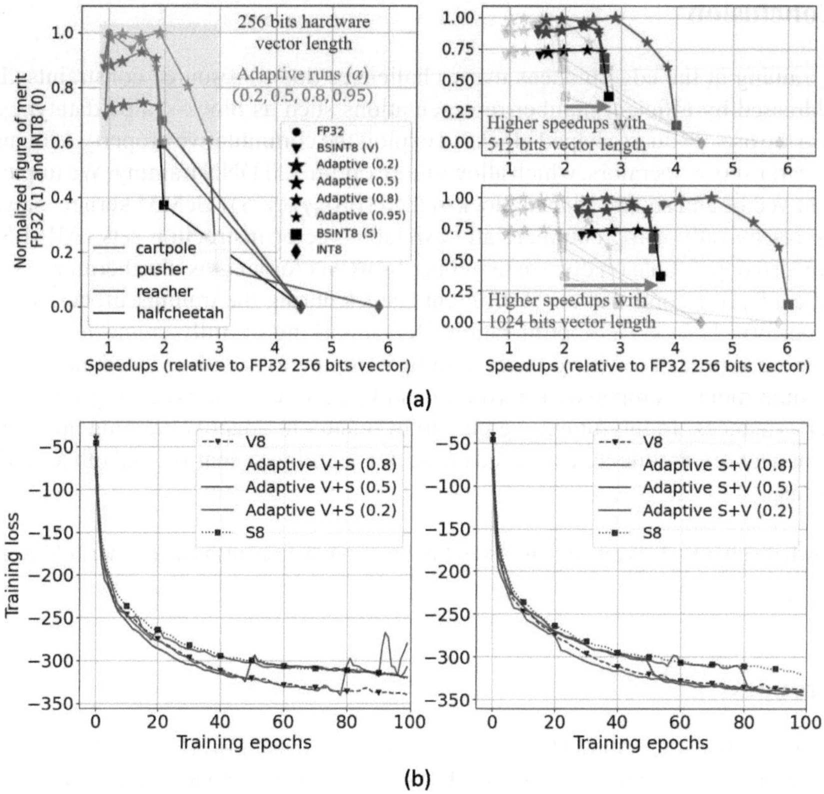

Fig. 8. (a) Accuracy vs speedup trade-offs demonstrating the benefits of our adaptive training approach. Impacts with different hardware vector lengths are also illustrated. (b) Comparisons of different adaptive runs for the reacher task.

Additionally, it should be noted that the specific configuration settings of the adaptive training also has an impact on the convergence quality. In the adaptive approach of [11], the block sizes are increased as training progresses, while however increasing the precision of the block operands. Since in our deployments we operate on fixed 8-bit operands, we explore 2 different settings with interchanged orders of performing square and vector block trainings, with the same α ratios. The results as shown in Fig. 8b further support our strategy, emphasizing the necessity of performing fine block quantizations only in the final stages, following an initial coarse training process. With more flexible deployment configurations, the adaptive approaches could push the boundaries further for co-optimization.

6 Conclusion

DNN training at the edge induces many challenges due to resource constraints. These are addressed by efficient number representations such as block-scaled datatypes. We propose the use of square shaped blocks to exploit the commutative property of quantization and transpose operators, which allows more optimized DNN training. We implement efficient vector and square shaped block-scaled ($BS_{INT8}(V/S)$) GeMM kernels on vector processors by only using commercially available vector instruction sets (ARM SVE), that are also deployable on diverse target hardware vector lengths. Furthermore, we propose the adaptive combination of different shapes during the training process to effectively perform HW-SW co-optimization. Benchmarking on fully-connected networks, our training approach can yield faster training computations with reduced memory footprint requirements, compared to conventional FP32 models while reaching similar training performances. In the future, we plan to evaluate our adaptive training approach on different network architectures, varied on-device learning scenarios, and other hardware platforms.

Acknowledgement. This research received funding from the Flemish Government (AI Research Program).

References

1. Lu, C.-H., Wu, Y.-C., Yang, C.-H.: A 2.25 tops/w fully-integrated deep CNN learning processor with on-chip training. In: 2019 IEEE Asian Solid-State Circuits Conference (A-SSCC), pp. 65–68. IEEE (2019)
2. Neuman, S.M., et al.: Tiny robot learning: challenges and directions for machine learning in resource-constrained robots. In: 2022 IEEE 4th International Conference on Artificial Intelligence Circuits and Systems (AICAS), pp. 296–299. IEEE (2022)
3. Chua, K., Calandra, R., McAllister, R., Levine, S.: Deep reinforcement learning in a handful of trials using probabilistic dynamics models. Adv. Neural Inform. Process. Syst. **31** (2018)
4. Krishnamoorthi, R.: Quantizing deep convolutional networks for efficient inference: a whitepaper. arXiv preprint arXiv:1806.08342 (2018)
5. Micikevicius, P., et al.: Mixed precision training. In: International Conference on Learning Representations (2018)
6. Alsuhli, G., Sakellariou, V., Saleh, H., Al-Qutayri, M., Mohammad, B., Stouraitis, T.: Number Systems for Deep Neural Network Architectures. Springer (2023)
7. Darvish Rouhani, B., et al.: Pushing the limits of narrow precision inferencing at cloud scale with microsoft floating point. Adv. Neural Inform. Process. Syst. **33**, 10271–10281 (2020)
8. Yang, G., Zhang, T., Kirichenko, P., Bai, J., Wilson, A.G., De Sa, C.: Swalp: stochastic weight averaging in low precision training. In: International Conference on Machine Learning, pp. 7015–7024, PMLR (2019)
9. Darvish Rouhani, B., et al.: With shared microexponents, a little shifting goes a long way. In: Proceedings of the 50th Annual International Symposium on Computer Architecture, pp. 1–13 (2023)
10. Zhang, S.Q., McDanel, B., Kung, H.: Fast: DNN training under variable precision block floating point with stochastic rounding. In: 2022 IEEE International Symposium on High-Performance Computer Architecture (HPCA), pp. 846–860. IEEE (2022)

11. Lee, S., Choi, J., Noh, S., Koo, J., Kung, J.: DBPS: dynamic block size and precision scaling for efficient DNN training supported by RISC-V ISA extensions. In: 2023 60th ACM/IEEE Design Automation Conference (DAC), pp. 1–6. IEEE (2023)
12. Rouhani, B.D., et al.:Microscaling data formats for deep learning. arXiv preprint arXiv:2310. 10537 (2023)
13. Nascimento, M.G.D., Prisacariu, V.A., Fawcett, R., Langhammer, M.: Hyperblock floating point: generalised quantization scheme for gradient and inference computation. In: Proceedings of the IEEE/CVF Winter Conference on Applications of Computer Vision, pp. 6364–6373 (2023)
14. Satya Murthy, N., Laubeuf, N., Bhattacharjee, D., Catthoor, F., Verhelst, M.: Adaptive block-scaled gemms on vector processors for DNN training at the edge. In: 2024 IFIP/IEEE 32nd International Conference on Very Large Scale Integration (VLSI-SoC), pp. 1–6. IEEE (2024)
15. Liang, T., Glossner, J., Wang, L., Shi, S., Zhang, X.: Pruning and quantization for deep neural network acceleration: a survey. Neurocomputing **461**, 370–403 (2021)
16. Fox, S., Rasoulinezhad, S., Faraone, J., Leong, P.,et al.: A block minifloat representation for training deep neural networks. In: International Conference on Learning Representations (2020)
17. Fan, H., Wang, G., Ferianc, M., Niu, X., Luk, W.: Static block floating-point quantization for convolutional neural networks on FPGA. In: 2019 International Conference on Field-Programmable Technology (ICFPT), pp. 28–35. IEEE (2019)
18. Das, D., et al.: "Mixed precision training of convolutional neural networks using integer operations. In: International Conference on Learning Representations (2018)
19. de Bruin, B., Zivkovic, Z., Corporaal, H.: Quantization of deep neural networks for accumulator-constrained processors. Microprocess. Microsyst. **72**, 102872 (2020)
20. Satya Murthy, N., Catthoor, F., Verhelst, M.: Optimization of block-scaled integer gemms for efficient DNN deployment on scalable in-order vector processors. J. Syst. Architect. 103236 (2024)
21. Stephens, N. et al.: The arm scalable vector extension. IEEE Micro **37**(2), 26–39 (2017)
22. Zhang, T., Lin, Z., Yang, G., De Sa, C.: Qpytorch: a low-precision arithmetic simulation framework. In: 2019 Fifth Workshop on Energy Efficient Machine Learning and Cognitive Computing-NeurIPS Edition (EMC2-NIPS), pp. 10–13. IEEE (2019)
23. Lowe-Power, J., et al.: The gem5 simulator: Version 20.0+. arXiv preprint arXiv:2007.03152 (2020)

Memory and Data Management

Application-Aware Memory Management for IPsec on Heterogeneous SoCs

Ayushi Agarwal[1(✉)], Radhika Dharwadkar[1], Isaar Ahmad[2], Krishna Kumar[1,2], P. J. Joseph[2], Sourav Roy[2], Prokash Ghosh[2], and Preeti Ranjan Panda[1]

[1] Indian Institute of Technology Delhi, New Delhi, India
anz188503@iitd.ac.in
[2] NXP Semiconductors, Noida, India

Abstract. SoC design has shifted towards heterogeneous architectures with CPUs and domain-specific accelerators to keep up with the growing computational demands of current-day applications. These accelerators demand high on-chip and off-chip memory bandwidth and require efficient management of shared system resources. We characterize Internet Protocol Security (IPsec), a high-throughput application, by collecting the memory traces of this application running on the accelerators and CPU cores of NXP LX2160A SoC. We use this characterization to design a simulation infrastructure for simulating IPsec on possible domain-specific architectural extensions and perform a design-space exploration across various general-purpose memory management policies. We propose APPAMM, an application-specific predictive packet-aware memory management policy using the knowledge of IPsec to improve performance for next-generation SoCs. Using our approach to manage memory for different input packet streams, we report improvements of up to 22x in the packet drop rate and peak throughput.

Keywords: Internet Protocol Security Accelerators · Data-flow Architectures · Application-Specific Memory Management

1 Introduction

Domain-specific accelerators (DSA) provide high-performance solutions for heavy computing applications such as machine learning [4, 10], and network security [11]. Complex systems-on-chip (SoCs) increasingly rely on heterogeneous processing components, such as CPUs and DSAs, to meet the performance requirements. Heterogeneous SoCs require high on-chip and off-chip memory bandwidth to meet heavy computational loads. Since the off-chip memory has not kept up with the rising bandwidth demand by applications, an on-chip memory shared by the cores and accelerators provides the necessary bandwidth. However, contention at this memory can cause severe performance bottlenecks. Intelligent on-chip memory management leads to significant performance improvement in homogeneous architectures [8, 17]. Memory management is crucial to mitigate contention in heterogeneous SoCs, especially for accelerators with strict Quality-of-Service (QoS) requirements.

Published by Springer Nature Switzerland AG 2026
E. -I. Vatajelu (Ed.): VLSI-SoC 2024, IFIP AICT 744, pp. 51–71, 2026.
https://doi.org/10.1007/978-3-032-09575-6_4

Internet Protocol Security (IPsec) is a computationally intensive, high-throughput application that provides network layer security for high-speed secured communication over insecure networks. It addresses security issues such as packet origin authentication via packet header checks and data confidentiality via high-quality encryption and decryption [7, 9]. The application demands heavy compute parallelism to guarantee the required throughput. Hence, it has always been a contender for hardware or software acceleration. However, its impact on the system resources has not been studied. We study the application on a high-performance heterogeneous SoC, NXP LX2160A [13], shown in Fig. 1.

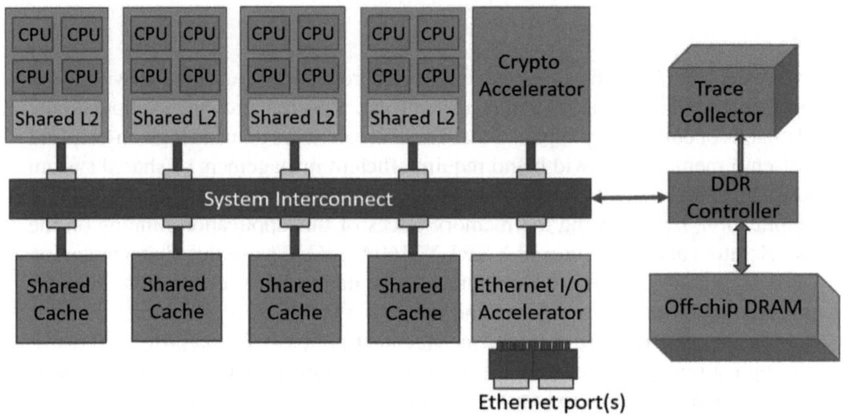

Fig. 1. LX2160A SoC [13] Architecture. The SoC has multiple CPU clusters with an Ethernet I/O and a Crypto Accelerator.

We collect the application's memory traces on the SoC to characterize the memory access patterns and design a simulation infrastructure based on the application's behavior to evaluate the impact on the shared memory resources. We perform a design-space exploration across various memory management policies on multiple architectural configurations to enable better performance and higher throughput on next-generation SoCs. We make the following major contributions:

1. We design a trace collection infrastructure to characterize the IPsec application by analyzing the memory access patterns and packet data flow.
2. We use the application's characteristics to design a simulation infrastructure with architectural flexibility and perform a design-space exploration across on-chip memory management policies to evaluate performance.
3. We propose an application-specific predictive packet-aware memory management policy to improve performance. The policy performs better than general-purpose policies on varied packet streams and can be generalized well to other architectures.

2 Related Work

Modern IPsec implementations in high-performance systems target sustained throughput [5, 13] with minimal computational overhead to achieve higher network bandwidth. Previous works have established that IPsec is a high-throughput computationally intensive workload [7, 9]. Domain-specific hardware or software implementations of IPsec can deliver high throughput. Guilford et al. [5] propose a fast, complete software implementation on multi-core processors. They propose highly optimized software implementations of the cryptographic operations in the IPsec protocol using custom-optimized CPU instructions to achieve high throughput on existing hardware. Strongswan [15] and Rockhopper [14] implement the IPsec Encapsulating Security Payload (ESP) protocol in the operating system's user space. Matching the throughput usually achieved by hardware-accelerated designs is difficult with complete software implementations. Niu et al. [12] propose a high-performance hardware accelerator to achieve high throughput. The accelerator uses a configurable multi-core architecture for cryptographic processing. The architecture can be configured with multiple Authentication Header (AH)/ESP and AES cores implemented in the design to achieve high throughput. Nam et al. [11] present an FPGA solution for IPsec ESP protocol to achieve high throughput and low latency from the IPsec core. They argue that software implementations cannot achieve the throughput demands of the application. They realize their system on an FPGA board and provide a complete hardware design to run IPsec on modern SoCs.

There has been an increasing interest in the hardware acceleration of IPsec by offloading operations to cryptographic accelerators already in the system. Chang et al. [6] design an IPsec accelerator as a co-processor to an ARM9 processor for running cryptographic algorithms. The network processor pre-processes the input packet and offloads the cryptographic operation to the IPsec accelerator. IPSecco [3] delivers a lightweight, low-footprint hardware implementation of IPsec cryptographic core that executes all cryptographic operations offloaded by a soft-core, performing protocol processing. Agrawal et al. [1] analyze the performance achieved by IPsec when offloaded to hardware-based accelerators on SoCs. They argue that protocol-aware offloading of IPsec to a cryptographic accelerator yields higher benefits than software offloading. Thoguluva et al. [16] suggest offloading the cryptographic operations from the SoC's host processor to a programmable security processor. They offer insights into the overheads of offloading the IPsec operations to other accelerators on the SoC. Doyle et al. [2] propose to offload the encryption and decryption operations to Intel QuickAssist Technology's a family of accelerators achieving 50 Gbps throughput.

Most of the above works show that offloading to cryptographic accelerators can meet the throughput requirements. Still, no detailed characterization of the application and the impact of this offloading on the system has been performed. In this work, we characterize the application to study its impact on the SoC's shared memory resources and enable efficient memory management to improve performance.

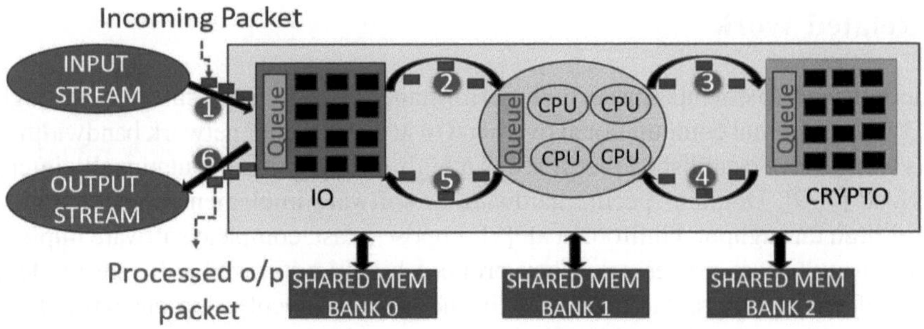

Fig. 2. Abstract Overview of the IPsec dataflow. I/O accelerators, Crypto accelerators, and CPUs have a packet queue and multiple computing resources for parallel computation.

3 IPsec Application Profiling on LX2160A SoC

We discuss the infrastructure used to collect traces for the application running on the SoC and analyze its memory access patterns. The SoC [13], as shown in Fig. 1, has four clusters of four ARM Cortex-A72 cores, each with private L1/L2 caches, two custom accelerators for the IPsec application, and a shared banked-cache. The application can achieve high throughput by software-managed offloading of the network packet processing to the Ethernet I/O accelerator and the encryption and decryption tasks to the Cryptographic accelerator on the SoC. A trace collector is connected to the SoC's DDR controller to snoop and collect DDR accesses as traces, which are later stored into a small on-chip memory called packet express buffer instead of DDR to minimize the instrumentation overhead and bandwidth contention between trace packets and the application's data. The traces are read and processed offline upon the application's completion.

3.1 IPsec Application Dataflow and Access Characteristics

We analyze the collected traces to study the IPsec workload properties, such as data locality and memory access patterns. Figure 2 shows that the packet dataflow sequence is I/P Stream $\rightarrow^{1}$ I/O Acc. $\rightarrow^{2}$ CPU $\rightarrow^{3}$ Crypto Acc. $\rightarrow^{4}$ CPU$\rightarrow^{5}$ I/O Acc. $\rightarrow^{6}$ O/P Stream. Figure 3 reveals the memory access pattern of a 390B packet stream at a 4 Gbps injection rate. It shows a regular and repeated sequence of memory accesses initiated by computing units plotted over time. Each unit sequence corresponds to a single IPsec packet and aligns with the IPsec dataflow. In the figure, we highlight the memory accesses of three such packets, each exhibiting the same memory access pattern. The sequence of memory accesses for all IPsec packets can be further divided into phases, which conform to the IPsec dataflow shown in Fig. 2. The memory access phases of a packet are as follows:

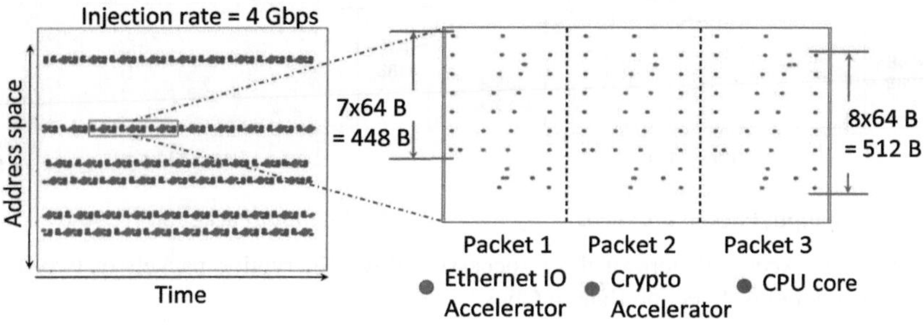

Fig. 3. IPsec memory traces for 390B packets at 4 Gbps Injection Rate.

1. *Write Access by IO accelerator*: A 390B packet received by the IO accelerator is written to the shared memory. Figure 3 shows that a 390B packet performs seven memory accesses in this phase.
2. *Read Access from CPU*: The packet data is read by the CPU, which processes the header to indicate the kind of cryptographic operation needed on the packet.
3. *Read and Write Access by Crypto Accelerator*: Crypto reads the packet data to perform the required cryptographic operations. It writes back the processed encrypted/decrypted packet to the memory. This is the most memory-intensive phase of the packet, as shown in Fig. 3.
4. *Read Access from CPU*: The processed packet header is read and updated by the CPU and marked ready for sending to the I/O accelerator.
5. *Read Access by IO accelerator*: The IO accelerator reads and processes the encrypted/decrypted packet and sends it out. We observe that for 390B packets, this phase performs eight memory accesses.

3.2 Memory Access Pattern Sensitivity to IPsec Workload Attributes

We profile the IPsec application by varying all the attributes that affect its memory access behavior. We discuss the sensitivity of IPsec's memory access pattern to these attributes.

1. *Input Packet Size:* IPsec packets can have different sizes - 86, 150, 250, 390, 162, and 466 bytes. The packet size determines the packet's total memory footprint and number of memory accesses needed to write/read the packet data to/from memory. Figure 4 shows that with a fixed injection rate of 4 Gbps on encryption packets, increasing the input packet size only marginally increases the packet processing time (1.22x with a 4.5x increase in packet size) but significantly increases its on-chip memory footprint and the number of memory accesses (up to 3x).

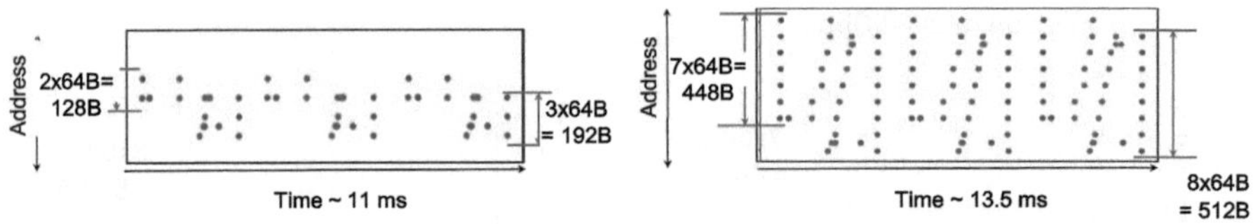

(a) Input Packet Size: 86 B (b) Input Packet Size: 390 B

Fig. 4. Memory Access Pattern of three successive IPsec Encryption packets of two different sizes - 86 B and 390 B. Injection Rate: 4 Gbps.

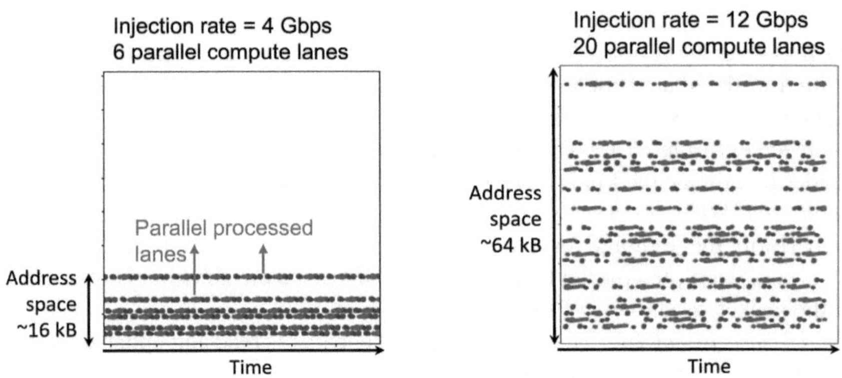

(a) Input Injection Rate: 4 Gbps (b) Input Injection Rate: 12 Gbps

Fig. 5. Increase in system parallelism with increasing injection rate. Input packet type ⇒ 390B Encryption.

2. *Workload/Packet Types:* The packets can be encrypted or decrypted depending on the cryptographic operation required. We observe from the traces that the memory access pattern has low sensitivity to the packet type. An 86 (162) bytes encryption packet differs marginally from a decryption packet of 162 (86) bytes in the number of memory accesses done by all the computational units and the total packet execution time.
3. *Input Injection Rate:* The packet injection rate is varied between 4–12 Gbps. The packet's injection rate, size, and type affect the system's peak throughput. Figure 5 shows that for a 390B packet, a 3x increase in the injection rate leads to a 3.3x increase in parallelism (facilitated by multiple compute resources). We observe a strong correlation between the packet injection rate and the degree of parallelism in the system.

4 Simulation Infrastructure for IPsec Application

We develop a simulation infrastructure by exploiting the dataflow characteristics and the memory access pattern, discussed in Sect. 3, to simulate the workload on future projected architectures and facilitate system-level design-space exploration to improve performance on next-generation SoCs.

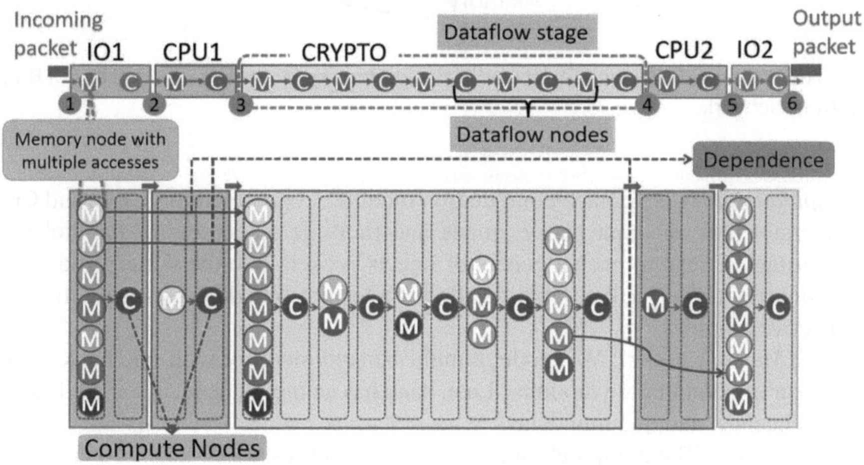

Fig. 6. Packet Dataflow Graph, Stage, and Nodes with an expanded view of M-nodes. Same color M-nodes: Dependent nodes with the same address.

4.1 Simulation Model

The IPsec simulation model, shown in Fig. 6, has multiple abstraction levels based on its trace characteristics.

1. *Dataflow Node*: This captures the most elementary task performed on a resource of any processing component. A compute node (C-type) represents a fixed-latency computation task. A memory node (M-type) represents multiple independent accesses to the shared memory.
2. *Dataflow Stage*: This is a directed sequence of multiple tasks or dataflow nodes scheduled in order of execution on a specific processing component. For any workload, the dataflow stage can capture any custom sequence of tasks.
3. *Packet Dataflow Graph (DFG)*: It is a directed sequence of multiple dataflow stages. The IPsec packet DFG has five dataflow stages, conforming to the dataflow discussed in Sect. 3. These dataflow stages have data dependencies and execute sequentially on different processing components. However, multiple packets' DFGs can be executed in parallel on the system and completed out of order.

4.2 Architecture Model

The architecture model, as shown in Fig. 7, has processing components such as CPUs, accelerators, shared memory, and communication networks.

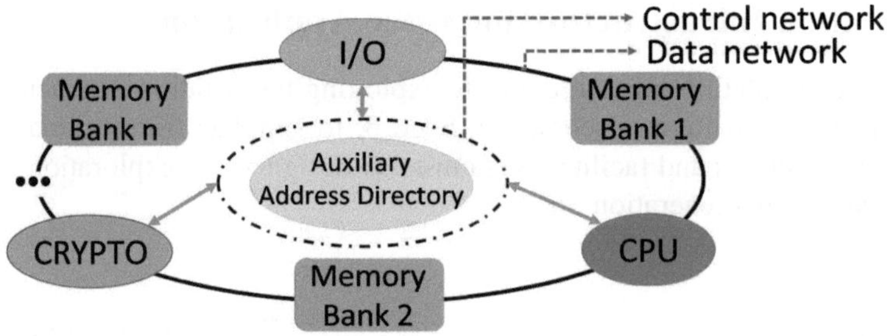

Fig. 7. Architecture Model with Computational and Memory Modules connected over a Bidirectional Ring Network.

1. *Computation Modules*: Each computation module, I/O accelerator, CPU, and Crypto accelerator, has an input packet queue and multiple resources for parallel packet processing. A custom packet generator injects packets into the system at a variable injection rate. The packet's five dataflow stages are scheduled sequentially on the respective modules.
2. *Shared Memory Model*: We model a multi-banked memory with one bank between each pair of computation modules. Each bank has an input queue, associated memory access latency, and queuing delay.
3. *Data Network*: The computation and memory modules are connected via a bidirectional ring network. The data transfer between a pair of computation and memory modules varies with the number of hops separating them.
4. *Control Network*: An Auxiliary Address Directory (AAD) is modeled to store the mapping between the memory addresses and banks for dynamic memory management. The control network provides uniform access to the AAD from all the computation modules. On query from a computation module, the AAD returns the mapping for an allocated memory node. An unallocated node is assigned to a bank using a memory management policy, which is then updated in AAD.

4.3 Comparison Against SoC Traces

As mentioned in Sect. 3.2, an increase in packet size from 86B to 390B increases execution time by 1.22x. We observe a similar trend for execution time in simulation with an error margin of up to 3%. We also reported that a 3x increase in injection rate increased the parallelism by 3.3x. We observe a similar trend in parallelism at multiple injection periods.

5 Application-Aware Memory Management for IPsec Workload

We evaluate the performance of traditional memory management policies using our simulation infrastructure on the architecture shown in Fig. 7. We leverage IPsec's deterministic memory access patterns to propose an application-specific memory management policy for performance optimization. Table 1 summarizes the policies explored for performance analysis and optimization.

Table 1. Design Space Exploration of Memory Management Policies for IPsec workload. STA: Static; DYN: Dynamic; UF: Uniform; NUF: Non-Uniform; GP: General-Purpose; AS: Application-Specific.

Policy Name	STA	DYN	UF	NUF	GP	AS
Fixed Map (FM)	✓		✓	✓	✓	
Round-Robin (RR)	✓		✓		✓	
Address Hash Map (AHM)	✓		✓		✓	
Link Latency-Aware (LLA)		✓		✓	✓	
Memory Queue-Aware (MQA)		✓		✓	✓	
Latency & Queue-Aware (LMQA)		✓		✓	✓	
APPAMM (proposed)		✓		✓		✓

5.1 Static GP Memory Management Policies

1. Fixed Map (FM): This policy maps all memory nodes from a computation module to a fixed memory bank.
2. Round-Robin (RR): This policy maps unallocated memory nodes to memory banks in a round-robin/circular manner independent of the source computation module.
3. Address Hash Map (AHM): This policy maps memory nodes to memory banks using an address hash function.

5.2 Proposed Dynamic GP Memory Management Policies

Figure 8 summarizes the proposed general-purpose dynamic memory management policies for IPsec workload.

1. Link Latency-Aware (LLA): This dynamic policy maps an unallocated memory node to the bank closest to the requester/source computation module.
2. Memory Queue-Aware (MQA): This dynamic policy maps an unallocated memory node to the bank with the smallest queue size (least contention), irrespective of the source computation module. Despite balancing inter-bank contention, this policy can lead to higher communication latency due to distant data placement, causing performance deterioration.
3. Latency and Memory Queue-Aware (LMQA): This dynamic policy maps an unallocated memory node to a bank based on its latency from the source computation module and queue size. Between the banks with equal latency from a computation module, the policy selects the bank with a smaller memory queue size for faster turn-around time.

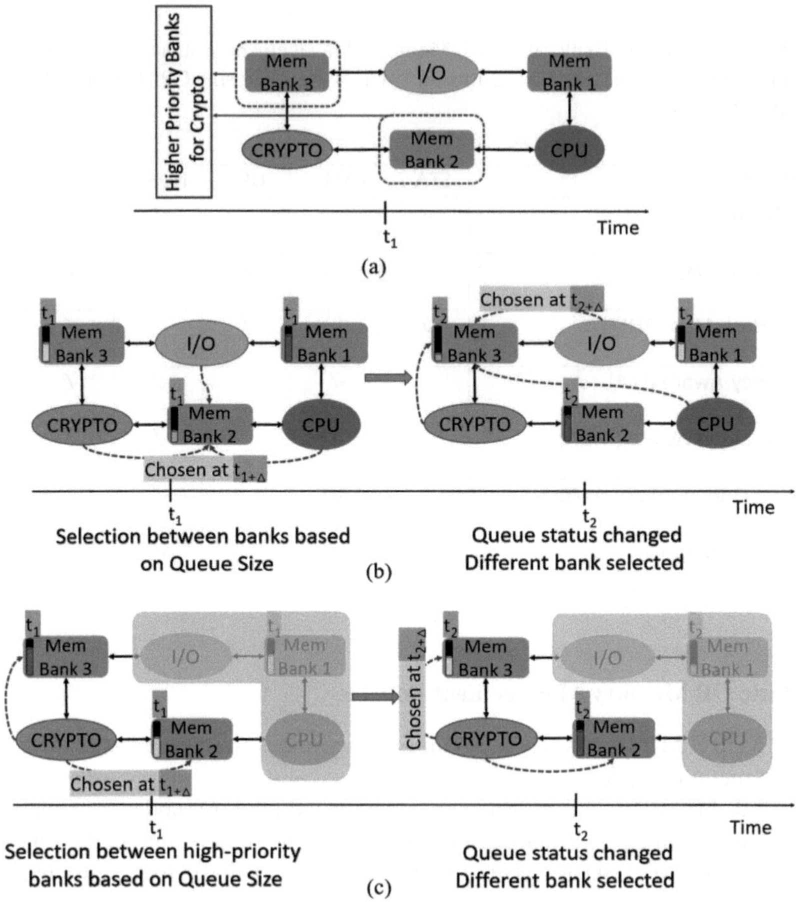

Fig. 8. Proposed Dynamic GP Memory Management Policies for IPsec. (a) LLA, (b) MQA, and (c) LMQA. Δ: Time taken to query the memory banks' queue sizes.

5.3 APPAMM: Application-Specific Predictive Packet-Aware Memory Management

We use the knowledge of the application's memory access patterns to propose APPAMM, an application-specific predictive packet-aware policy for memory management to improve performance. The knowledge of all dependent memory accesses across the packet's dataflow stages provides *packet awareness* to predict the impact on the future state of memory queues and the total packet execution time for efficient memory management.

Equation 1 shows the policy formulation for estimating the cost, in terms of total execution time, of choosing a memory bank k from a computation module i at time t. The equation has the following variables: CM = Number of Computation Modules; B = Number of Memory Banks; $\hat{Q}_{kt}$ = Estimated queue size of bank k at time t; Q_{kt} = Observed queue size of bank k at time t; MAT_{ik} = Total memory access time (memory + network) to access data for computation module i from the bank k; N_{ij} =

Number of dependent accesses between computation module i and computation module j for a packet; W = Window length for computing the average queue size; T = Total number of times the queue size has been sampled (every S cycles until time t); $\hat{\text{Cost}}_{ik}$ = Predicted cost of choosing bank k to place data from computation module i. At the source computation module i, the policy evaluates two main latency components:

1) *Total Memory Access Time (MAT)*, including queuing delay, witnessed by the packet if a memory node is placed in a particular bank. The first term of Eq. 1 shows that this is a function of this bank's access latency and future queue size prediction, as it will process all accesses to this node.
2) *Total network latency*, the second term of Eq. 1, is the time needed for accessing the chosen bank from all the computation modules according to the number of *dependent* memory accesses to this bank.

$$\hat{\text{Cost}}_{ik} = (\hat{\text{Q}}_{kt} \times \text{MAT}_{ik}) + \sum_{j=1}^{\text{CM}} \text{N}_{ij} \times \text{MAT}_{jk} \tag{1}$$

$$\forall i \in [1, 2, 3, ..., \text{CM}]\ \forall k \in [1, 2, 3, ..., \text{B}]$$

$$\hat{\text{Q}}_{kt} = \frac{1}{W} \sum_{y=T-W}^{T} \text{Q}_{k(y \times S)} \tag{2}$$

The chosen bank for the computation module i, Chosen $\text{Bank}_i = k \mid \hat{\text{Cost}}_{ik}$ is minimum over $k \in [1, 2, \ldots, \text{B}]$. Figure 9 shows the policy's bank allocation from the I/O module. We compute the cost of placing data from the I/O module into each memory bank and choose the bank with the minimum predicted cost (in this case, Bank 3).

Queue Size Prediction: We experimented with several strategies to predict the memory bank queue size, capturing the effect of all dependent accesses on the queue. Equation 2 proposes a history-based queue size prediction strategy that uses the average queue size in a window large enough to capture the queue state history. Our experiments show that using $W = 10$ and $S = 500$ cycles for the IPsec workload provides the best trade-off between performance achieved and implementation overhead. For $10 < W \leq 100$, the performance improves by up to 0.05% but with significant sampling and storage overhead. Our experiments show that $W = 1$, or Q_{kt}, differs in performance by up to 0.1% compared to the history-based queue size prediction ($W = 10$). Therefore, $\hat{\text{Q}}_{kt} = \text{Q}_{kt}$ is a good reactive estimate of the future queue state.

Implementation overhead: The policy runs whenever an unallocated memory node is encountered during the packet execution. APPAMM is implemented in each computation module with four 8-bit multipliers and three 10-bit adders for estimating the cost for one bank. Three 10-bit comparators compare the cost across banks to make the final decision. For Synopsys 40 nm technology, APPAMM shows an area overhead of 0.044 mm^2. Additionally, AAD incurs a storage overhead of at most 30 KB for all packet streams and sizes. With minimum implementation overhead, APPAMM can easily be integrated into SoC architectures.

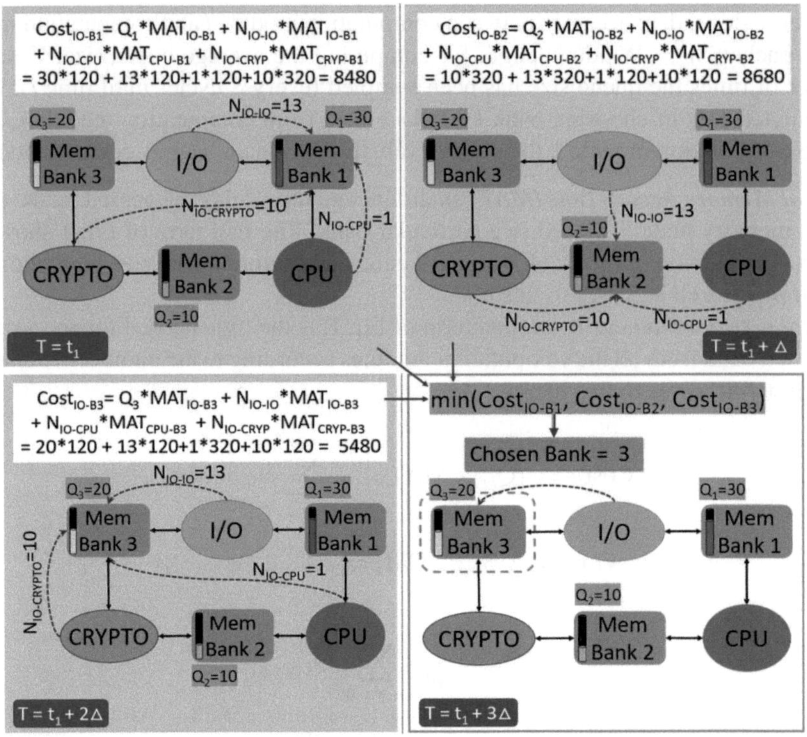

Fig. 9. APPAMM Memory Management Policy; In this example, $i, j \in$ [I/O, CPU, CRYPTO] and $k \in [1, 2, 3]$; $\hat{Q}_{kt} = Q_{kt}$; Memory Access Latency $= 20$ cycles; 1 hop network turn-around time $= 100$ cycles; Total MAT for 1 hop $= 120$ cycles.

6 Experiments and Results

6.1 Experimental Setup

We evaluate the performance of the policies using the simulation infrastructure discussed in Sect. 4 for the IPsec workload. The architecture has three computation modules (resources), namely I/O (20), CPU (16), and Crypto (40), connected to three shared memory banks by a bidirectional ring network. The packet generator can generate packets with different parameters discussed in Sect. 3. We model additional packets different from the collected traces by changing the memory access patterns to generalize the packets that can be received from a network. For completeness, we model *status* IPsec packets processed only in CPU, PKT14, and PKT15, which are not seen in the SoC traces. Table 2 summarizes the simulated packets based on their type and size.

Table 2. Summary of IPsec packets with their Memory Nodes (M_1, M_2, M_3, M_4, M_5) in each Dataflow Stage. Monochromatic entries represent address dependency within a packet. PKTn : Packets modeled accurately from traces.

Packet	Size	Type	IO1	CPU1	CRYPTO	CPU2	IO2
PKT1	390B	enc	7	1	(7, 2, 2, 3, 5)	1	(6, 2)
PKT2	390B	enc	7	1	2	1	(6, 2)
PKT3	466B	dec	8	3	(8, 2, 2, 3, 6)	(2, 4)	(1, 6)
PKT4	466B	dec	8	2	(8, 2, 1, 2, 6)	(2, 3)	(1, 6)
PKT5	390B	enc	7	5	(3, 1, 1, 2, 4)	(3, 1, 1, 4)	(2, 1, 1, 4)
PKT6	390B	enc	7	5	(4, 2, 2, 3, 6)	5	(2, 6)
PKT7	390B	enc	7	6	(1, 2, 1, 2, 6)	(4, 3)	(5, 3)
PKT8	390B	enc	7	1	(7, 2, 2, 3, 5)	1	(3, 5)
PKT9	466B	dec	8	1	(8, 2, 2, 3, 2)	1	(5, 2)
PKT10	86B	enc	2	1	(2, 2, 1, 2)	2	(1, 2)
PKT11	150B	enc	3	1	(3, 1, 7)	1	(2, 2)
PKT12	250B	enc	4	1	(2, 2, 6, 2)	1	(3, 2)
PKT13	162B	dec	3	1	(3, 2, 2)	1	2
PKT14	86B	status	2	1	-	1	2
PKT15	390B	status	7	1	-	1	7

We generate large packet streams with 10k–100k packets motivated by real use cases described below. The packet injection period varies around a fixed period ranging from 500–2500 cycles. We show in Sect. 6.2 that APPAMM's performance is insensitive to these values. We report the number of packets dropped at a given mean injection period. We choose one of the traditional GP policies as a baseline for comparison due to the lack of a proper baseline from prior works on IPsec. To evaluate the peak throughput, we consider a 1 GHz operating frequency.

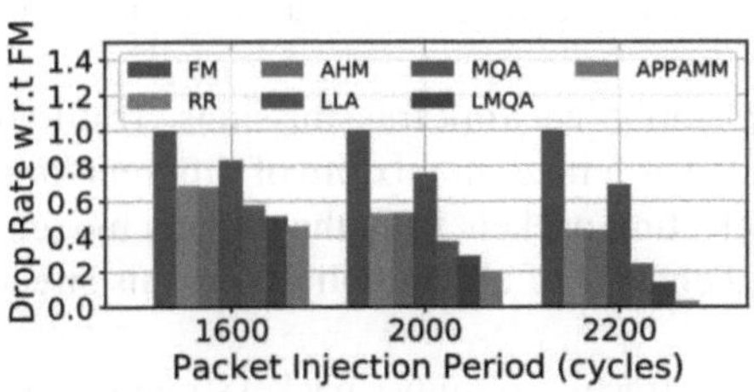

Fig. 10. Case 1: Relative Drop Rates for policies compared to FM.

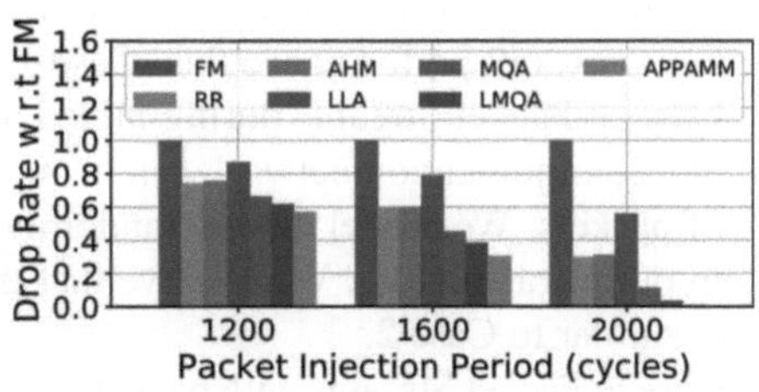

Fig. 11. Case 2-3: Relative drop rates for different policies compared to FM.

We summarise the performance of the policies in Table 3 for different packet streams. APPAMM performs consistently better than FM and the best-performing general-purpose policy, such as LMQA. Some observations are consistent for all types of packet streams discussed further in this section. The difference between the packet injection and packet completion rate increases at low injection periods, causing contention at the I/O module. Hence, the system performs poorly at low injection periods. APPAMM achieves better *resource utilization*, almost 90%, by efficiently exploiting parallelism across packets.

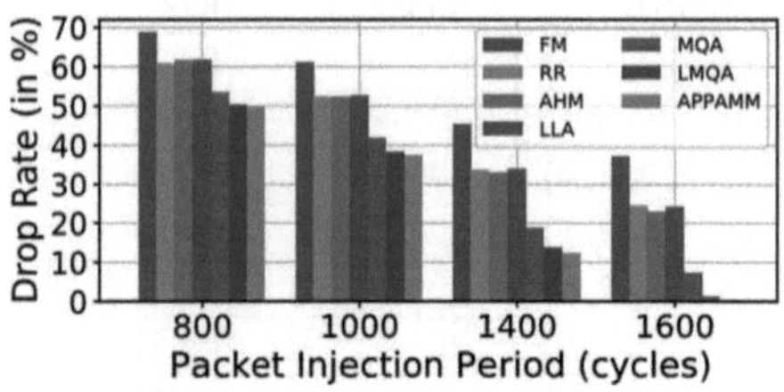

Fig. 12. Case 4: Drop rate (in % for n = 10000) achieved by various policies.

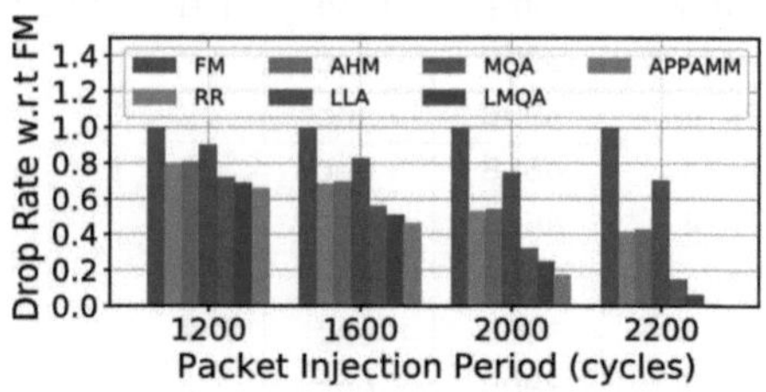

Fig. 13. Case 5: Relative drop rates for policies compared to FM.

1. Case 1: Packet Streams for Streaming Applications. Streaming network traffic usually consists of bursts of large packets mixed with status packets for regular handshaking. We randomly mix multiple large packets (PKTs 1–9) with one status packet (PKTs 14, 15). Figure 10 shows that at an injection period of 2200 cycles, APPAMM achieves a peak throughput of 1.4 Gbps with a 31x, 7.5x, and 4.3x improvement in drop rate compared to FM, MQA, and LMQA policy, respectively. At an injection period of 2000 cycles, APPAMM achieves a 5.8x improvement in drop rate over FM and up to 2x improvement over the GP policies.
2. Case 2: Packet Streams for Browsing Applications. Search engines generate network traffic with alternating bursts of large packets (PKTs 19) and small packets (PKTs 10–13). Figure 11 shows that at an injection period of 2000 cycles, APPAMM achieves no packet drops and shows a 57x and 7.2x reduction in drop rate compared to MQA and LMQA. This packet stream has smaller packets with fewer total and dependent memory accesses, which pose lower system contention, complete fast, achieving better overall performance than Case 1.
3. Case 3: Packet Streams during mixed application network transmissions. Traffic on any communication network can be modeled as a random mixture of different kinds of packets. We model this by randomly selecting packets from the packets modeled in our infrastructure. We observe that the behavior of all the policies on this stream is similar to Case 2.
4. Case 4: Packet Streams with packets from real traces. To study a packet stream similar to the one we generated our traces on, we create a packet mixture by randomly mixing the packets modeled accurately from the traces (PKTs 1, 9–13) to observe the performance of our policy. Figure 12 shows that at an injection period of 1600 cycles, APPAMM achieves a 73x and 12.6x reduction in packet drop rate compared to MQA and LMQA policy, respectively. We also observe that in this case, APPAMM achieves high performance at lower injection periods compared to other cases.

Table 3. Comparison between memory management policies for various packet mixes at different Injection Periods (IP). '-' in a cell signifies no packet drops with APPAMM at that injection period.

Pkt. Mix/IP	APPAMM vs FM				APPAMM vs LMQA				APPAMM vs MQA			
	2200	2000	1600	1200	2200	2000	1600	1200	2200	2000	1600	1200
Case1	31x	5.1x	2.1x	1.5x	4.3x	1.5x	1.1x	1.1x	7.5x	1.9x	1.3x	1.1x
Case 2 & 3	-	-	3.5x	1.8x	-	7.2x	1.3x	1.1x	-	57x	1.5x	1.2x
Case 4	-	-	-	3.7x	-	-	12.6x	1.2x	-	-	73x	1.5x
Case 5	-	5.8x	2.2x	1.5x	23x	1.5x	1.1x	1.1x	60x	1.9x	1.2x	1.1x

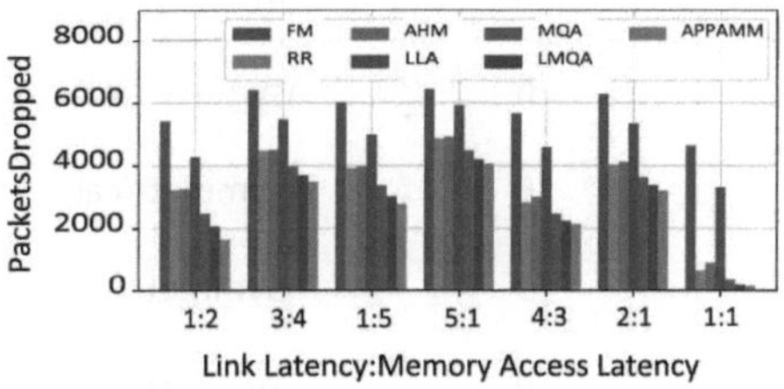

Fig. 14. Packets dropped out of 10000 packets with variable latency ratios.

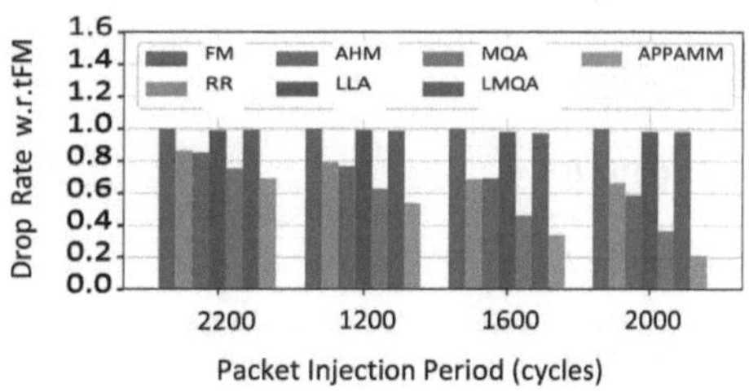

Fig. 15. Relative drop rates with unequal hops between CM and banks.

5. Case 5: Packet Streams during End-to-End Secured Communications. Most data-sharing and user communication applications provide end-to-end secured communication for data security and privacy. Network traffic on such a channel consists of bursts of encryption and decryption packets (PKTs 1–13). Figure 13 shows that at an injection period of 2200 cycles, APPAMM achieves 60x and 23x reduction in drop rate compared to MQA and LMQA policy, respectively. At an injection period of 2000 cycles, APPAMM achieves a 5.8x improvement in packet drop rate over the FM policy and up to 2x improvement over the GP policies, achieving a peak throughput of 1.1 Gbps.

6.2 Generalization to Other Architectural Configurations

Varying Memory Access and Network Delay Ratio. Our experiments assume constant network and memory model delays. Figure 14 shows the performance of different policies on a random packet stream by varying the hop link and memory access latency ratio. The ratio used in all the previous experiments is 5:1 (100:20 cycles). APPAMM performs consistently better than the GP policies for all delay ratios and is therefore insensitive to the absolute delays modeled.

Table 4. Architecture configurations used to test the generalization and performance of the proposed policies. Symmetrical placement: Equal number of memory banks between all compute nodes. Asymmetrical placement: Unequal number of memory banks between all compute nodes.

Architecture Config	Bidirectional Ring	Unidirectional Ring	No. of Memory banks	Banks Placement
Config 1	✓		3	Symmetrical
Config 2		✓	3	Symmetrical
Config 3	✓		6	Symmetrical
Config 4		✓	6	Symmetrical
Config 5	✓		6	Asymmetrical
Config 6		✓	6	Asymmetrical
Config 7	✓		9	Symmetrical
Config 8		✓	9	Symmetrical
Config 9	✓		9	Asymmetrical
Config 10		✓	9	Asymmetrical

Varying Network Latencies between Compute Nodes. Our experiments assume a constant network latency of 1 hop between compute units and memory banks. We modify the number of hops between the compute units and the memory banks so that each compute unit has a different latency to all neighbor banks. The modified latencies are as follows: *IO* - *Bank 1*: 1 hop; *Bank 1* - *CPU*: 1 hop, *CPU* - *Bank 2*: 2 hops; *Bank 2* - *Crypto*: 2 hops; *Crypto* - *Bank 3*: 1 hop; *Bank 3* - *IO*: 2 hops. Figure 15 shows that APPAMM achieves up to 5x and 2x improvement in drop over FM and MQA, respectively, for a random packet stream on this architecture. APPAMM, MQA, RR, and AHM perform better than LLA and LMQA because they can distribute accesses to distant banks and efficiently exploit system-level parallelism.

Varying Number of Memory Banks and Network Type. We evaluate the performance of APPAMM on multiple architecture configurations by varying the network type and the number of banks between the compute nodes. We vary the number (3, 6, 9 banks) and placement (symmetrical/equal or asymmetrical/unequal) of banks between the compute nodes and the network type (bidirectional or unidirectional ring). Table 4 summarizes all these ten different architectural configurations from Config 1 to Config 10. Figure 16 and 17 show the relative performance of different placement policies compared to the Fixed Map policy on a random packet stream simulated on architectures with different number of memory banks connected to the compute nodes by a bidirectional ring network and a unidirectional ring network, respectively. Table 5 summarizes the improvement in performance achieved by APPAMM over FM, LMQA, and MQA policy at various packet injection periods on different architectural configurations.

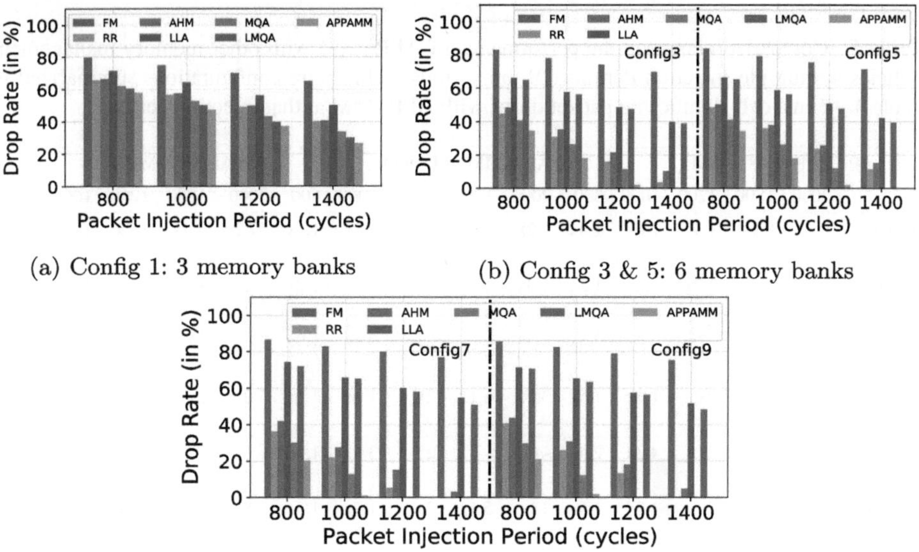

(a) Config 1: 3 memory banks

(b) Config 3 & 5: 6 memory banks

(c) Config 7 & 9: 9 memory banks

Fig. 16. Packet drop rate (in % for N = 10000) for all policies on a random packet stream at different injection periods on architectures with different numbers of memory banks; Network: Bidirectional Ring Network.

- Configurations with Bidirectional Ring Network:
  1. *Three Memory Banks (Config 1)*: This architectural configuration is used in our experimental evaluation, discussed in Sect. 6.1. Figure 16(a) and Table 5 show that on this architecture, APPAMM achieves up to 57x and up to 7.2x reduction in packet drop rate compared to the MQA policy and the LMQA policy, respectively. APPAMM performs 10%-70% better than LMQA at lower injection periods because the bottleneck is resource contention at the IO compute node rather than memory contention.
  2. *Six Memory Banks (Config 3 and Config 5)*: Figure 16(b) and Table 5 show that at 1200 cycles, APPAMM achieves 23.5x and 25x reduction in drop rate compared to LMQA, 5.86x and 6.1x reduction compared to MQA policy with symmetrical and asymmetrical bank placement respectively. LMQA cannot utilize all the memory banks efficiently and, therefore, performs poorly. APPAMM efficiently exploits a higher degree of parallelism with more memory banks and performs better than MQA (best-performing GP policy).
  3. *Nine Memory Banks (Config 7 and Config 9)*: Figure 16(c) and Table 5 show that APPAMM achieves 35x and 61x reduction in drop rate compared to LMQA, 7x and 12x reduction compared to MQA policy with symmetrical and asymmetrical

bank placement, respectively. APPAMM achieves up to 50% benefit over other policies at a low injection period of 800 cycles, which is significantly better than Config 1, 3, and 5.

Table 5. Comparison between the performance of APPAMM with other memory management policies at multiple Injection Periods (IP) on various architecture configurations summarized in Table 4. '-' in a cell signifies no packet drops with APPAMM at that injection period.

Arch./IP	APPAMM vs FM					APPAMM vs LMQA					APPAMM vs MQA				
	2000	1800	1200	1000	800	2000	1800	1200	1000	800	2000	1800	1200	1000	800
Config 1	-	8.9x	1.9x	1.6x	1.4x	7.2x	1.7x	1.1x	1.1x	1.1x	57.2x	2.4x	1.2x	1.2x	1.1x
Config 2	1.8x	1.7x	1.3x	1.2x	1.2x	1.9x	1.7x	1.3x	1.2x	1.2x	1.2x	1.2x	1.1x	1.1x	1.1x
Config 3	-	-	37x	4.4x	2.5x	-	-	23x	3.1x	1.9x	-	-	5.9x	1.5x	1.2x
Config 4	30x	6.1x	2x	1.6x	1.5x	30x	6.1x	2x	1.6x	1.5x	6.2x	2x	1.3x	1.2x	1.1x
Config 5	-	-	39x	4.3x	2.4x	-	-	25x	3.1x	1.9x	-	-	6.1x	1.9x	1.2x
Config 6	18x	5.6x	2x	1.7x	1.5x	18x	5.6x	2x	1.7x	1.5x	3.8x	1.7x	1.2x	1.1x	1.1x
Config 7	-	-	-	45x	4.1x	-	-	-	35x	3.4x	-	-	-	7x	1.5x
Config 8	-	32x	2.6x	2x	1.7x	-	32x	2.6x	2x	1.7x	10x	3.7x	1.3x	1.2x	1.1x
Config 9	-	-	-	77x	4.3x	-	-	-	61x	3.6x	-	-	-	12x	1.6x
Config 10	-	22x	2.6x	2x	1.7x	-	22x	2.6x	2x	1.7x	4.8x	2.6x	1.3x	1.2x	1.1x

APPAMM performs increasingly better than all the GP policies on architectures with more memory banks. We observe that APPAMM performs better with a bidirectional ring network and asymmetrical placement of memory banks compared to symmetrical placement. Hence, we conclude that APPAMM uses parallelism in the architecture and the application more efficiently. As the number of memory banks increases, the throughput achieved by APPAMM for the IPsec application increases.

– Configurations with Unidirectional Ring Network:

The performance of GP policies like LLA and LMQA is similar to FM policy on architectures with unidirectional ring networks since all the memory banks are at unequal distances from the compute nodes. Hence, only one memory bank is the minimum latency contender for each compute node. MQA is the best-performing GP policy for architectures with this network.

1. *Three Memory Banks (Config 2)*: Figure 17(a) and Table 5 shows that on this architecture, APPAMM achieves up to 2x reduction in packet drop rate compared to the FM policy and 1.2x reduction in packet drop rate compared to the MQA policy.

2. *Six Memory Banks (Config 4 and Config 6)*: Figure 17(b) shows that at an injection period of 2000 cycles, APPAMM achieves a 30x reduction in drop rate compared to the FM, and LMQA policy. It achieves a 6x and 3.8x reduction compared to MQA policy with the symmetrical and asymmetrical placement of memory banks, respectively. APPAMM performs consistently better than other policies at lower injection periods.
3. *Nine Memory Banks (Config 8 and Config 10)*: Figure 17(c) shows that at an injection period of 1600 cycles, APPAMM achieves up to 3.7x and 2.6x reduction in drop rate compared to MQA policy with symmetrical and asymmetrical memory bank placement, respectively. It performs an order of magnitude better than the FM and LMQA policy, as shown in Table 5.

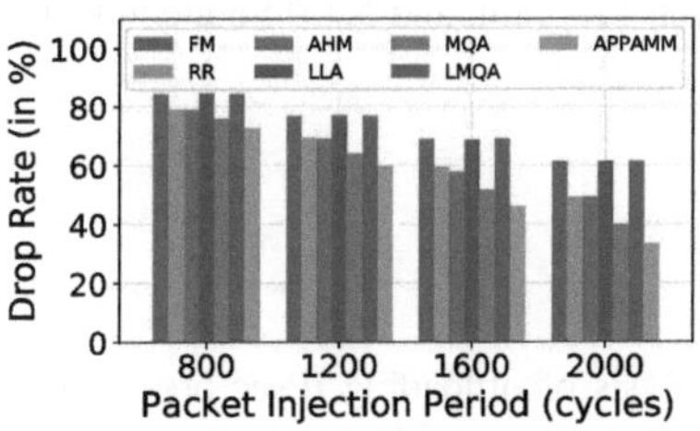

(a) Config 2: 3 memory banks

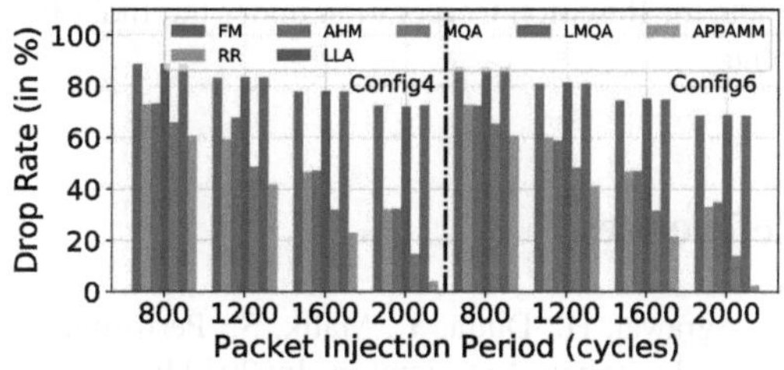

(b) Config 4 & 6: 6 memory banks

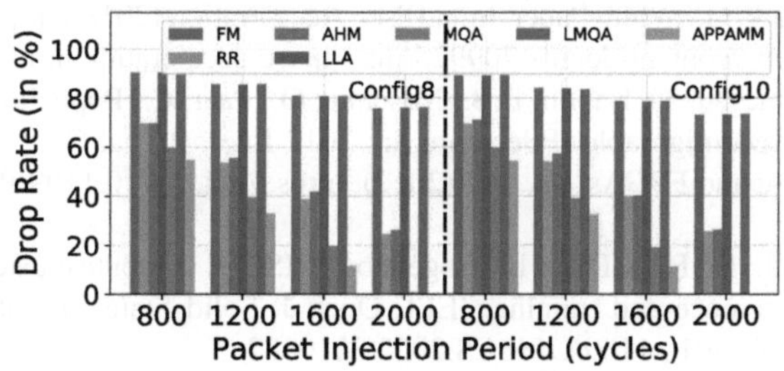

(c) Config 8 & 10: 9 memory banks

Fig. 17. Packet drop rate (in % for N = 10000) for all policies on a random packet stream at different injection periods on architectures with different numbers of memory banks; Network: Unidirectional Ring Network.

APPAMM performs consistently better than other GP policies on architectures with more memory banks. On architectures with a unidirectional ring network, symmetrical placement of banks performs better than asymmetrical placement. However, the performance of all the memory management policies on these architectures is lower as compared to the bidirectional network architectures.

These experiments show that general-purpose policies do not adapt well to different architectures. APPAMM, on the other hand, performs consistently better on different architectures with different number of memory banks and networks. It efficiently manages memory to enable a higher degree of parallelism in the system, thereby improving application throughput.

7 Conclusions

We characterized the IPsec application by collecting and analyzing the memory access pattern on a commercial SoC platform. We developed a simulation infrastructure based on these characteristics and explored the design space on heterogeneous architectures. The application has deterministic and regular memory access patterns. These helped formulate an application-specific predictive packet-aware policy that significantly improves the performance achieved on next-generation architectures. Such policies can be further enhanced by adding packet-level priorities for efficient arbitration to achieve the required QoS while maintaining high throughput.

Acknowledgments. This work was supported by research grant 2017-SD-2738 from Semiconductor Research Corporation under the India Research Program, and NXP Semiconductors, India.

References

1. Agrawal, H., Dutta, Y., Malik, S.: Performance analysis of offloading IPsec processing to hardware based accelerators. In: 2012 International Symposium on Electronic System Design (ISED), pp. 291–294 (2012). https://doi.org/10.1109/ISED.2012.53
2. Doyle, S., Tkachuk, G.: White Paper, Intel IPsec Acceleration (2018). https://www.intel.com/content/www/us/en/content-details/709925/intel-ipsec-acceleration.html?wapkw=IPSEC
3. Driessen, B., Güneysu, T., Kavun, E.B., Mischke, O., Paar, C., Pöppelmann, T.: IPSecco: a lightweight and reconfigurable IPSec core. In: 2012 International Conference on Reconfigurable Computing and FPGAs, pp. 1–7 (2012). https://doi.org/10.1109/ReConFig.2012.6416757
4. Garofalo, A., et al.: DARKSIDE: a heterogeneous RISC-V compute cluster for extreme-edge on-chip DNN inference and training. IEEE Open J. Solid State Circuits Soc. **2**, 231–243 (2022). https://doi.org/10.1109/OJSSCS.2022.3210082
5. Guilford, J., Gulley, S., Ozturk, E., Yap, K., Gopal, V., Feghali, W.: White Paper | Fast Multi-buffer IPsec Implementations on Intel Architecture Processors (2012). https://www.intel.com/content/dam/www/public/us/en/documents/white-papers/fast-multi-buffer-ipsec-implementations-ia-processors-paper.pdf
6. Ha, C.S., Lee, J.H., Leem, D.S., Park, M.S., Choi, B.Y.: ASIC design of IPSec hardware accelerator for network security. In: Proceedings of 2004 IEEE AsiaPacific Conference on Advanced System Integrated Circuits, pp. 168–171 (2004). https://doi.org/10.1109/APASIC.2004.1349439
7. Harkins, D., Carrel, D.: RFC2409: The Internet key exchange (IKE) (1998)
8. Holtryd, N.R., Manivannan, M., Stenström, P., Pericàs, M.: CBP: coordinated management of cache partitioning, bandwidth partitioning and prefetch throttling. In: 2021 30th International Conference on Parallel Architectures and Compilation Techniques (PACT), pp. 213–225 (2021). https://doi.org/10.1109/PACT52795.2021.00023
9. Kent, S., Atkinson, R.: RFC2402: IP Authentication Header (1998). IETFRFC, 1998. http://www.ietf.org/rfc.html
10. Liu, Z., Li, G., Cheng, J.: Hardware acceleration of fully quantized BERT for efficient natural language processing (2021). https://arxiv.org/abs/2103.02800

11. Nam, T.S., Thuc, H.V., Long, N.V.: A high-throughput hardware implementation of NAT traversal for IPSEC VPN. Int. J. Commun. Netw. Inf. Secur. (IJCNIS) **14**(1) (2022). https://doi.org/10.17762/ijcnis.v14i1.5260. https://ijcnis.org/index.php/ijcnis/article/view/5260
12. Niu, Y., Wu, L., Zhang, X.: An IPSec accelerator design for a 10 Gbps in-line security network processor. J. Comput. **8** (2013). https://doi.org/10.4304/jcp.8.2.319-325
13. NXP Semiconductors: Layerscape LX2160A Processors (2019)
14. [Online] Rockhopper: IPsec/IKEv2-based VPN software for Linux (2012). https://rockhoppervpn.sourceforge.net/
15. [Online] Strongswan: Open-source, modular and portable IPsec-based VPN solution (2005). https://www.strongswan.org/
16. Thoguluva, J., Raghunathan, A., Chakradhar, S.T.: Efficient software architecture for IPSec acceleration using a programmable security processor. In: 2008 Design, Automation and Test in Europe, pp. 1148–1153 (2008). https://doi.org/10.1109/DATE.2008.4484833
17. Tiwari, S., Tuli, S., Ahmad, I., Agarwal, A., Panda, P.R., Subramoney, S.: REAL: REquest arbitration in last level caches. ACM Trans. Embed. Comput. Syst. **18**(6) (2019). https://doi.org/10.1145/3362100

Scalable Design Techniques for Expanding Ferroelectric-Based Non-volatile SRAMs Applications

Lucas Rhetat[1(✉)], Jean-Philippe Noel[1], Bastien Giraud[1], Laurent Grenouillet[1], Julie Laguerre[1], Cédric Marchand[2], and Ian O'Connor[2]

[1] CEA LIST, Univ. Grenoble Alpes, Grenoble, France
lucas.rhetat@cea.fr
[2] INL, CNRS, Ecole Centrale de Lyon, Univ. Lyon, Écully, France

Abstract. Static Random Access Memories (SRAM) are fast and efficient circuits used as the main working memory of processing units. However, associating these volatile memories with external non-volatile memories leads to energy consumption and area penalties, while leading to security issues. Ferroelectric-based NVSRAMs are one of the most promising ways of combining the high efficiency of SRAMs with nonvolatile operations to tackle these challenges. In this work, several design parameters of the bitcell are optimized to ensure error-less data transfer between 6T SRAM internal nodes and ferroelectric capacitors (4C). We present a first detailed study in 130 nm bulk technology then we explore the scalability of this design in a thinner 22 nm FDSOI technology. These NVSRAM circuits presents STORE and RECALL energies ranging from 3fJ/bit to 200fJ/bit. A high reliability is achieved on both technology nodes from −40 °C to +85 °C for SS, TT and FF fabrication corners. We quantify the area overhead as well as the time and energy increases in SRAM operations resulting from the integration of FeCAPs into the bitcell. A previously developed Fast-Erase design technique has also been integrated for countering cold-boot attacks and improving the RECALL operation. Combining design optimizations and Fast-Erase technique enables error-less RECALL while permitting WRITE operations into SRAM part between STORE and RECALL, leading to new applications for NVSRAM circuits.

Keywords: Non-Volatile SRAM · reliable & secure data · ferroelectric capacitor

1 Introduction

SRAM are the fastest and most energy-efficient commercial memories. However, they are volatile, which means that data disappear quickly from SRAM after power-off. The simplest solution to avoid volatility could be to use a BatteryBacked SRAM (BBSRAM), i.e. maintaining the SRAM supplied permanently using an embedded battery [21]. However, this solution has the major disadvantage of requiring a bulky battery, with limited

Published by Springer Nature Switzerland AG 2026
E. -I. Vatajelu (Ed.): VLSI-SoC 2024, IFIP AICT 744, pp. 72–90, 2026.
https://doi.org/10.1007/978-3-032-09575-6_5

energy capacity and lifespan. Carrying a battery in the system may also limit its deployment due to the environmentally hazardous substances it contains. If the battery solution is excluded, data can be transferred to an off-chip non-volatile (NV) memory (often EEPROM or Flash memory) before power-off, which is both time-consuming and energy-intensive. Moreover, this can provide an attack window, for example, by probing the bus connections between the two memories. Non-Volatile SRAMs (NVSRAM) overcome theses problems by finely co-integrating non-volatile storage elements into SRAM bitcell. In this work, NV Ferroelectric CAPacitors (FeCAPs) components presenting a promising combination of write speed and energy as well as endurance among others NV memories are used. More precisely, we focus on $HfZrO_2$ (HZO) ferrelectrics that can be highly scaled to be integrated on recent CMOS technology nodes, contrary to PZT ferroelectrics, which have limited scalability below the 130 nm node. The resulting circuit can then perform four different operations: reading from SRAM (op. READ), writing to SRAM (op. WRITE), copying data from SRAM to FeCAPs (op. STORE) and moving data from FeCAPs to SRAM (op. RECALL) [16]. Using these four operations permits to obtain a fast, efficient and non-volatile memory. NVSRAMs have gained interest [10, 18, 22] and are especially good candidates for intermittent applications with either (i) unreliable power supplies (e.g. energy harvesting applications) or (ii) strict energy quota where it could be appropriate to power-off parts of the system avoiding stand-by current consumption (particularly relevant in advanced fabrication processes where the I_{on}/I_{off} currents ratio is reduced). These memories are also suitable for secure critical systems that need to quickly restart after a power supply interruption. NVSRAMs can in particular be integrated in Non-Volatile Processors (NVPs) [11].

On the security side, storing sensitive data in FeCAPs appears to be safer than in Flash [4]. For example, it has been shown that a method based on Scanning Electron Microscopy (SEM) in Passive-Voltage-Contrast mode permits to quickly retrieve the whole content of floating-gate based memories [2]. Retrieving data in HZO ferrelectric memories is much more challenging and implies the use of Scanning-Probe Microscopy (SPM) techniques that are far slower and more expensive [20]. In general, ferroelectric memories are expected to be one of the least sensitive to attacks among emerging non-volatile memories [7].

Still in a security point of view, SRAM memories are prone to cold-boot attacks, enabling attackers to recover data previously stored in the memory just after it has been shut down [1]. To counter this, a fast erasing technique has recently been developed [17]. This system enables data to be erased very quickly (in the nanosecond time scale, reduction of more than 1000x) when a tampering event is detected, at the cost of an additional area of less than 5%.

In terms of reliability, the RECALL operation is sensitive to mismatches between the cross-coupled inverter transistors and that seems to be a main factor limiting the development of these circuits. In [13, 23] the robustness of 6T2C and 6T4C bitcells against threshold voltage mismatches have already been studied, showing that a better RECALL reliability is achieved with 6T4C bitcells with an optimal FeCAPs sizing ratio. However, theses experiments only concerned the case where no WRITE operation was performed between STORE and RECALL.

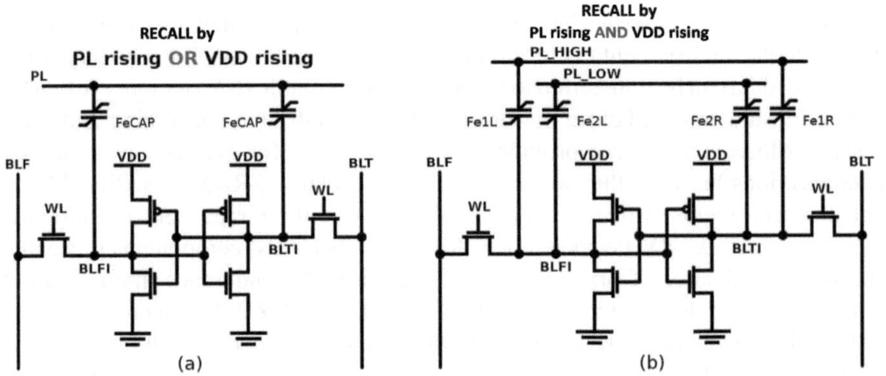

Fig. 1. (a) Conventional 6T2C bitcell implementing one of the two RECALL methods from Fig. 2, (b) 6T4C bitcell with separated Plate-Lines (PL), combining both RECALL methods.

In this paper, we demonstrate that combining these previous results with the Fast-Erase technique permits a reliable NVSRAM circuit with WRITE operations between STORE and RECALL, leading to new applications of these circuits (see Subsect. 6).

The remainder of the paper is organized as follow: Sect. 2 describes the proposed FeCAP-based NVSRAM architecture and its implementation. Section 3 presents our simulation setup and the FeCAP model, in the 130 nm node. Section 4 presents the simulation results in 130 nm node. Section 5 describes a projection of the results in 22 nm FDSOI technology node. Section 6 opens a discussion about the potential applications of the proposed NVSRAM and Sect. 7 summarizes the paper.

2 Proposed 6T4C NVSRAM Architecture

2.1 6T2C vs 6T4C NVSRAM Bitcells

Figure 1(a) shows the conventional NVSRAM 6T2C bitcell. It is composed of a 6T SRAM bitcell in which 2 FeCAPs have been added, one on each internal node BLTI/BLFI, both connected to a common Plate-Line (PL). By correctly driving PL, the data can be copied from the SRAM internal nodes to the FeCAPs (STORE op.) or transferred from the FeCAPs to the SRAM internal nodes (RECALL op., destructive for the FeCAPs data).

Figure 2 shows that data transfer from FeCAPs to SRAM bitcells (RECALL operation) can be achieved in several ways. Firstly, V_{DD} can be set from ground to its nominal value (Fig. 2(a)) [8]. However, this method is sensitive to the transistor mismatch. To improve the robustness of the RECALL operation, a second method involves first applying a pulse to the PL, which inverts one of the two FeCAPs. This will inject a different amount of charge into the SRAM internal nodes, thereby creating a potential difference on these nodes before raising V_{DD} to the nominal value (Fig. 2(b)). Both techniques can be used with 6T2C bitcells. However, these two RECALL methods can be advantageously combined by using 6T4C bitcells (Fig. 1(b)) and separated PLs, PL_{HIGH} (rising at RECALL) and PL_{LOW} (staying at 0 V at RECALL). Indeed, by correctly adjusting the

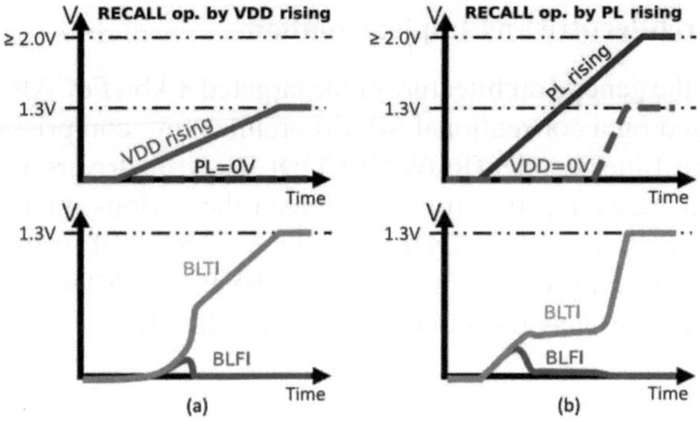

Fig. 2. Simulated waveforms of the two existing RECALL methods: (a) by only pulling up V_{DD} or (b) by applying a pulse on PL before.

sizes of the FeCAPs connected to PL_{HIGH} and PL_{LOW}, it is possible to reach an optimal configuration [23].

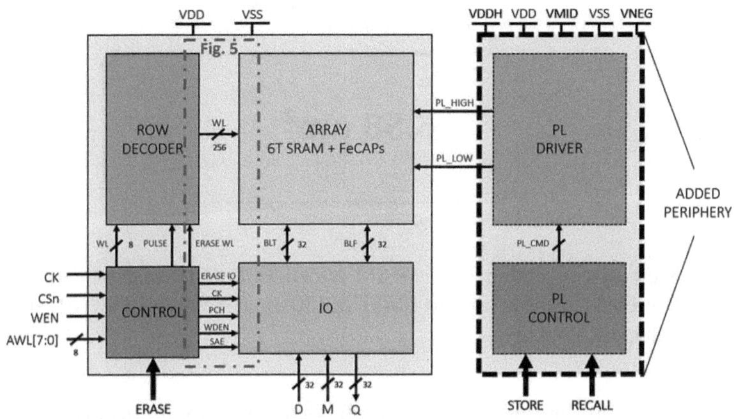

Fig. 3. Internal architecture of the proposed 8kbit FeCAP-based 6T4C NVSRAM.

2.2 Fast-Erase Technique

When switched off, SRAM bitcell retains its data for some time due to the leakage current path (pull-up PMOS) from the internal nodes, up to several minutes if the circuit is cooled, leading to two issues. First, a security issue: it is possible to read the remanent data in SRAM by quickly restoring power to the circuit after shutdown (e.g. cold-boot attack [1]). Secondly, this makes difficult to quickly RECALL the data stored in FeCAPs in case their data are different from the last written data in SRAM. Indeed, remanent charges in BLTI and BLFI corresponding to the previous data makes an additional bias to counter for a correct sensing of the FeCAPs from the SRAM bitcell. For these reasons, a previously-developed Fast-Erase technique is implemented into our circuitry [17].

2.3 Memory Architecture and Implementation

Figure 3 presents the general architecture of the targeted 8-kbit FeCAP-based NVSRAM. The circuit is based on a conventional SRAM architecture, comprising a bitcell matrix (ARRAY), a Word-Line decoder (ROW DECODER), write drivers and sense amplifiers (IO) and a circuit managing the timings between the various internal control signals (CONTROL). IO and ROW DECODER blocks are modified to implement the Fast-Erase circuitry, according to [17] (see Fig. 5). The PL CONTROL and PL DRIVER blocks are also added to generate control signals for the PLs.

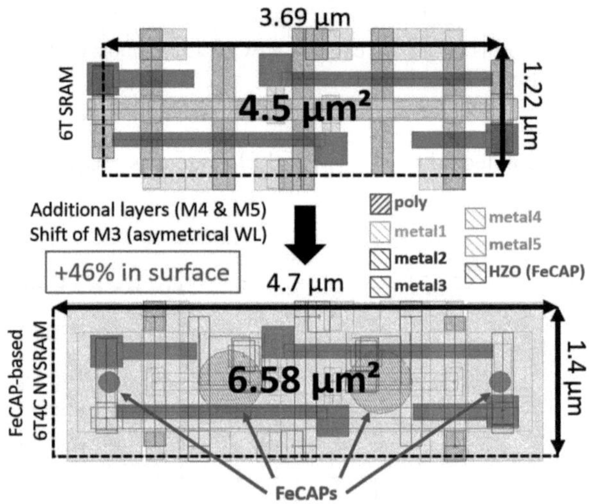

Fig. 4. Layout view of conventional 6T SRAM bitcell vs FeCAP-based 6T4C SRAM bitcell (including the additional back-end level M4/M5), in 130 nm node. The 4 FeCAPs are represented by the red round shapes.

Figure 4 shows the layout view of the physical implementation of the FeCAPs in the SRAM bitcell. Integrating them in the BEOL level permits to limit the bitcell area overhead. The presented 6T4C bitcell area is roughly increased by 46% with respect to initial 6T SRAM bitcell. FeCAPs are integrated between M4 and M5 levels and the Word-Line is off-center to free enough space to add the M1–M4 vias in the upper part. The Plate-Lines are placed vertically at the M5 level. The layers below M2 have not been modified. A second version of this layout could be designed to reduce the surface overhead, e.g. by relaxing the BEOL rules or using 3D FeCAPs.

3 Testbench and Simulation Setup

3.1 Testbench

The circuit is designed using ST 130 nm HCMOS9A design plateform (GF 22 nm FDSOI for the part 5) and SPICE simulations are carried out with Synopsys XA. The results being quite sensitive to the precision of the simulations, these were carried out with high precision settings. The following error-related results were obtained from Monte-Carlo simulations in different foundry process corners.

Figure 5 presents the simulated circuit and its peripheral circuitry. To keep simulation times acceptable at high precision, the choice was made to restrict the simulation to a 32-bit column only. Our simulated circuit also contains a precharge circuit (PCH), a Write Driver (WD) and a Sense-Amplifier (SA). The Fast-Erase circuit is shown in blue and consists in shorting the two Bit-Lines (BL) of each column while activating all the Word-Lines (WL) and powering-off the write drivers. In our simulation, the ERASE op. is carried out by directly activating the Word-Lines and the ERASE_IO signal, with $V_{DD} = 0$ V.

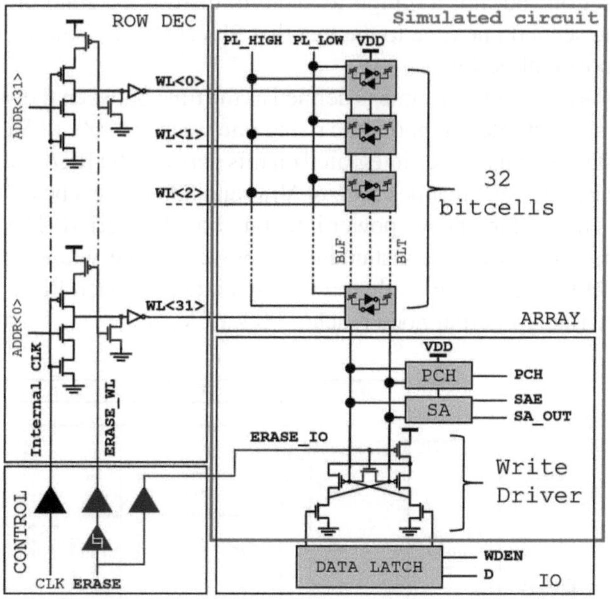

Fig. 5. Schematic view of the simulated circuit and its periphery, including the FastErase circuit [17].

Figure 6 shows the overall timing diagram of RECALL and STORE ops. between SRAM READ and WRITE ops. PL_{HIGH} and PL_{LOW} behave the same during the STORE, READ and WRITE operations but differ during the RECALL (see [13, 23]). The PLs are kept at $V_{MID} = V_{DD}/2$ during normal SRAM operations in order to limit the amplitude of voltage variations across each FeCAP, thereby limiting their aging. The main contribution of the proposed circuit regarding the prior art is the blue part of the diagram: SRAM operations after STORE and the addition of the ERASE signal that equalizes the bitcell internal nodes (see Fig. 8 for details). The goals of this Fast-Erase circuit are (i) countering cold-boot attacks and (ii) ensuring correct RECALL ops. even with READ and WRITE ops. after the last STORE. At the next RECALL, the last data stored in the FeCAPs (which is not necessarily the last written in SRAM; this correspond to a worst case) is going to be transferred to the SRAM. In the RECALL operation, PL and V_{DD} rising edges are shifted by 195 ns and their rising times are 30 ns and 50 ns, respectively. The RECALL is then achieved in 245 ns in our simulations, time mainly defined by the delay between the PL_{HIGH} and V_{DD} rising edges. This delay must be neither too short, to take into account a reasonable FeCAP response time, nor too long, to minimize charge leakage from the SRAM internal nodes (leading to the vanishing of the potential difference |BLTI − BLFI|) before the V_{DD} rising edge. The STORE op. is carried out in a comfortable time of 480 ns but this cold probably be reduced.

The nominal supply voltage of the HCMOS9A technology is 1.2 V but we choose to over-supply (+10%) this circuit at $V_{DD} = 1.3$ V to obtain a sufficient FeCAP programming voltage of $2V_{DD} = 2.6$ V. The PLs vary between $V_{NEG} = -1.3$ V and $V_{DDH} = 2.6$ V. These voltages are chosen to be sufficiently high to ensure maximal inversion of the FeCAPs polarizations but not too high to avoid to disturb the state of the first FeCAP while writing the second one (due to the fact that PLs are each common to two FeCAPs polarized in opposite directions).

In the following, the WRITE time is defined as the time between the WL reaches 50% of V_{DD} and the slowest internal node (the rising one) reaches 90% of V_{DD}. The WRITE energy is the instantaneous power integrated on this period. The READ time is measured as the time between the WL reaches 50% of V_{DD} and SA_{OUT} reaches 90% of V_{DD}. The READ energy is the instantaneous power integrated on this period. The STORE energy is defined as the integral of the instantaneous power on the whole operation pattern period and the RECALL energy is the power integrated between PL_{HIGH} reaches 10% of V_{DDH} and the rising internal node reaches 90% of V_{DD}.

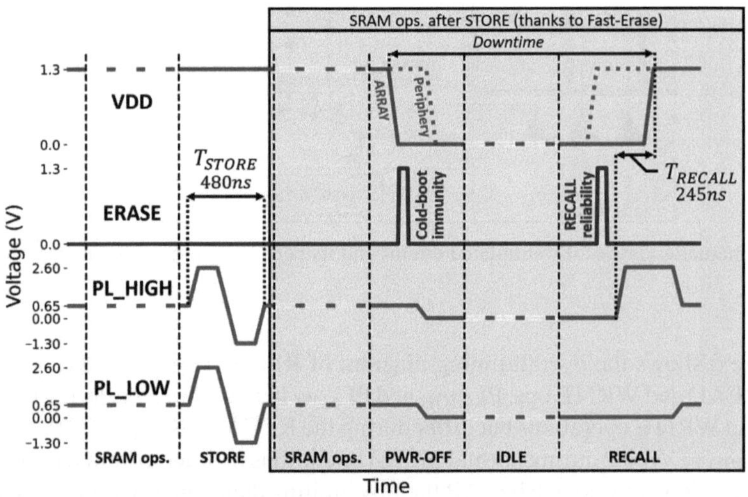

Fig. 6. Chronogram of NVSRAM operations.

3.2 FeCAP Model

For the FeCAPs simulation, a Preisach-based VerilogA model is used [14, 15]. This model simulates both the ferroelectric part of polarization and the paraelectric part. It also takes into account the capacitive effect between the two electrodes and the leakage current.

Figure 7 presents the FeCAPs considered in this circuit and their main characteristics: the saturation polarization (P_{sat}), the remanent polarization (P_r) and the coercive voltage (V_c). To ensure that our model matched the real components, a model calibration phase was carried out. This involved adjusting the model's hysteresis cycle in relation to that measured on real components representative of the technology (average P-V curve on 10nm thick HZO BEOLintegrated scaled FeCAPs) (Fig. 7) [3, 5].

4 Simulation Results in 130 nm

4.1 Fast-Erase Benefits

Figure 8 shows the ERASE operation principle, which presents two objectives. First of all, it takes part in the RECALL operation. Indeed, if the system restarts very quickly after a shutdown, it may be difficult to perform a RECALL while the data stored in the FeCAPs is different than the last written data in SRAM. In the example given in Fig. 8, the stored data in the FeCAPs is '1' (BLTI = 1, BLFI = 0) (Fig. 8(a)). The system then performs WRITE ops. in SRAM. Figure 8(b) shows that if the system restarts after a short downtime, the residual charges on BLFI (corresponding to the last written bit in SRAM) prevent the SRAM (that acts like a sense amplifier) from performing a correct RECALL of the stored state '1'. This phenomenon is especially significant at low temperature (40 °C) and slow corners (SS) where the leakage currents are weaker. Furthermore, performing WRITE operations after STORE means maintaining PL_{HIGH} and PL_{LOW} at $V_{DD}/2$ to improve the FeCAPs endurance. When the PLs fall down to 0 V after power-off, they can inject charges in the internal nodes. These charges constitute an other voltage bias disturbing the RECALL op. Performing an ERASE pulse just before the RECALL permits to equalize the internal nodes potentials, that greatly improves the reliability of the RECALL in all corners (Fig. 8(c)). For example, for 1000 Monte-Carlo runs of the 32-bit column without ERASE in the −40 °C/SS corner, we obtain 30343 RECALL errors for a downtime of 1 μs and still 660 errors for a downtime of 1ms. However, there are no errors in either case with the ERASE pulse just before the RECALL. Furthermore, the memory is still vulnerable to cold-boot attacks between the power-off and the RECALL op. due to the data remanence, especially when the downtime is long. In order to ensure cold-boot attack immunity, we use another ERASE pulse, just after the power-off (Fig. 8(d)), making cold-boot attacks far more tricky [17].

The duration of these ERASE pulses doesn't matter as long as it is greater than the erasing time of the internal nodes (in the order of some nanoseconds, see [17]). The minimal downtime, mainly limited by the RECALL sequence, is on the order of a hundred nanoseconds.

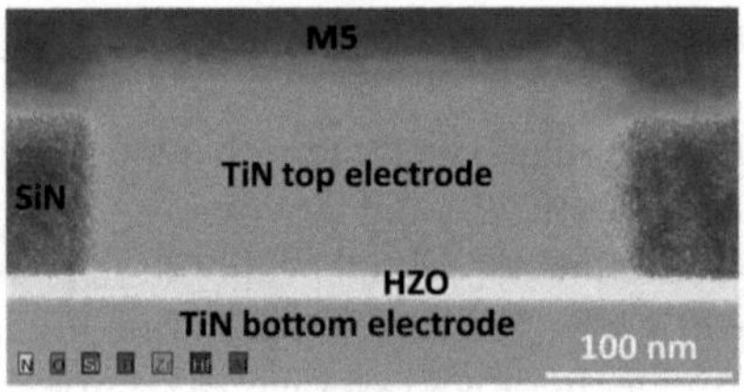

(a)

$$\begin{cases} P_{sat} = 28\,\mu\mathrm{C/cm}^2 \\ P_r = 13\,\mu\mathrm{C/cm}^2 \\ V_c = 1.1\,\mathrm{V} \end{cases}$$
(b)

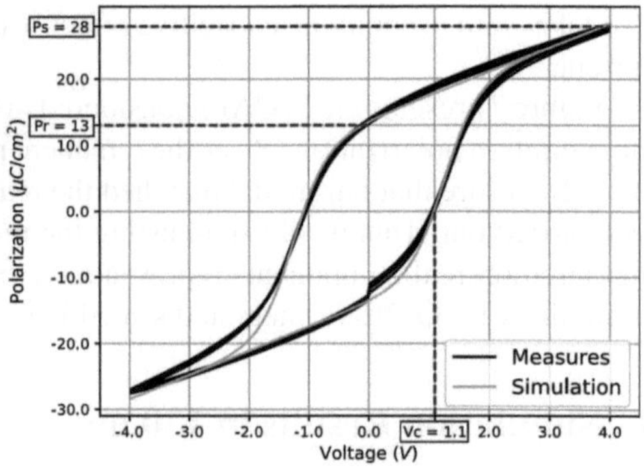

(c)

Fig. 7. (a) STEM-EDX cross section image of a BEOL-integrated TiN/HZO/TiN ferroelectric capacitor from CEA, revealing the different materials (reproduced with permission from [5]), (b) Main characteristics of the considered FeCAPs, (c) Comparison between measured (black) and simulated (orange) FeCAP's P-V hysteresis cycle.

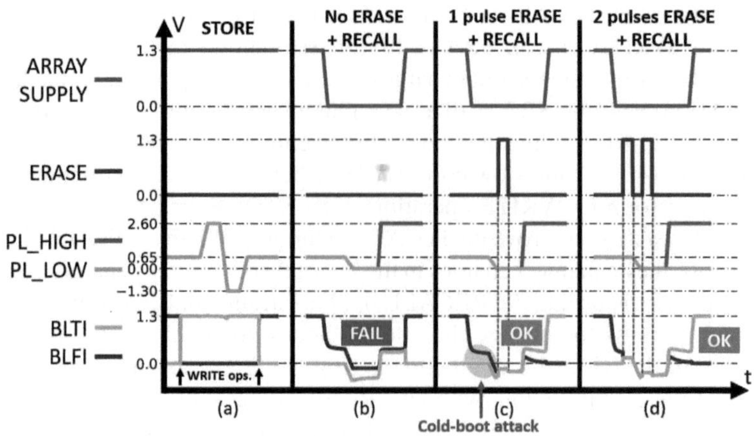

Fig. 8. Comparison of the waveforms of the internal nodes of the SRAM bitcell, with stored data in (a), between RECALL without ERASE pulse (b), with one ERASE pulse (c), with 2 ERASE pulses (d).

4.2 FeCAP Sizing Optimization

In the following, we define A_{FeX} as the area of the FeCAP "X". We define as well:

$$A_{\mathrm{HIGH}} = A_{\mathrm{Fe1L}} + A_{\mathrm{Fe1R}} \quad A_{\mathrm{LOW}} = A_{\mathrm{Fe2L}} + A_{\mathrm{Fe2R}}$$

$$A_{\mathrm{tot}} = A_{\mathrm{HIGH}} + A_{\mathrm{LOW}} \quad R = \frac{A_{\mathrm{HIGH}}}{A_{\mathrm{HIGH}} + A_{\mathrm{LOW}}}$$

Figure 9 shows the number of RECALL errors for 100 Monte-Carlo runs in each corner with respect to the R ratio, for $A_{tot} = 6\mathrm{e}{-13}\ \mathrm{m}^2$. At $R = 0$, the four FeCAPs are

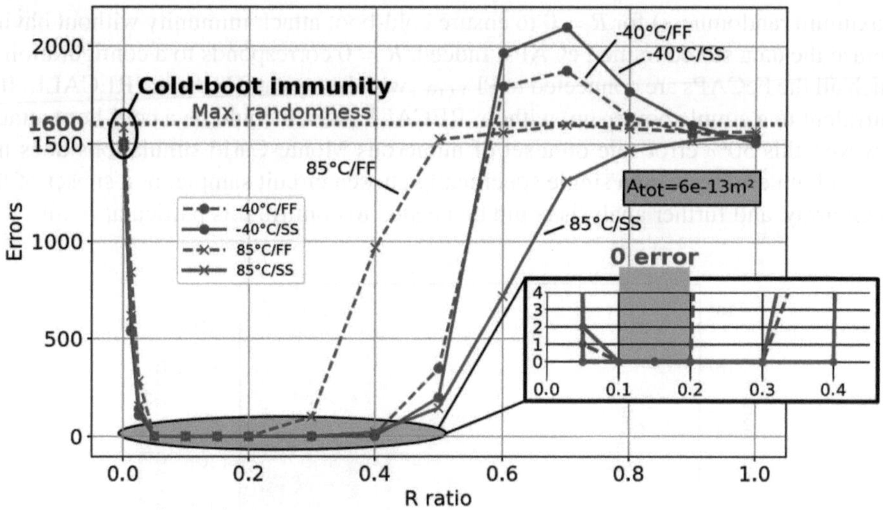

Fig. 9. Number of RECALL errors w.r.t. the R ratio (100 Monte-Carlo runs of the 32-bit column for each corner) in 130nm technology. This RECALL op. follows the sequence of operations of Fig. 6, with last WRITE in the opposite state to the last STORE state (worst-case).

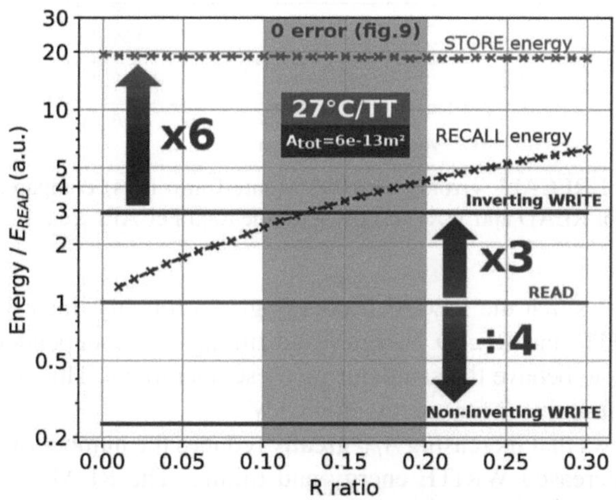

Fig. 10. STORE and RECALL energies w.r.t. the R ratio.

connected to PL_{LOW} (staying at 0 V at RECALL): the RECALL operation is performed only thanks to the rising edge of V_{DD} (Fig. 2(a)). At $R = 1$, the four FeCAPs are connected to PL_{HIGH} (rising at RECALL): the RECALL is performed by the rising edge of PL_{HIGH} (Fig. 2(b)). All the intermediate values correspond to configurations where the FeCAPs are connected to PL_{HIGH} and PL_{LOW} in the surface ratio R. A low error rate can be achieved with $R \in [0.1; 0.4]$ with an optimum for $R \approx 0.1$, corroborating the results of [23]. From a security point of view, the RECALL error rate must be close to 50%

(maximum randomness) for $R = 0$ to ensure cold-boot attack immunity without having to erase the data stored in the FeCAPs. Indeed, $R = 0$ corresponds to a configuration in which all the FeCAPs are connected to PL_{LOW}, which stays at 0 V during RECALL. It is equivalent to a simple power-up, without RECALL, which could be a cold-boot attack. However, this 50% error rate on a set of numerous Monte-Carlo simulations does not imply a high error rate on a single specifically chosen circuit sample, or a subset of the bitcell array, and further analysis could be needed to confirm this particular point.

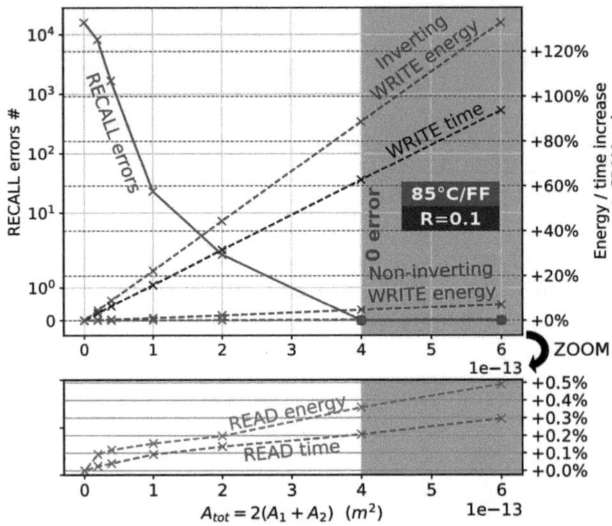

Fig. 11. Number of RECALL errors (for 1000 Monte-Carlo runs) compared to the impact in energy and timing of READ and WRITE ops. w.r.t. the total FeCAPs area A_{tot}.

Figure 10 shows that the RECALL energy grows roughly linearly with increasing R. STORE, WRITE and READ energies and timings are independent on R because PL_{HIGH} and PL_{LOW} behave the same during these operations. This figure shows that it is preferable to minimize R for energy efficiency.

Figure 11 shows that increasing A_{tot} greatly reduces the number of RECALL errors, at the price of increased WRITE energy and timing. The READ energy and timing stay roughly constant (increase very slightly) with increasing A_{tot}. We obtain 0 error with $A_{tot} = 4e{-}13\ m^2$ for 1000 Monte-Carlo simulations of the 32bit column, in the 85 °C/FF corner. However, $A_{tot} = 6e{-}13\ m^2$ can be considered as a better configuration, taking into account a design margin. This corresponds to an increase of roughly 94% in WRITE time compared to the SRAM bitcell without FeCAP. The WRITE energy penalty is 133% for an inverting WRITE and 7% for a non inverting WRITE, both cases with an opposite value stored in the FeCAPs. Assuming that 20% of the data change between two consecutive WRITE ops., the FeCAPs impact on the WRITE energy is reduced to 32% on average.

The combination of $A_{tot} = 6e{-}13\ m^2$ with $R = 0.1$, which is the best case presented here, corresponds to circular FeCAPs of diameters $D_1 \approx 200$ nm and $D_2 \approx 600$ nm, whose can be integrated in the existing SRAM bitcell through an increase of 46% of the initial bitcell area (see Fig. 4). In this configuration, at 85 °C in FF corner, storing data in FeCAPs consumes 191fJ/bit or 153fJ/bit, depending if the FeCAPs polarizations are inverted or not, respectively. If we assume that 20% of the SRAM data change between two STORE ops., this operation consumes 161fJ on average. Recalling data in SRAM consumes 27fJ/bit in this corner.

5 Projection in 22 nm

To go one step further, we have studied the scalability of this circuit in a more advanced Global Foundries 22 nm FDSOI technology node. To achieve this, we build on recent advances in FeRAM technology, which recently demonstrated a good scalability in 22 nm [12] (Fig. 12).

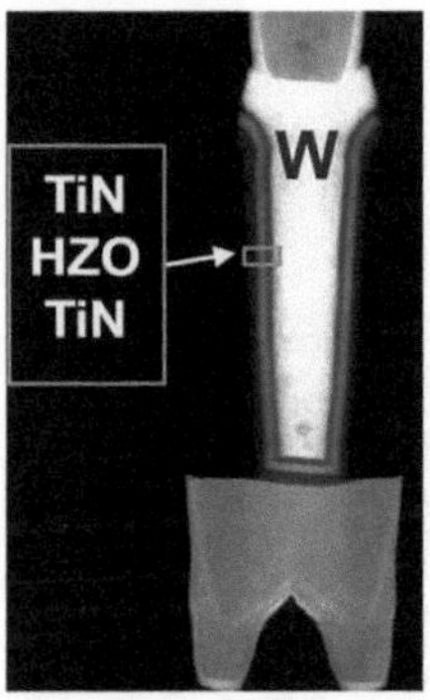

$$\begin{cases} P_{sat} = 11\,\mu\text{C/cm}^2 \\ P_r = 10\,\mu\text{C/cm}^2 \end{cases}$$

V_c = 0.66V

Fig. 12. (left) HAADF-STEM cross section of 3D-based BEOL-integrated HZO FeCaps from CEA (reproduced with permission from [12]) (right) main characteristics of the considered 22 nm node compatible BEOL FeCAPs.

In this part, we base our simulations on a 22 nm-compatible FeCAP Preisach model calibrated by the CEA. We simulate a 32 bitcell column connected to a Write-Driver and a precharge circuit. The nominal voltage is $V_{DD} = 0.8$ V. We use a pushed-rules GF22FDSOI 6T SRAM bitcell in which all of the 6 transistors of the bitcells are in a flip-well configuration (pMOS in a p-well tied to 0 V).

The FeCAPs we consider in this section are optimized for use in classic FeRAM arrays. This means that their Hafnium-Zirconium-Oxide (HZO) layer thickness is quite thin ($T_{fe} = 6$ nm versus $T_{fe} = 10$ nm in the 130 nm node) in order to reduce their coercive voltage and thus enables lower operating voltages. In our case, this is a constraint due to the fact that (i) we have only a single PL for writing several FeCAPs in opposite states and (ii) we must not lose the FeCAPs polarizations during WRITE ops. on the internal SRAM nodes to which they are connected. To take these considerations into account, we make two adjustments to the previous case. Firstly, we have to reduce the amplitudes of PL_{HIGH} et PL_{LOW} during the STORE op. to avoid excessive disturbance of the first written FeCAP during the writing of the second one. We therefore reduce the amplitude of the PL from $V_{NEG} = -1.3$ V to $V_{NEG} = -0.4$ V and from $V_{DDH} = 2.6$ V to $V_{DDH} = 1.2$ V. Secondly, due to the fact that the reduced coercive voltage $V_c = 0.66$ V becomes lower than the nominal voltage of the circuit $V_{nom} = 0.8$ V, maintaining the PL at $V_{MID} = V_{DD}/2$ during the SRAM ops. is not only an option to reduce the FeCAPs fatigue, but becomes mandatory to avoid loosing the previously stored polarizations. In this 22 nm variant, the STORE and RECALL ops. are achieved in 50 ns and 75 ns, respectively.

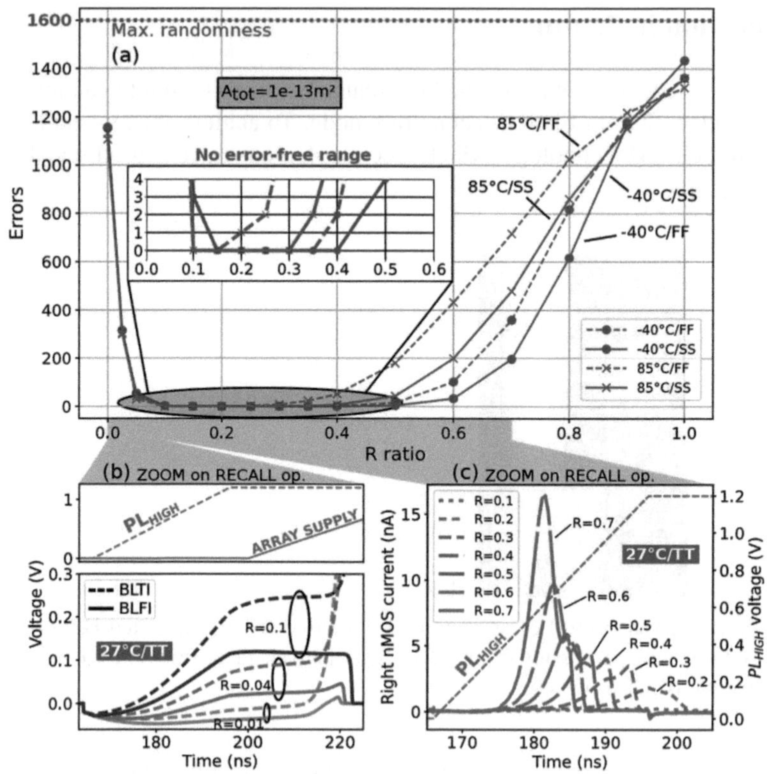

Fig. 13. (a) Number of RECALL errors w.r.t. the R ratio (100 Monte-Carlo runs of the 32-bit column for each corner) in 22nm technology, following the sequence of operations of Fig. 6, with last WRITE in the opposite state to the last STORE state (worst-case), (b) Internal nodes voltage during the PL_{HIGH} rise in the RECALL op., for low R values, (c) Right nMOS channel transient current during the PL_{HIGH} rise in the RECALL op., for high R values.

Like in 130 nm technology node, we explore the FeCAPs total area A_{tot} and the R ratio. A_{tot} should be carefully chosen to be sufficient to overcome transistor mismatch during RECALL but not too high to avoid disturbing the SRAM WRITE operation.

In Fig. 13(a) we present the RECALL error rate with respect to the R ratio with $A_{tot} = 1\text{e}{-13}\ \text{m}^2$, for the 22 nm circuit. A low error rate is obtained for $R \in [0.1;0.5]$, a result comparable to the 130 nm circuit. However, we do not obtain an error-free zone in all the considered corners. The 85 °C/FF case seems to be the most problematic corner, as its minimum error zone is shifted from those of the other corners. Furthermore, we get some writing errors in several corners, thus it seems difficult to increase A_{tot} further without losing reliability on the WRITE op. We see in Fig. 13(b) that errors that occur at low R values mainly come from the fact that the potential difference |BLTI − BLFI| is too low to overcome transistor mismatch during the V_{DD} rise. On the other end, the errors due to too high R values are correlated to high transient currents in the bitcell inverters transistors, especially the nMOS during the PL_{HIGH} rise.

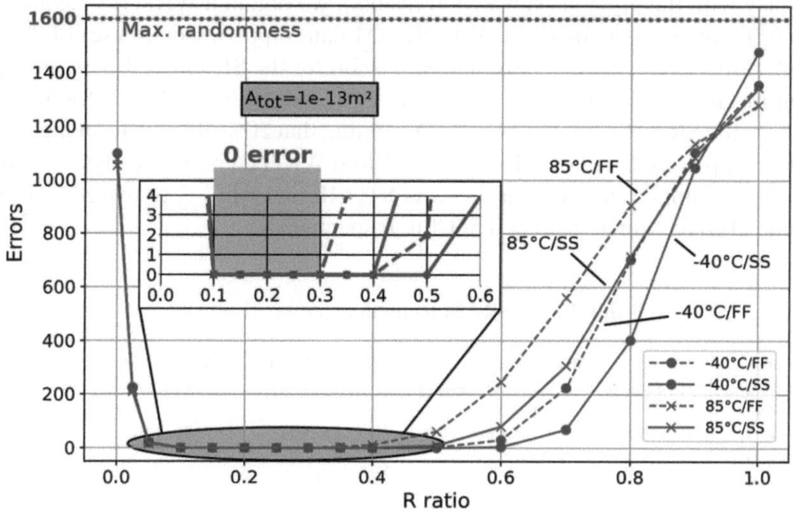

Fig. 14. Number of RECALL errors w.r.t. the R ratio (100 Monte-Carlo runs of the 32-bit column for each corner) for the modified bitcell in 22nm technology. This RECALL op. follows the sequence of operations of Fig. 6, with last WRITE in the opposite state to the last STORE state (worst-case).

The higher these currents are, the more important the mismatches among these transistors will disturb the internal nodes balance during PL_{HIGH} rise. It appears that the low error zone corresponds to configurations where |BLTI − BLFI| is maximized before the V_{DD} rise and the transient current during PL_{HIGH} rise is minimized. Figure 13(b–c) are given for the intermediate 27 °C/TT corner for the sake of clarity but the results in the other corners are similar. In order to improve the Fig. 13 results, we have slightly increased the pull-up and pull-down MOS lenghts, from 24 nm to 32 nm. This increase has two goals. First, this reduces the transient current in the transistors (especially the pull-down nMOS transistors) during the rise of the PLs. This permits to reduce (i) the charges leakage from the internal nodes and (ii) the impact of transistors mismatches on the RECALL op. Secondly, it slightly increases the SRAM write margin, ensuring reliable WRITE ops. with larger FeCAPs. This modification also slightly reduces the SRAM READ margin, but the READ op. is still always valid. Indeed, we make sure that a voltage between BLs |BLT − BLF| of at least 100 mV is achieved after activating one WL, with equivalent metallic capacitance on the BLs of 0.1fF/bitcell, i.e. 3.2fF for this 32-bit column. In Fig. 14 we present the RECALL error rate with respect to the R ratio for the modified SRAM bitcell, with A_{tot} = 1e–13 m^2. In this case, we get no WRITE and READ errors in any corner over the whole R range. For $R = 0.2$, the configuration in the middle of the 0-error zone for all the corners, can be considered as the optimal configuration. The corresponding planar FeCAPs diameters are approximately $D_1 \approx 115$ nm and $D_2 \approx 230$ nm. To optimize surface overhead, we could use 3D FeCAPs (which have also been demonstrated in [12]) with the same equivalent developed area. Admitting a 15-fold footprint reduction according to [12] the equivalent horizontal diameters are $D_{1,eq} \approx 30$ nm and $D_{2,eq} \approx 60$ nm. For this optimal configuration, in 85°/FF corner (for consistency with the previous subsection results), we obtain a WRITE time and energy (first WRITE after an opposite STORE, SRAM data flipped, worst-case) of 290ps and 2.6fJ/bit, respectively, against 68ps and 0.53fJ/bit for the SRAM cell without FeCAPs. The non-inverting WRITE results in an energy of 53aJ/bit for the NVSRAM against 41aJ/bit for the SRAM without FeCAPs. Assuming that 20% of the data change between two WRITE ops., the four FeCAPs lead to a 2-fold WRITE energy overhead, in average. Finally, this 22 nm circuit version presents STORE and RECALL energies of 20fJ/bit (inverting STORE, worst-case) and 3fJ/bit, respectively.

Table 1. NVSRAM technology comparison table

Reference	This Work		Infineon 2016 [19]	VLSI 2015 [9]	ISSCC 2023 [18]
CMOS bitcell technology	6T | 22nm FDSOI	6T | 130nm	10T | 40nm	7T | 90nm	6T | 22nm FDSOI
NVM technology	4C | BEOL HZO	4C | BEOL HZO	2T | SONOS	1R | BEOL HfO_x	2T | Charge-Trap Transistors
SRAM ops. after STORE	Yes		No	No	No
Cold-boot immunity	High		Low	Low	Low
Physical attack cost	High		Medium	High	High
Technology scalability	High		Low	Medium	Low
Endurance	High		Medium	Medium	Low
STORE energy	fJ/bit		nJ/bit	fJ/bit	uJ/bit
STORE time	ns		ms	ns	ms
RECALL time	ns		us	ns	Not specified

We obtain an error-free window similar to the 130 nm circuit. However, the FeCAPs integration leads to larger energy and timing overheads on the WRITE op. Nevertheless, these can be mitigated. Indeed, regarding the WRITE time, the NVSRAM memory presented here is mainly indicated for a circuit operating on a sub-GHz operating frequency, corresponding to a clock period on the order of ns. A WRITE time of the order of few hundreds ps is not a limiting timing on the main clock frequency. Moreover, regarding the WRITE energy overhead, this one is here assessed at the bitcell level but will be lower at the top circuit level. Finally, we can note that contrary to the 130 nm circuit, for a configuration with $R = 0$ (i.e. only FeCAPs connected to PL_{LOW} that stays at 0 V during RECALL) that could correspond to a cold-boot attack (see Subsect. 4.2), the error rate is quite far away from the max. randomness level. This means that during an attack, the state of a part of the bitcells will be correlated with the polarization of the FeCAPs above them, corresponding to the last stored data. This mitigates the robustness of this circuit against this kind of attack and additional optimizations could be necessary to improve this feature.

Table 1 presents comparisons between this work and several recently presented NVS-RAMs, in various memory and CMOS technologies. Ferroelectric memory technology is competitive with other non-volatile memory technologies in many aspects, and our solution offers unique advantages in terms of safety and functionality.

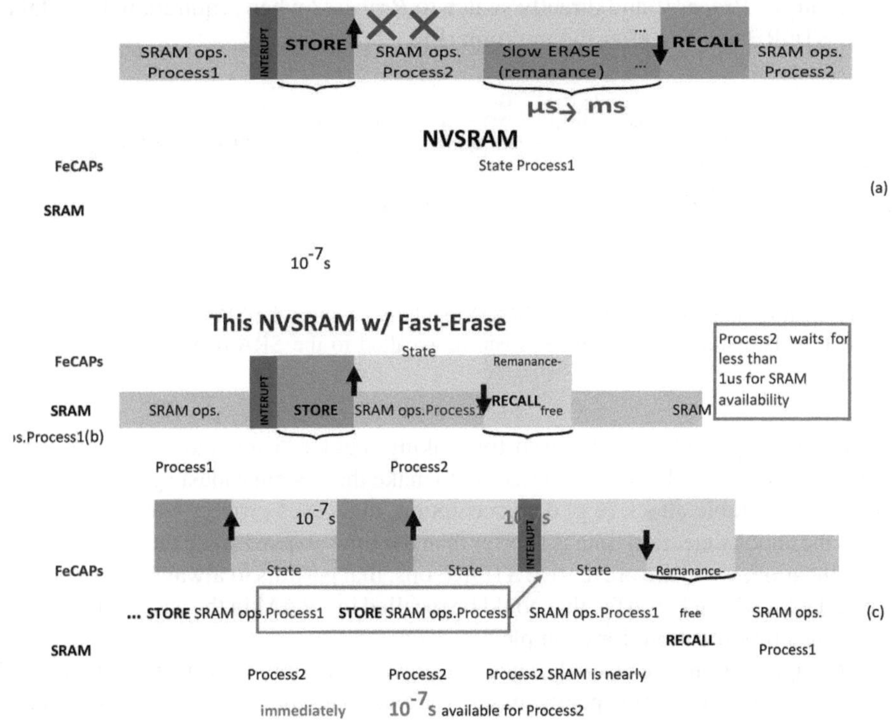

Fig. 15. Fast context switching application: (a) State-of-the-art NVSRAM cannot reliably address this application due to destructive WRITE after STORE ops. and long RECALL op. (b, c) Fast context switching application in STORE-on-Interrupt and Preventive-STORE fashions, respectively

6 Application Perspectives

The Fast-Erase circuit and WRITE operations between STORE and RECALL enable this NVSRAM solution to address new applications. For example, Fig. 15 presents a fast context switching application.

In this use case, a main process *Process1* is running. Suddenly, another urgent process *Process2* asks for SRAM availability. In a classical NVSRAM (Fig. 15(a)), we cannot easily manage this process transition because (i) we may loose the previously stored *Process1* state while performing *Process2* WRITE ops. and (ii) we would have to wait a variable (hardly estimable, temperature and process dependent) long time after the array power-off to succeed to RECALL correctly the *Process1* data, waiting for the remaining charges in the internal nodes to escape. With the Fast-Erase circuitry and correctly sized FeCAPs (Fig. 15(b–c)), we demonstrated that we succeed to correctly RECALL the stored data even with WRITE ops. after the last STORE op. and can perform this RECALL nearly instantaneously after the ARRAY power-off. If the recover of the very last state of *Process1* is not mandatory, we can even make preventive regular checkpoints of *Process1* and directly switch to *Process2* when required, without taking time to STORE the data after the interrupt (Fig. 15(c)).

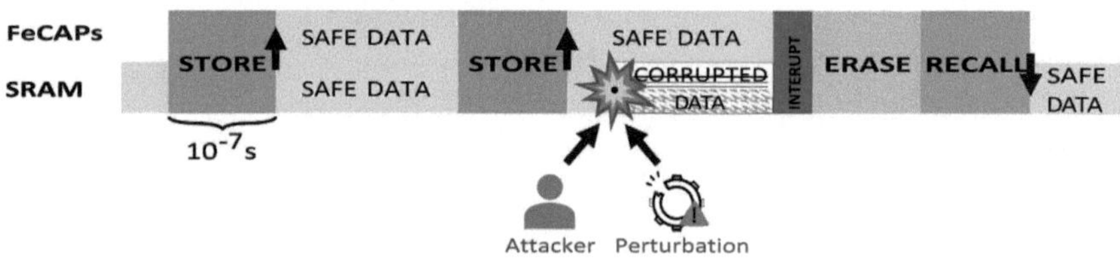

Fig. 16. Snapshot application: the NVSRAM regularly backups the SRAM state in the FeCAPs and the last state stored in the FeCAPs can be recalled to the SRAM when a perturbation is detected.

This memory could also be used for making regular "safe-state snapshots" of the system (Fig. 16) [24]. This could be useful to make the system robust against not instantaneously detectable attack (e.g. data corruption, malicious process execution, etc.), as long as the attack detection time is shorter than the time elapsed since the last STORE. In this application, we make preventive STORE ops. that permits to always keep a previous state of the SRAM in FeCAPs, that could be recalled in SRAM in the case of a suspicious SRAM data modification, for example.

Other applications are possible, such as using this memory to perform regular SRAM checkpoints only in certain specific cases, for example when all cache lines are invalidated and the whole system state is contained in the main memory. We could also use this NVSRAM as a Physical Unclonable Function (PUF) [6]. These circuits use CMOS process variabilities to associate a unique key signature to each circuit. Using an SRAM as a PUF usually means reserving this SRAM to this application only. However, the proposed circuit can be used as a classical SRAM PUF then store the PUF response as a key in the FeCAPs that permits to continue to use the entire SRAM for other applications, keeping the PUF key available at any time. In all of these applications, we benefit from the proximity of the two memories in terms of energy, time and safety. More generally, any application requiring fast snapshots of a part of its memory at a given time could benefit from this solution.

7 Conclusion

The presented design techniques demonstrate a good scalability in simulation down to the 22 nm node at least, with a few design adjustments. The proposed ferroelectric-based 6T4C NVSRAM circuits demonstrate the ability to both STORE data in non-volatile part of memory, for an energy of about 200fJ/bit (130 nm node) and 20fJ/bit (22nm node), and RECALL it to the SRAM memory, for an energy of about 30fJ/bit (130 nm node) and 3fJ/bit (22 nm node), with a high reliability. In return, we observe worst-case inverting WRITE energy and timing overheads of a factor 2x (130 nm node) and 5x (22 nm node) at the array level, that can be acceptable in the targeted applications and in sub-GHz context. In this work, the combination of FeCAPs sizing optimization with the previously developed Fast-Erase technique demonstrates the ability to continue using the SRAM after storing data in the FeCAPs and recalling data different from that previously written in the internal nodes of SRAM, without having to wait for a significant amount of time. The integration of the FastErase technique also enhances robustness against cold-boot attacks. This design combination leads to new, previously unaddressed use cases of ferroelectric-based NVSRAMs, e.g. in critical systems, including fast context switching or safe-state checkpointing.

Acknowledgments. This work was supported by funding from the French government managed by the National Research Agency under the France 2030 program with the reference "ANR-23-PEEL-0003".

Disclosure of Interests. The authors have no competing interests to declare that are relevant to the content of this article.

References

1. Anagnostopoulos, N.A.: Attacking SRAM PUFs using very-low-temperature data remanence. Microprocess. Microsyst. (2019)
2. Courbon, F.: Reverse engineering flash EEPROM memories using scanning electron microscopy. In: Smart Card Research and Advanced Application Conference (2016)
3. Francois, T.: Demonstration of BEOL-compatible ferroelectric Hf0.5Zr0.5O2 scaled FeRAM co-integrated with 130nm CMOS for embedded NVM applications. In: IEDM (2019)
4. Fujitsu: FRAM MCU key strengths and applications (2010)
5. Grenouillet, L.: Performance assessment of BEOL-integrated HfO2-based ferroelectric capacitors for FERAM memory arrays. In: IEEE Silicon Nanoelectronics Workshop (SNW) (2020)
6. Holcomb, D.E.: Power-up SRAM state as an identifying fingerprint and source of true random numbers. IEEE Trans. Comput. (2009)
7. Khan, M.N.I.: Comprehensive study of security and privacy of emerging non-volatile memories. JLPEA (2021)
8. Kobayashi, M.: Experimental demonstration of a nonvolatile SRAM with ferroelectric HfO2 capacitor for normally off application. JEDS (2018)
9. Lee, A.: RRAM-based 7t1r nonvolatile SRAM with 2x reduction in store energy and 94x reduction in restore energy for frequent-off instant-on applications. In: VLSIC (2015)
10. Li, Y.: Working principles and performance optimization of nonvolatile 6T2C-SRAM with hafnia-based ferroelectric capacitors. IEEE Trans. Electron Dev. (2024)
11. Liu, Y.: 4.7 a 65nm ReRAM-enabled nonvolatile processor with 6× reduction in restore time and 4× higher clock frequency using adaptive data retention and self-write-termination nonvolatile logic. In: ISSCC (2016)

12. Martin, S.: $Hf_{0.5}Zr_{0.5}O_2$ FeRAM scalability demonstration at 22nm FDSOI node for embedded applications. In: IEDM 2024 (2024)
13. Masui, S.: A ferroelectric memory-based secure dynamically programmable gate array. JSSC (2003)
14. Miller, S.L.: Device modeling of ferroelectric capacitors. J. Appl. Phys. (1990)
15. Miller, S.L.: Modeling ferroelectric capacitor switching with asymmetric nonperiodic input signals and arbitrary initial conditions. J. Appl. Phys. (1991)
16. Miwa, T.: NV-SRAM: a nonvolatile SRAM with back-up ferroelectric capacitors. In: CICC (2000)
17. Noel, J.P.: A near-instantaneous and non-invasive erasure design technique to protect sensitive data stored in secure SRAMs. In: ESSCIRC (2021)
18. Nouri, S.: An 8T eNVSRAM macro in 22nm FDSOI standard logic with simultaneous full-array data restore for secure IoT devices. In: ISSCC (2023)
19. Prakash, R.: Nonvolatile SRAM (nvSRAM) basics (2016)
20. Quadir, S.E.: A survey on chip to system reverse engineering. J. Emerg. Technol. Comput. Syst. (2016)
21. Shivendra, S.: Nonvolatile SRAMs (nvSRAMs) in gaming applications (2015)
22. Shuto, Y.: HZO-based nonvolatile SRAM array with 100% bit recall yield and sufficient retention time at 85°c. In: VLSI Technology and Circuits (2024)
23. Takeuchi, K.: A feasibility study on ferroelectric shadow SRAMs based on variability-aware design optimization. JEDS (2019)
24. Thevenon, P.H.: iMRC: Integrated monitoring & recovery component, a solution to guarantee the security of embedded systems (2022)

Reliability and Trustworthiness

Verification and Debugging of Modular ($2^n - 1$) Multipliers Using Linear Algebra Technique

Jiteshri Dasari[1(✉)], Cunxi Yu[2], and Maciej Ciesielski[1]

[1] University of Massachusetts Amherst, Amherst, MA, USA
{jdasari,ciesiel}@umass.edu
[2] University of Maryland, College Park, MD, USA
cunxiyu@umd.edu

Abstract. The paper presents a novel approach to formal verification and debugging of modular ($2^n - 1$) multipliers. It takes advantage of the regular array structure of such multipliers and models them as a system of linear equations. The method is significantly more effective than the popular symbolic computer algebra and algebraic rewriting techniques, allowing verification of 512-bit multipliers in single minutes. Furthermore, it naturally enables debugging as an integral part of the verification process, an important feature not offered by other known approaches.

1 Introduction

Verification and debugging of digital circuits, especially of arithmetic circuits, pose serious challenges in the design of reliable and efficient hardware systems. Multipliers in particular are fundamental components in many digital systems, used in applications ranging from digital signal processing and machine learning to cryptography. Modular multipliers, an important class of multipliers, are essential in systems that rely on modular arithmetic for functions like cryptography, homomorphic encryption, and error correction [1, 2]. Despite their importance, verification and debugging of these circuits pose a significant challenge due to their complexity and regular, but intricate structures.

Formal verification methods, which aim to mathematically prove correctness of a circuit, have been widely employed in verifying digital designs. Traditional approaches, such as SAT solvers [3] and symbolic techniques based on Boolean methods and BDDs, [4] have been successfully used for simpler circuits, including adders and multipliers. However, when applied to large-scale arithmetic circuits, such as modular multipliers, these methods face significant scalability issues. Bt construction, Boolean methods require bit-blasting, i.e., flattening the design into a bit-level netlist, a process that is computationally expensive and impractical for arithmetic designs [3]. Moreover, these techniques rely on the availability of a reference circuit, which may not always be available.

An alternative approach that has gained popularity in verifying complex circuits is based on Symbolic Computer Algebra (SCA) and Groebner basis theory. SCA techniques

Published by Springer Nature Switzerland AG 2026
E. -I. Vatajelu (Ed.): VLSI-SoC 2024, IFIP AICT 744, pp. 93–108, 2026.
https://doi.org/10.1007/978-3-032-09575-6_6

represent circuits in the algebraic rather than Boolean domain by modeling the logic gates and their operation with pseudo-Boolean polynomials. One common method is based on algebraic rewriting [5], in which the input operands, represented as polynomials, are transformed using algebraic representation of the internal gates into an output polynomial and checking if it matches the expected specification of the circuit. Such a rewriting, however, suffers from the problem of generating large numbers of redundant (*vanishing*) monomials, which can lead to memory explosion. Several strategies have been developed to cope with this issue, such as those described in the work of [6]. Despite it being capable of eliminating millions of vanishing monomials in large multipliers, the method is not scalable.

Another widely used method in formal verification, especially applied in industrial designs, is Theorem Proving. Theorem provers use mathematical reasoning and induction to prove that a circuit's implementation satisfies its specification [7, 8]. While powerful, theorem proving systems are highly specialized and require in-depth domain knowledge and user expertise. Moreover, they may not guarantee termination, making them less practical for verifying large and complex circuits like modular multipliers.

Despite the effectiveness of these methods for standard circuits, modular multipliers present unique verification challenges due to their complex architectures. These multipliers are used in systems that perform computations on encrypted data, such as homomorphic encryption [1]. The structure of modular multipliers, whether parallel or digit-serial as in Montgomery multiplication [2], adds complexity to their verification. Although the verification of certain modular multipliers using theorem proving has been explored [9], such methods do not apply to the types of modular multipliers considered in this work, and the existing techniques are computationally expensive.

An important exception in this field is the work of [10], which investigates the verification of modular multipliers using an SCA-based approach combined with SAT procedures to remove vanishing monomials. This method, although innovative, requires significant computational resources and processing time. For instance, it takes about two hours to verify a 512-bit modular multiplier. In contrast, the technique proposed in this work leverages the regular structure of modular multipliers to reduce verification time drastically. Our approach, applied to a modulo $(2^n - 1)$ multiplier, verifies large multipliers in a matter of minutes, making it significantly more efficient.

A particularly critical aspect of design verification is *debugging*, the task of identifying and locating a source of design errors, followed by its fixing. While fault detection methods are well-established in the context of manufacturing defects, debugging in digital circuit design is concerned with finding and fixing logical errors. Debugging techniques used in other domains, such as detecting stuck-at faults in logic circuits, do not directly apply to arithmetic circuits like multipliers, where the error space is far larger. The work by [11] addresses fault detection through test generation, but this method is limited to specific fault models, such as gate replacement or signal inversion.

Several approaches have attempted to tackle the debugging of complex multiplier circuits. The work by [12] combines SCA techniques with Boolean satisfiability (SAT) to detect faults but suffers from the problem of generating a large number of intermediate polynomials during rewriting, leading to memory overload. Similarly, [13] uses corrector polynomials to compensate for errors, but this technique also involves expensive computational steps, such as Groebner basis computation, making it impractical for large circuits.

Debugging of arithmetic dividers has received some attention in the literature, focusing on reverse-engineering techniques to extract individual components of divider circuits to match them against the known circuit structures [14]. However, this approach is highly dependent on the circuit's structure, limiting its applicability to more general architectures. A notable exception is the debugging approach proposed in [15], as it does not rely on any specific fault model or internal structure of the circuit. Instead, it applies the controllability and observability techniques commonly used in testing, to identify the source of an error, without assuming any particular type of fault.

In contrast to the existing work on divider debugging, the debugging of modular multipliers is almost non-existent. There are no specialized techniques for identifying and correcting logical errors in modular multiplier circuits. This lack of dedicated methods for modular multiplier debugging represents a significant gap in the field. This work addresses this need by introducing a novel debugging approach that does not rely on a fault model, but is an inherent part of the verification process.

This paper focuses on advancing techniques for the verification and debugging of modular multipliers. While formal verification methods, such as SCA and theorem proving, have been successful in some contexts, they are often computationally expensive or inefficient for large modular multipliers. Our approach simplifies the verification process by exploiting the regular structure of modular multipliers, reducing the time and resources required for verification. Furthermore, the proposed debugging method offers a scalable solution for detecting and fixing logical errors in large modular multiplier circuits, making it a valuable tool for designers of complex arithmetic systems.

2 Background

2.1 Modular Multipliers

A modular multiplier computes the product of two integers under a given modulus m, producing an output: $Z = (A \times B) \bmod m$ with inputs and output satisfying the constraints: $A, B, Z < m$.

There are two primary methods for implementing modular multiplication in hardware. The first involves computing the product $A \times B$ followed by a mod m reduction. The second, and more efficient method, integrates the modular reduction into the multiplier structure. This minimizes hardware area and delay, making it preferable for high-performance circuits. A modular $(2^n - 1)$ multiplier follows the structure of a conventional binary multiplier and consists of three key components: Partial Product Generation; Partial Product Accumulation; and Final Carry Propagation with Modular Reduction.

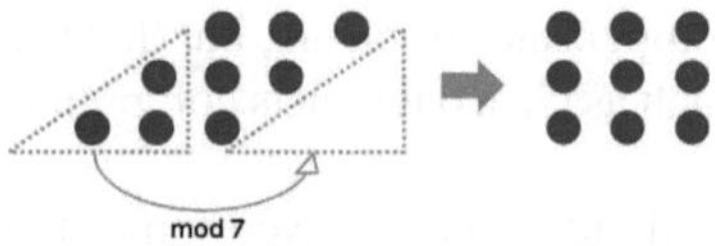

Fig. 1. Computational scheme of a 3bit modulo 7 multiplier.

The fundamental difference between a standard binary multiplier and a modular (2^n – 1) multiplier lies in the handling of the carry-out from the most significant bit (MSB) position. Figure 1 illustrates the principle of computation modulo $m = 2^n - 1$ for $n = 3$ and $m = 7$. The three heavy dots enclosed by the gray triangle in the left corner represent those partial products whose weights (determined by the respective bit position) exceed $m = 7$. Modulo 7 reduction is accomplished by repositioning those partial products from MSB to LSB at the corresponding row, resulting in a rectangular array with $n = 3$ columns. This wrap-around carry is a key feature of the modular computation.

Figure 2 shows the architecture of a 3-bit modular multiplier modulo $m = 7$. Inputs to the multiplier are partial products, $p_{ij} = a_i b_j$, generated by AND gates. In a conventional multiplier, the carry-out from column $n - 1$ propagates to the next layer within the same column. However, in a modular multiplier shown here, the MSB carry-out in each row is wrapped around and fed back into the least significant bit (LSB) position of the next row at column 0, thus enforcing the modulus constraint. This architecture can be generalized to different values of *n*, creating a regular, structured form that simplifies verification and debugging. Since the modular reduction is integrated within the circuit, verifying such a design involves ensuring that both the adder structure and the carry wrap-around mechanism function correctly.

2.2 Verification Challenges

The state-of-the-art approach for verifying arithmetic circuits is based on Symbolic Computer Algebra (SCA), which uses algebraic rewriting with logic gates and arithmetic structures represented as polynomial expressions. This method replaces complex Boolean expressions with equivalent algebraic forms by applying predefined rewriting rules. However, traditional SCA-based approaches face significant scalability challenges due to exponential growth in expression complexity.

In standard SCA-based verification, each gate in the circuit is represented as an algebraic equation. The fundamental Boolean operations (*AND, OR, XOR*) are encoded as polynomial expressions using algebraic models of logic gates as shown in Table 1. The verification process involves backward rewriting, where gate expressions are progressively substituted starting at the primary outputs and working towards the primary inputs. To speed up the rewriting process, the half-adders (HA) and full-adders (FA) are also modeled with their characteristic equations, shown below, instead of treating the sum and carry terms separately.

$$\text{HA}: a + b = 2C + S \quad \text{FA}: a + b + c = 2C + S \tag{1}$$

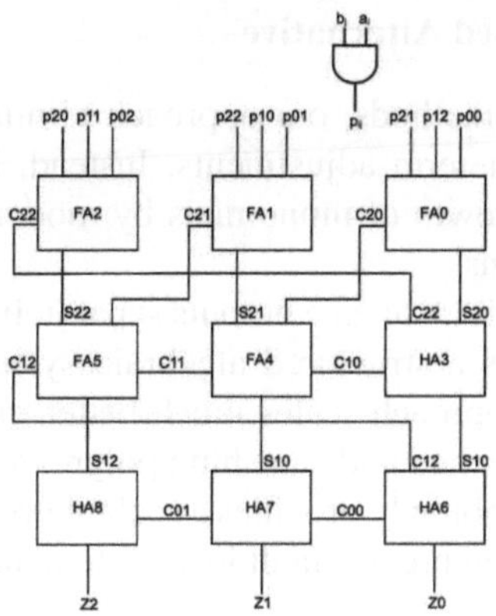

Fig. 2. Modular 3-bit mod 7 multiplier.

During rewriting, the size and the number of intermediate polynomials (including the redundant and vanishing monomials) grow uncontrollably, making the process computationally expensive.

Table 1. Algebraic models of basic logic functions.

Operation	Boolean model	Algebraic model
INV (a)	$\neg a$	$1 - a$
AND (a, b)	$a \wedge b$	ab
OR (a, b)	$a \vee b$	$a + b - ab$
XOR (a, b)	$a \oplus b$	$a + b - 2ab$
XOR3 (a, b, c)	$a \oplus b \oplus c$	$a + b + c - 2ab - 2ac - 2bc + 4abc$
MAJ3 (a, b, c)	$a \wedge (b \vee c) \vee b \wedge c$	$ab + ac + bc - 2abc$

Modular arithmetic verification introduces additional complexities that make direct rewriting even harder. Consider verifying a modulo-17 multiplier, as described in [10]. At bit position 3 (where weight $k = 8$), the rewriting process encounters an expression $-c_3 + 8s_3$. In conventional binary arithmetic, $-c_3$ and s_3 can be rewritten independently, but modular constraints prevent such a straightforward substitution. To facilitate rewriting, $-c_3$ is adjusted using modular equivalence: $-c_3 + 17c_3 = 16c_3$ This transformation results in expression $16c_3 + 8s_3$, matching with the expected adder structure. More generally, [10] proposes searching for a constant p, such that $p = 2k + m \cdot q$, for some integer q, and the modulus m. If such a p exists, rewriting reduces the expression to $8(2c_3 + s_3)$; otherwise, individual terms must be handled separately, leading to an explosion in monomial complexity and high computational overhead.

2.3 A Linear Algebra-Based Alternative

Unlike traditional rewriting methods, our approach eliminates the need for nonlinear term expansion and modular term adjustments. Instead, it leverages Linear Algebra, avoiding the uncontrolled growth of monomials by modeling the verification problem as a system of linear equations.

Rather than rewriting individual gate outputs separately, our method treats the entire modular multiplier circuit as a structured algebraic system, extracting and verifying equations efficiently. This approach scales much better than backward rewriting, as it avoids the expansion of redundant and vanishing polynomials. By leveraging structured linear algebra, our approach not only provides a scalable verification framework but also simplifies debugging, ensuring precise fault localization and correction within a unified mathematical model.

3 Verification Approach

As described in our previous work [16], verification of modular multipliers can be efficiently performed using a linear algebraic approach that takes advantage of the regular structure of these circuits. The circuit is conceptually divided into two sections. The first section consists of the non-linear components, responsible for computing the initial partial product terms using AND gates. The second section is a structured network of adders, forming a linear array that adds the partial products. The verification goal is to demonstrate that the output polynomial derived from this structure is equivalent to the expected product modulo m.

To illustrate this approach, consider a 3-bit modulo 7 multiplier array, shown in Fig. 2. The inputs to the array are partial products, computed as $p_{ij} = a_i b_j$, where a_i and b_j are individual bits of operands A and B, respectively. With this, one can compute the *specification* of the mod 7 multiplier as follows:

$$
\begin{aligned}
&(A \times B)\ mod\ 7 = \\
&\quad (4a_2 + 2a_1 + a_0)(4b_2 + 2b_1 + b_0)\ mod\ 7 = \\
&\qquad [16p_{22} + 8(p_{12} + p_{21}) + 4(p_{11} + p_{02} + p_{20}) + 2(p_{01} + p_{10}) + p_{00}]\ mod\ 7 = \\
&\quad 4(p_{11} + p_{02} + p_{20}) + 2(p_{22} + p_{01} + p_{10}) + (p_{00} + p_{12} + p_{21})
\end{aligned}
\tag{2}
$$

The terms in red are those whose coefficients have been reduced *modulo* 7 (namely, $16p_{22} \rightarrow 2p_{22}$ and $8p_{12}+8p_{21} \rightarrow p_{12} + p_{21}$). With this, in a functionally correct mod 7 multiplier, the relation between the primary inputs and outputs should be as follows:

$$
4z_2 + 2z_1 + z_0 = 4(p_{11} + p_{02} + p_{20}) + 2(p_{22} + p_{01} + p_{10}) + (p_{00} + p_{12} + p_{21})\ mod\ 7 \tag{3}
$$

This expression forms the *Specification* or the *Reference Signature* against which the verification process compares the extracted circuit behavior.

3.1 Constructing a Linear System

The following linear system can be constructed for the 3-bit mod 7 multiplier from its array structure, shown in Fig. 2:

$$[p_{00} + p_{12} + p_{21} - 2 * c_{20} - s_{20}] = 0$$

$$[p_{01} + p_{10} + p_{22} - 2 * c_{21} - s_{21}] = 0$$

$$[p_{02} + p_{11} + p_{20} - 2 * c_{22} - s_{22}] = 0$$

$$[s_{20} + c_{22} - 2 * c_{10} - s_{10}] = 0$$

$$[c_{10} + c_{20} + s_{21} - 2 * c_{11} - s_{11}] = 0$$

$$[c_{11} + c_{21} + s_{22} - 2 * c_{12} - s_{12}] = 0$$

$$[s_{10} + c_{12} - 2 * c_{00} - z_0] = 0$$

$$[s_{11} + c_{00} - 2 * c_{01} - z_1] = 0$$

$$[s_{12} + c_{01} - z_2] = 0$$

While the above linear equations can be trivially derived from the array structure in Fig. 2, such a network of adders needs to be extracted from the initial description (a *netlist*) of the multiplier. Such a netlist is typically available in a BLIF (Berkeley interchange format) or an AIG (And-Inverter Graph) format, traditionally used in industry and academia to describe logic and arithmetic circuits. Such an extraction can be readily performed by parsing the AIG or BLIF netlist with the ABC tool [17] using command & *show* − *a*, which generates a list of interconnected adders, intermediate logic gates and I/O signals. Figure 3 shows the resulting logic network for a 3-bit mod 7 multiplier, originally provided in the AIG format. It is composed of HAs, FAs, product terms, p_{ik}, and the operand bits, a_i, b_i.

The next step of the procedure is to find the multiplicative constant α_i for each equation i, in an attempt to eliminate the internal variables and relate the input and output polynomials to each other. In the case of our 3-bit mod 7 multiplier, the output polynomial (signature) $Z = 4z_2 + 2z_1 + z_0$ immediately dictates the weights α_i of the last three equations to be 1, 2, 4, respectively. Similarly, the input polynomial (specification) that is expressed by Eq. 3 imposes weight 4, 2, and 1 on the first three equations, involving the respective partial product term. The weights are computed by a separate procedure, described next.

A similar approach has been proposed for conventional (standard) multipliers in [18]. The goal there was to find integer coefficients α_i for each equation i that would reduce the weighted sum of the equations to an expression containing only the primary inputs (in this case, partial product terms p_{ij}) and output variables (z_i). The intention was to eliminate the internal variables, resulting in an expression relating the input (partial products) and output variables (Z_i). Subsequently, the presence of any *residual expression*, containing any of the internal signals, would be an indication of a bug in the circuit. This approach, however, does not directly apply to modular multipliers considered here, since some of the variables in the final sum should be reduced modulo m; and all the intermediate variables (the connecting *sum* and *carry* signals) should be eliminated by reducing them modulo 7 to zero. These intermediate signals can be viewed as analogous to the "vanishing monomials" that plague the SCA and algebraic rewriting.

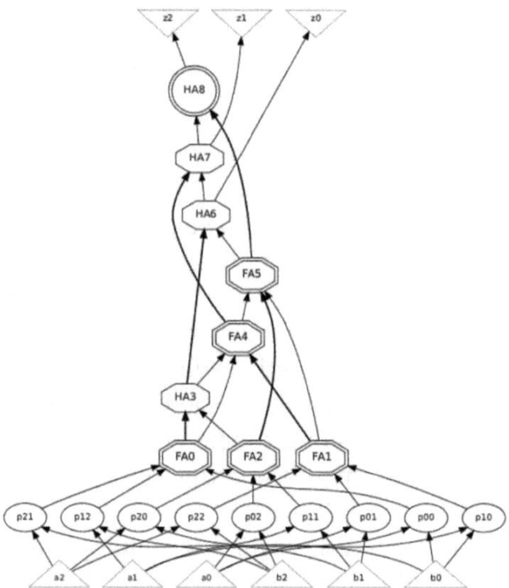

Fig. 3. Network of a 3-bit modulo 7 multiplier.

3.2 Computing the Weights and Solving the Linear System

In our approach, instead of solving the linear system for α, we compute these coefficients based on the topology of the network of interconnected adders. Figure 3 shows such a network obtained by the ABC adder extraction tool. Starting with the least significant bit z_0 of the network, we can trace the *Sum* outputs of the adders leading to the primary inputs (product terms), namely: $z_o \rightarrow HA_6 \rightarrow HA_3 \rightarrow FA_0$ and $z_1 \rightarrow HA_7 \rightarrow FA_4 \rightarrow FA_1$; $z_2 \rightarrow HA_8 \rightarrow FA_5 \rightarrow FA_2$.

All the equations associated with adders in column z_0 (LSB) will have coefficient $\alpha = 1$. Similarly, the equations associated with adders HA_7, FA_4, FA_1 will have coefficient $\alpha = 2$, corresponding to column z_1; and those associated with adders HA_8, FA_5, FA_2 will have coefficient $\alpha = 4$, corresponding to column z_2. In summary, the computed coefficients α correspond to the respective columns of the array, even if the array structure is not directly available from the input file. The linear system with properly computed weights is then constructed as follows:

$$1 * [p_{00} + p_{12} + p_{21} - 2 * c_{20} - s_{20}] = 0$$

$$2 * [p_{01} + p_{10} + p_{22} - 2 * c_{21} - s_{21}] = 0$$

$$4 * [p_{02} + p_{11} + p_{20} - 2 * c_{22} - s_{22}] = 0$$

$$1 * [s_{20} + c_{22} - 2 * c_{10} - s_{10}] = 0$$

$$2 * [c_{10} + c_{20} + s_{21} - 2 * c_{11} - s_{11}] = 0$$

$$4 * [c_{11} + c_{21} + s_{22} - 2 * c_{12} - s_{12}] = 0$$

$$1 * [s_{10} + c_{12} - 2 * c_{00} - z_0] = 0$$

$$2 * [s_{11} + c_{00} - 2 * c_{01} - z_1] = 0$$

$$4 * [s_{12} + c_{01} - z_2] = 0$$

$$\text{SUM: } 4 * (p_{11} + p_{02} + p_{20}) + 2 * (p_{22} + p_{01} + p_{10}) + (p_{00} + p_{12} + p_{21})$$

$$+ 7 * c_{12} + 7 * c_{22} - 4 * z_2 - 2 * z_1 - z_0 = 0$$

Since the terms $7c_{12}$ and $7c_{22}$ reduce modulo 7 to zero, the final result confirms that the circuit correctly implements modular multiplication.

3.3 Final Validation and Output Constraints

As a last step, the correctness of the output must be verified against the condition $Z < m = 2^n - 1$. This can be efficiently checked using a SAT solver by ensuring that the condition $Z \geq m$ remains unsatisfiable under valid input constraints. Additionally, an alternative method involves checking if the product of all output bits is not equal to 1, providing a simple yet effective verification condition.

4 Debugging Approach

Debugging is a critical part of this approach, as it identifies functional errors and localizes the source of the fault within the circuit. As shown in Eq. 3, a functionally correct modulo 7 multiplier exhibits a direct relationship between its inputs (product terms, p_{ij}) and outputs Z, with no presence of internal variables, such as sum or carry bits of intermediate adders. This structural property serves as the foundation of our debugging methodology. If, after reduction modulo m, the resulting equation retains some of the internal variables, their presence signifies existence of an error in the circuit; it also provides information about its location. By analyzing the residual terms, it is possible to trace the error back to the specific adder or another module responsible for this discrepancy. This systematic identification process facilitates efficient debugging and enables circuit correction. Identification of a fault in the circuit can be illustrated with the 3-bit mod 7 multiplier example in Fig. 2 by swapping the carry-out bits c_{20} and c_{21} of adders FA_0 and FA_4, respectively. As a result, adder FA_4 incorrectly receives c_{21} instead of c_{20}, while FA_5 receives c_{20} instead of c_{21}. This is shown in Fig. 4, with part a) showing the netlist of a functionally correct circuit, and part b) the faulty circuit with signals c_{20} and c_{21} swapped, as described above. To highlight the difference between the two circuits, the faulty signal connections are shown in red.

Introduction of such a fault leads to incorrect computations within the adder network that can be identified by analyzing and solving the resulting linear system. The differences between the functionally correct system, derived in Sect. 3.2, and the one with the introduced fault, are highlighted in red. This discrepancy not only confirms the presence of a fault, but also indicates the location of the fault within the adder network. In this case, the difference involves the carry-out signals c_{20} and c_{21}. The resulting system of linear equations is then modified by introducing weights α, as described earlier. The modified linear system with the inserted fault is shown, with the weighted sum provided at the bottom.

$$
\begin{aligned}
&1 * [p_{00} + p_{12} + p_{21} - 2 * c_{20} - s_{20}] = 0\\
&2 * [p_{01} + p_{10} + p_{22} - 2 * c_{21} - s_{21}] = 0\\
&4 * [p_{02} + p_{11} + p_{20} - 2 * c_{22} - s_{22}] = 0\\
&1 * [s_{20} + c_{22} - 2 * c_{10} - s_{10}] = 0\\
&2 * [c_{10} + c_{21} + s_{21} - 2 * c_{11} - s_{11}] = 0\\
&4 * [c_{11} + c_{20} + s_{22} - 2 * c_{12} - s_{12}] = 0\\
&1 * [s_{10} + c_{12} - 2 * c_{00} - z_0] = 0 \qquad (4)\\
&2 * [s_{11} + c_{00} - 2 * c_{01} - z_1] = 0\\
&4 * [s_{12} + c_{01} - z_2] = 0
\end{aligned}
$$

SUM:

$$
\begin{aligned}
&4(p_{11} + p_{02} + p_{20}) + 2(p_{22} + p_{01} + p_{10}) + (p_{00} + p_{12} + p_{21})\\
&-7c_{12} - 7c_{22} + 2c_{20} - 2c_{21} - 4z_2 - 2z_1 - z_0 = 0
\end{aligned}
$$

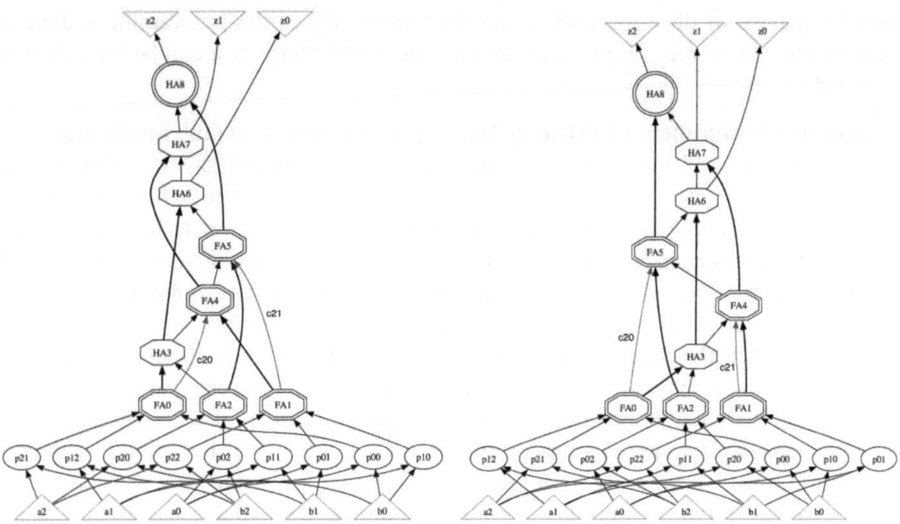

(a) Functionally correct multiplier. (b) Faulty multiplier: c_{20}, c_{21} swapped.

Fig. 4. Extracted network of a 3-bit mod 7 multiplier

4.1 Localizing the Error

It is important to note the terms highlighted in blue and red within the final *SUM* expression. Since the system is computed under modulo 7 arithmetic, the terms that are marked in blue, namely $7c_{12}$ and $7c_{22}$, are reduced modulo 7 to zero. However, the terms in red, namely $2c_{20}$ and $-\ 2c_{21}$, cannot be reduced mod 7 any further. These residual terms appear as a result of the bug introduced into the system, indicating the source of the fault: the swapped carry-bit signals c_{20} and c_{21}. That is, the red terms in the final equation point to the location of the bug. In order to fix the bug, the designer ought to examine the netlist, paying attention to the connections of the two residual signals (in red).

While the above example demonstrates the effect of a cross-wiring fault, other types of faults can also occur within the circuit and can be identified with this debugging approach. Some of the common fault scenarios include:

- **Multiple Cross-Wiring Faults:** In some cases, multiple input or output signals may be cross-wired at different locations within the circuit. This can introduce additional errors that propagate through the network, leading to unexpected terms in the final equation. The debugging approach outlined earlier can still be applied to detect and isolate such errors by analyzing the residual terms that appear in the final computed signature.
- **Mislabeling of Output Signals:** The specific example discussed in this paper focused on cross-wiring faults occurring at the carry-out bits of adders.

However, a similar issue can arise if the outputs are mislabeled at the very input stage of the circuit. This mislabeling can lead to incorrect signal associations, producing a similar pattern of discrepancies in the final result. By carefully examining the extra terms that appear in the computed equations, the mislabeling error can be identified and corrected.

- **Incorrect Assignment of Primary Inputs:** Another possible fault involves an incorrect assignment of primary input signals, such as partial products (p_{ij}). For instance, if a partial product term such as p_{00} is mistakenly connected to column 1 instead of column 0, the weight associated with that term in the final computation will be incorrect. This misplacement alters the final computed signature, indicating an error. By comparing the erroneous signature with the expected reference signature, the location of the fault can be identified, allowing for a targeted correction.
- **Errors within the Adder Modules:** The debugging method described here mainly targets the interconnection errors in the adder netlist. If the error appears inside an adder, the logic netlist obtained by parsing with the ABC tool will contain modules or logic gates different than adders. In this case other types of functional verification techniques will need to be employed. The case of a modulo $(2^n + 1)$ multiplier, discussed next, falls in this category, if the parsing (adder extraction) tool is incapable of properly extracting "clean" adders.

In summary, the debugging methodology presented in this paper is not limited to cross-wiring faults alone but can be extended to various types of circuit errors. By leveraging the algebraic properties of the computed equations, discrepancies introduced by different types of faults can be systematically detected and traced back to their source.

4.2 Other Modular Architectures

In more complex modular multipliers, such as those based on Booth encoding or other reduction strategies (e.g., $(2^n + 1)$ modular multipliers), the nonlinear section may involve multiple layers of logic beyond simple AND gates. However, as long as the nonlinear portion remains structurally separable from the linear adder array and feeds its outputs directly into the accumulation stage, the principles of verification and debugging described here can be extended to those designs as well.

We tried to evaluate our verification approach on a small modulo $(2^n + 1)$ multiplier. Such a multiplier calculates the product of two $(n + 1)$-bit unsigned integers, followed by a reduction modulo $(2^n + 1)$. In these designs, the partial products corresponding to bit position n (which represent the MSB carry-out in each row, except for the final output) have a weight of 2^n, and are fed *inverted* into bit position 0. While these circuits have similar linear array structure as modulo $(2^n - 1)$ multipliers, their nonlinear component is significantly more complex. This by itself is not a problem since all these nonlinear components will actually reduce to linear expressions under the mod 2^n+ 1 condition. The main problem is the inversion of the carry-out signals that are fed to lower bit positions. This makes it hard for the extraction tools, such as ABC and others [19, 20] to correctly extract the adders. We believe that the complication comes mostly from the inversion of the carry out signal between the MSB cell of a given row of adders and the LSB cell of the next row. Some of the inversion is probably being used during logic synthesis to the point that it cannot be mapped into clean adders. As a result, our attempts to solve this problem were unsuccessful due to a lack of reliable reverse-engineering techniques to produce such an array structure. Knowing the exact structure, instead of deriving it from the lower-level Verilog, AIG, or Blif netlists, would solve this problem.

5 Results

The verification framework was implemented as a Python-based software program interfaced with the ABC logic synthesis & verification tool [21]. The input to the program is an arithmetic modular circuit in the AIG or BLIF format; it is parsed by ABC to extract key structural components, such as adders and logic gates, using the & *show* – *a* command. The extracted network, such as the one illustrated in Fig. 3, is further parsed by a Python program to derive algebraic expressions that form the basis of the verification process. The program systematically constructs a system of linear equations for the circuit, with properly computed weights. The system is solved symbolically using the *SymPy* library, the results are analyzed and modified by reducing terms modulo ($2^n - 1$) and compared against the expected specification polynomial.

The verification method was tested on benchmarks ranging from 4-bit to 512-bit modular multipliers, provided by the authors of [10]. Our approach successfully verified a 512×512-bit modular multiplier in a matter of minutes, with the results shown in Table 2, published in our initial work on verification [16]. Since debugging is an integral part of verification, the process of localizing the faults to the exact location will take approximately the same amount of time as for the verification.

Debugging uses the same framework as in verification for equation-solving and reduction to detect discrepancies in the linear system of equations in the presence of faults. Any deviation from the expected algebraic structure of the circuit signals a fault. The only additional time to be accounted for is the process of analyzing and correcting these faults. This should be done by analyzing discrepancies in the linear system, interpreting them in the context of the design and correcting them accordingly. This task is left to the designer, who is in the best position to interpret the faults and find the way to fix them. For example, the presence of residual expression $c_{20} + c_{21}$ in our 3-bit mod 7 circuit indicates that there is a wiring problem involving these signals and should be handled by the designer.

Table 2. Verification results for $2^n - 1$ modular multiplier (in CPU seconds).

Size	Nodes	Extract adders	Compute weights	Solve linear sys.	Total time	Verif. time [10]
4×4	160	<0.01	<0.01	<0.01	<0.01	<0.01
8×8	744	<0.01	<0.01	<0.01	<0.01	0.01
16×16	3,096	<0.01	<0.01	0.01	0.02	0.05
32×32	12,344	0.02	0.01	0.05	0.08	0.21
64×64	49,784	0.07	0.09	0.19	0.35	1.40
128×128	197,880	0.29	0.62	0.81	1.71	15.16
256×256	787,960	1.15	4.81	3.44	9.40	384.39

(continued)

Table 2. (*continued*)

Size	Nodes	Extract adders	Compute weights	Solve linear sys.	Total time	Verif. time [10]
512 × 512	3,152,888	4.58	38.26	12.78	55.62	6,948.99

6 Discussion and Conclusions

This work introduces a novel approach to solve the verification and debugging of modular arithmetic circuits by modeling them as system of linear equations. It partitions the design into two distinct components: a nonlinear Boolean section that consists of partial product generation and an array of adders that can be modeled using linear equations.

In modular $(2^n - 1)$ multipliers, the nonlinear portion is relatively simple, comprising a single layer of AND gates. In other modular multipliers, such as modulo $(2^n + 1)$ multipliers or Booth multipliers, the nonlinear section can be significantly more complex, incorporating multiple layers of logic. In principle, as long as the nonlinear portion remains separable from the adder array and serves purely as input to the array, the proposed methodology can still be applied. The key advantage of this approach is its ability to transform the verification problem into a system of linear equations, bypassing the computational difficulties encountered in traditional algebraic methods such as SAT- and CSA-based verification.

Unlike the SCA verification methods that rely on extensive polynomial manipulations, our approach avoids the exponential explosion of terms and vanishing monomials by structuring the verification process around multiple-output components that can be conveniently represented by linear equations. Instead of treating logic gates such as Majority-3, XOR, and AND as isolated elements with nonlinear characteristics, these logic components are grouped into full- and half-adders, allowing the entire adder structure to be analyzed in a linear algebraic framework. This transformation enables an efficient and scalable verification, where the internal computation of the adder array is reduced to solving a system of linear equations, significantly improving the verification performance. A crucial part of this approach is the efficient computation of weights, which eliminates the need for costly modulo reductions and backward rewriting.

An important aspect of this methodology is its direct applicability to debugging. Since the verification process itself systematically constructs and solves linear equations that describe the circuit behavior, any deviation from the expected specification signals a fault. The ability to localize errors is integrated into the framework, as the inconsistencies in the system of equations directly point to specific components of the design. The time required for fault localization is therefore nearly identical to that of verification, making debugging as efficient as verification itself.

Despite its advantages, this method is limited to designs with a structured, regular architecture that can be naturally decomposed into linear and nonlinear sections. It relies on the availability of the adder array and may not generalize to arbitrary modular multipliers unless a similar structure is present. In contrast, traditional rewriting-based verification techniques, such as those in [10], are more general and can be applied to a broader range of arithmetic circuits. However, their flexibility comes at the cost of a significantly higher computational complexity.

Given the increasing complexity of modern arithmetic circuits, verification methodologies must prioritize simplicity and efficiency. This aligns with the philosophy of "design for verification," where circuits are constructed with verification in mind, even at a cost of area or delay deficiency. This perspective is closely related to the concept of "polynomial-time verification" emphasized in [22], advocating for verification-friendly design choices that ensure scalability in formal verification methodologies.

Acknowledgment. This work has been supported by a grant from the National Science Foundation, Award No. CCF-2006465.

References

1. Zimmermann, R.: Efficient VLSI implementation of modulo (2/sup n//spl plusmn/1) addition and multiplication. In: Proceedings 14th IEEE Symposium on Computer Arithmetic (Cat. No. 99CB36336), pp. 158–167. IEEE (1999)
2. Fatemi, S., Zare, M., Khavari, A.F., Maymandi-Nejad, M.: Efficient implementation of digit-serial montgomery modular multiplier architecture. IET Circuits Dev. Syst. **13**(7), 942–949 (2019)
3. Ganai, M., Gupta, A.: SAT-Based Scalable Formal Verification Solutions. Springer, New York (2007). https://doi.org/10.1007/978-0-387-69167-1
4. Bryant, R.E.: Graph-based algorithms for Boolean function manipulation. IEEE Trans. Comput. **100**(8), 677–691 (1986)
5. Yu, C., Brown, W., Liu, D., Rossi, A., Ciesielski, M.: Formal verification of arithmetic circuits by function extraction. IEEE Trans. Comput. Aided Des. Integr. Circuits Syst. **35**(12), 2131–2142 (2016)
6. Mahzoon, A., Große, D., Drechsler, R.: REVSCA-2.0: SCA-based formal verification of non-trivial multipliers using reverse engineering and local vanishing removal. IEEE Trans. Comput. Aided Des. Integr. Circuits Syst. (2021)
7. Temel, M., Slobodova, A., Hunt, W.A.: Automated and scalable verification of integer multipliers. In: Lahiri, S., Wang, C. (eds.) CAV 2020. LNCS, vol. 12224, pp. 485–507. Springer, Cham (2020). https://doi.org/10.1007/978-3-030-53288-8_23
8. Kaufmann, D., Biere, A.: AMulet 2.0 for verifying multiplier circuits. In: TACAS, vol. 2, pp. 357–364 (2021)
9. Walther, C.: Formally verified Montgomery multiplication. In: Chockler, H., Weissenbacher, G. (eds.) CAV 2018. LNCS, vol. 10982, pp. 505–522. Springer, Cham (2018). https://doi.org/10.1007/978-3-319-96142-2_30
10. Mahzoon, A., Große, D., Scholl, C., Konrad, A., Drechsler, R.: Formal verification of modular multipliers using symbolic computer algebra and Boolean satisfiability. In: Proceedings of the 59th ACM/IEEE Design Automation Conference, pp. 1183–1188 (2022)
11. Farahmandi, F., Mishra, P.: Automated test generation for debugging arithmetic circuits. In: 2016 Design, Automation & Test in Europe Conference & Exhibition (DATE), pp. 1351–1356 (2016)
12. Mahzoon, A., Große, D., Drechsler, R.: Combining symbolic computer algebra and Boolean satisfiability for automatic debugging and fixing of complex multipliers. In: 2018 IEEE Computer Society Annual Symposium on VLSI (ISVLSI), pp. 351–356 (2018)

13. Sabbagh, N.A., Alizadeh, B.: Arithmetic circuit correction by adding optimized correctors based on groebner basis computation. In: 2021 IEEE European Test Symposium (ETS), pp. 1–6 (2021)
14. Haghbayan, M.H., Alizadeh, B.: A dynamic specification to automatically debug and correct various divider circuits. Integr. VLSI J. **53**, 100–114 (2016)
15. Dasari, J., Ciesielski, M.: Combining formal verification and testing for debugging of arithmetic circuits. In: 2024 Design, Automation & Test in Europe Conference & Exhibition (DATE), pp. 1–6 (2024)
16. Dasari, J., Yu, C., Ciesielski, M.: Linear algebra approach to verification of modular $(2^n - 1)$ multipliers. In: 2024 IFIP/IEEE 32nd International Conference on Very Large Scale Integration (VLSI-SoC), pp. 1–6 (2024)
17. Brayton, R., Mishchenko, A.: ABC: an academic industrial-strength verification tool. In: Proceedings of the International Conference on Computer-Aided Verification, pp. 24–40 (2010)
18. Basith, M.A., Ahmad, T., Rossi, A., Ciesielski, M.: Algebraic approach to arithmetic design verification. In: Formal Methods in CAD. FMCAD, , pp. 67–71 (2011)
19. Soeken, M., et al.: The EPFL logic synthesis libraries, June 2022. arXiv:1805.05121v3
20. Yin, J., Song, Z., Chen, C., Hu, Q., Yu, C.: BoolE: exact symbolic reasoning via Boolean equality saturation. In: Design Automation Conference (DAC 2025) (2025)
21. Mishchenko, A., et al.: ABC: a system for sequential synthesis and verification (2007). http://www.eecs.berkeley.edu/~alanmi/abc
22. Drechsler, R., Mahzoon, A.: Preserving design hierarchy information for polynomial formal verification. In: 2022 IFIP/IEEE 30th International Conference on Very Large Scale Integration (VLSI-SoC), pp. 1–7. IEEE (2022)

Challenges in FPGA Resource Allocation and Placement for Efficient EM Fault Attack Detection Strategies

Sami El Amraoui(✉), Régis Leveugle, and Paolo Maistri

Univ. Grenoble Alpes, CNRS, Grenoble INP, TIMA, 38000 Grenoble, France
{sami.el-amraoui,regis.leveugle, paolo.maistri}@univ-grenoble-alpes.fr

Abstract. The integration of FPGAs into security-critical systems entails a thorough evaluation of their vulnerability to fault injection attacks. ElectroMagnetic Fault Injection (EMFI) represents a particularly concerning threat vector due to its non-invasive characteristics, affordability, and capacity for precisely inducing transient faults. Our research examines the susceptibility to single EM pulsed attacks of Ring Oscillators (ROs), which can serve as a building block for both security primitives and EMFI sensors. By conducting different experiments on 28 nm Xilinx FPGAs, we reveal that RO harmonic responses significantly vary based on the spatial configuration and routing constraints of the ring within the FPGA die. Additionally, we demonstrate the paramount importance of evaluating the EM pulse polarity and injection timing effects as they critically influence the fault distribution pattern while enabling a full control over the induced harmonic errors. These findings underscore the critical role of the FPGA resource utilization in security, providing valuable insights for the design of effective EMFI countermeasures and robust RO-based hardware implementations.

Keywords: Ring oscillators · Pulsed EM Fault Injection · FPGA · Place & Route · Harmonic locking

1 Introduction

In today's digital landscape, ensuring the security of electronic systems is paramount, as they can be targeted by malicious entities seeking to compromise data confidentiality and system integrity. To this end, physical attacks and notably fault attacks have become a prevalent method for circumventing the security mechanisms of embedded devices, with a large arsenal of techniques at the attackers' disposal. These techniques range from disrupting clock signals to inducing sudden variations in temperature, supply voltage or substrate bias, along with injecting parasitic currents using powerful electromagnetic (EM) disturbances [1]. Other sophisticated techniques using laser or X-rays can be

---

Grenoble INP—Institute of Engineering Univ. Grenoble Alpes.

Published by Springer Nature Switzerland AG 2026
E. -I. Vatajelu (Ed.): VLSI-SoC 2024, IFIP AICT 744, pp. 109–126, 2026.
https://doi.org/10.1007/978-3-032-09575-6_7

more efficient but very expensive and risky for the attackers as they can damage the target device. Among these methods, ElectroMagnetic Fault Injection (EMFI) has gained prominence due to the optimal balance between the attack effectiveness and its low cost and device preparation requirements. In a recent paper [2], an open-source design 'PicoEMP' was introduced whereby an EM pulsed fault injection can be mounted for less than 100$. On one hand, this makes EMFI attacks more accessible in both academia and industry, which will help improve our understanding of its fault mechanisms. On the other hand, this render the attack easier and more accessible for malicious entities as well, therefore extending the threat on several applications.

EMFI alters the behavior of a target device by inducing ground bounces or voltage drops as a result of the magnetic flux created by the EM probe [3]. The EM coupling can be performed either through harmonic or pulsed Fault Injection. In the context of our study, we are interested in the second method involving powerful EM pulses.

After recognizing the inherent threat of EMFI, extensive research efforts have been targeted in recent years to fully understand and mitigate its impact on diverse devices, ranging from microcontrollers to FPGAs and Application-Specific Integrated Circuits (ASICs). Our focus in this work will be directed towards FPGAs as they represent good candidates for implementing cryptographic algorithms and security primitives such as Physical Unclonable Functions (PUFs) and True Random Number Generators (TRNGs). Since these primitives employ ROs as an essential building block in their design, assessing their response to EMFI is important to improve their robustness.

Within this context, this paper aims to enhance the understanding of the harmonic locking impact on ROs with pulsed EMFI in FPGAs. This effect was introduced in [4] where the authors were able to lock the RO frequency into one of its harmonics through a single properly tuned EM pulse. The RO harmonic response was characterized as a function of its placement in the FPGA chip, the EM pulse width (PW) and amplitude, and the position of the probe relative to the FPGA package. In [5], the investigation sought to understand how multiple pulses and the placement and routing (P&R) constraints of both the inverters and the input/output (IO) pins influence the sensitivity of the ring. In this study, we advance from the groundwork of these papers and our recent work [16] to elaborate on the influence on the harmonic errors of other parameters related to the EM pulse timing and polarity, the manufacturing properties of the FPGA and the RO layout and density within the FPGA die. In more detail, the main contributions of this paper consist of:

- Assessing the impact of the FPGA structure (Spartan7 vs. Artix7-100T) and its type of packaging (Wire-bond vs. Flip-Chip) on the fault distribution and its magnitude on different modern FPGA platforms.
- Investigating the pulse polarity effect on faults to emphasize its significance when evaluating the efficiency of EMFI across various FPGAs.
- Investigating the influence of P&R constraints on maximizing the harmonic response while varying the density and the layout of the RO with a constant number of inverters.
- Highlighting the importance of optimal utilization of interconnects to enable an efficient RO-based detector with minimal overhead.
- Analyzing the injection timing impact on the control over the range of induced harmonic errors to verify the attacker's ability to circumvent the detectors.

The remainder of this paper is organized as follows. Section 2 introduces the related works on EMFI as well as the locking phenomenon on ROs. The experimental setup and methodology for the tests are described in Sect. 3. Section 4 reports and analyzes the experimental results. Finally, Sect. 5 draws conclusions and perspectives.

2 Background

2.1 Electromagnetic Fault Injection

EMFI corrupts the normal operation of an integrated circuit (IC) through parasitic currents that are induced in all wire loops of the IC after a sudden variation of the magnetic or electric field generated by a probe. The EM coupling can be achieved through two different methods: harmonic EMFI and pulsed EMFI. The former consists of exposing the ICs to continuous EM waves to usually target analog blocks of ICs whose operation is continuous in time like clock generators and TRNGs as studied in [17] and [18]. On the other hand, pulsed EMFI disrupts the behavior of ICs during a few clock cycles by generating sudden variations of the magnetic field in a reduced volume close to the IC surface that induce parasitic currents in the closed loops of the power and ground networks of the DUT. In this study, we are mainly interested in single short perturbations; therefore, our EMFI attack will be focused on EM pulses.

It should be noted that mounting a successful EMFI attack includes multiple steps and identifying the optimal sensitive location on the die is the critical one. To achieve that, one can leverage EM side-channel to find the maximum leakage observed on the target chip. Within this context, a recent paper [6] investigated the design optimization of a hybrid EM probe that can efficiently enable both capturing EM emissions and injecting EM perturbations. This can help reduce the time and complexity of the evaluation that still includes other parameters related to the pulse such as the injection timing, and the width, amplitude, and polarity of the pulse.

2.2 Related Works

EM Fault Models & Countermeasures. Considering all these challenges, ensuring full protection of different devices against EMFI requires accurate fault models describing the mechanism involved in EM-induced faults. Several works [7–9] have been carried out to explain their nature. They suggested that these faults can be explained either by the Timing or by the Sampling fault model, depending on the clock frequency of the target and the strength of the EM coupling within the circuit. A recent study by Nabhan et al. [10] highlighted that two underlying mechanisms are involved within the timing fault model. The first one relates to the target's clock distribution network which becomes highly susceptible to voltage glitches on the clock tree at low or moderate frequencies. However, at high frequencies associated with small slack, the power distribution network (PDN) is the most sensitive on-chip network as EM perturbation leads to violations in timing constraints. In another paper [11] trying to uncover the complexity of the EM injection and its interaction with circuits at a low physical level, the authors conducted EMFI experiments from the substrate backside of a 180 nm CMOS technology equipped with six crypto cores of 128-bit AES and an on-chip voltage waveform monitor. Their results showed a key finding emphasizing that depending on the polarity of the probe, significant negative voltage drops can be induced at specific locations within the PDN originating from injection positions that are not necessarily close to the impacted point.

Previous works studied the implementation of EMFI countermeasures on FPGAs such as [12] and [13]. However, the optimal number and location of the sensors to guarantee security against EM perturbations with the lowest overhead is still an open question. This primarily stems from the fact that the customization of placement and routing is challenging in FPGA design tools as they are designed by default to guarantee the best performance and resource optimization but do not take into account the circuit's EM emissions or susceptibility issues during the P&R process. To this end, our work will try to give more insights into the effects of P&R constraints on EMFI susceptibility to determine the best strategy for implementing detectors in different FPGA platforms.

Locking of Ring Oscillators. A RO is harmonically locked when it is forced to oscillate at a harmonic frequency (i.e., a multiple of the fundamental frequency). Previous studies on ROs focused mainly on the locking phenomenon happening due to radiofrequency interference on the power supply [19] or sinusoidal perturbation signals passed across a delay line placed near the RO [20], which makes them lock onto a signal with a frequency close to their natural oscillation frequency or its harmonics. This can render the confidential key generated using RO-based TRNGs partially or even fully deterministic by controlling the bias as demonstrated in [17, 21] through EM harmonic injections.

Sustained Harmonic Errors. This phenomenon was achieved with both laser experiments on a custom-designed 40nm Bulk CMOS ring oscillator, and electrical experiments on a RO constructed with discrete components in [14]. The authors were able to conclude that when one or several Single Event Transients (SETs) with a pulse width smaller than the total loop delay are induced during one oscillation period T of the RO, it deviates from its fundamental frequency and locks to one of its odd harmonics depending on the induced number of extra rising edges. In [4], the authors were able to validate this behavior through the injection of a single positive EM pulse into a RO composed of 1200 (50×24) inverters and implemented in an Artix7-100T FPGA. In their work, the ring was placed either on the top or bottom clock region and used 1 Look-Up Table (LUT) per Slice. The results showed that the placement of the RO in the chip, and the location and intensity of the injection affect the fault occurrence: when placed on the top clock region, the RO was more vulnerable to harmonic errors. Also, it was shown that in order to force higher harmonics with higher probabilities, one can increase the PW and amplitude of the pulse.

In [5], the characterization included a first analysis of the impact of routing constraints on the harmonic response of the RO. The findings suggested that for the same placement of the ring, favoring short vertical connections (called 'vertical snake') between LUTs results in higher harmonic sensitivity, while the lowest vulnerability was reported with long horizontal connections. Conducting similar tests on Spartan7 and Kintex7 FPGAs enabled the confirmation of this conclusion. Therefore, in this work, we will adopt the most sensitive routing 'vertical snake' to investigate further parameters: how the pulse polarity, the density, the layout of the RO and the injection timing impact the fault distribution and the harmonics intensity on different FPGAs.

3 Experimental Setup and Methodology

3.1 EMFI Setup

The following setup shown in Fig. 1 was used to perform the EMFI experiments:

- Pulse Generator: We used the ChipShouter pulse generator for this work to perform EM pulsed fault injection. It can generate pulses with amplitudes from 150 V up to 500 V and variable pulse widths depending on the probe's diameter and the voltage amplitude.
- XYZ Motorized Table: The motors are used to precisely control the position of the EM probe. They can set the X, Y, and Z positions via an RS-232 serial interface.
- EM Probes: We used two of the EM probes provided with the ChipShouter and consisting of a 1 mm wire coiled either clockwise (CW) or counter-clockwise (CCW) around a 4 mm ferrite core to induce positive or negative pulse polarity, respectively.
- Control PC: controls the whole platform through serial ports.
- Digital Oscilloscope: A Picoscope of 200 MHz bandwidth monitored the frequency of the RO and the synchronization between its oscillations and the pulse injection.
- Targets: Our characterization has been achieved on four types of AMD-Xilinx
- FPGAs all manufactured in 28 nm process technology: a Spartan7 (xc7s251CSGA225) in a Cmod-S7 board; two Artix7 FPGAs (xc7a100T-1CSG324 & xc7a200T-1SBG484) within Nexys-A7 and Nexys-Video boards respectively, and finally a Kintex7 (xc7k160T-1FBG676) embedded in a SAKURA-X board. Their characteristics are summarized in Table 1.

It should be noted that each FPGA die covers only a portion of the package. The die sizes of Kintex7 and Artix7-200T were measured since both were decapsulated in their boards. For Spartan7, this information was revealed through X-ray imaging while it was reported in [15] for Artix7-100T. Both Spartan7 and Artix7-100T use a wire-bond packaging technology, where the die is attached to the substrate face up and the connections are made with wires. On the other hand, the Kintex7 and Artix7-200T are flipped over and placed face down, which eliminates wire bonds and results in lower inductance and better thermal performance. All these differences will be leveraged to explore how they will affect the outcome of EMFI.

Fig. 1. Experimental setup

Table 1. Characteristics of the targeted FPGAs

FPGA	Packaging	Package Size (mm^2)	Die Size (mm^2)	Logic Slices
Spartan7	Wire-bond chip-scale	13 × 13	5 × 5.1	3650
Artix7100T	Wire-bond chip-scale	15 × 15	6.5 × 10	15850
Artix7200T	Flip-Chip lidless	19 × 19	10.66 × 11.95	33650
Kintex7	Flip-Chip lidless	27 × 27	9 × 12	25350

3.2 RO Design

Ring Oscillator. The oscillating frequency of a RO depends on various parameters but its simplified computation can be done with the following formula, where D_i is the propagation delay of each delay element in the RO, D_r is the average delay related to the routing between them, and N is the number of these elements:

$$F = \frac{1}{2 \times (D_i + D_r) \times N}$$

Figure 2 shows the architecture of our implemented RO with an even number N = 1200 of inverters and a Nand gate used as an activation gate. After the Enable signal moves from a logical low level to a logical high level, oscillations start. Then if we force the Enable signal to move low, the oscillations stop.

Placement and Routing Constraints. In all targeted FPGAs, the Configurable Logic Block (CLB) tile contains two slices. Each slice includes 4 LUTs and 8 flip-flops. Depending on the density that we want to achieve, our RO was formed by configuring either one or all of the 4 LUTs within each slice as an inverter. This makes the ring more or less compact in the FPGA. Also, to explore the effect of different RO layouts, we customized the placement and routing of the LUTs in Vivado tool to enable either a horizontal, vertical, or square shape. It should be noted that in all our experiments, we used the same number of inverters (N = 1200 to constrain the RO to one clock region) for each different P&R implementation of the RO in all three FPGAs.

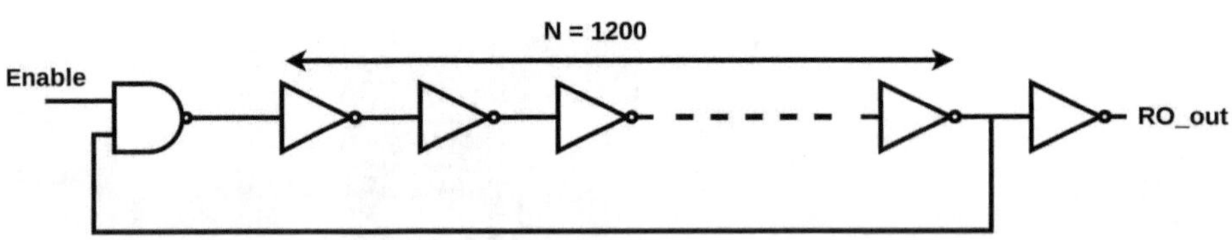

Fig. 2. Architecture of the ring oscillator

3.3 Methodology

After a single EM pulse injection, the RO frequency may change or not, as follows:

- Unchanged frequency: In that case, after the attack, the RO still oscillates at the same fundamental frequency. If we disable the RO and it keeps oscillating, we know that the 'Enable' configuration was corrupted, and the FPGA must be reprogrammed for the next test.
- Harmonic locked frequency: After the attack, the RO frequency can be locked into one of its odd harmonics (3, 5, 7….). Therefore, a reset of the 'Enable' is mandatory to restore the original oscillation frequency of the ring. However, as in the previous case, lack of control over the 'Enable' means that the board must be reprogrammed.
- Noise signal: the attack forces the RO output signal to noise, which means the bitstream was corrupted as resetting the enable signal does not restart oscillations. Therefore, reprogramming the bitstream is always mandatory before the next test.

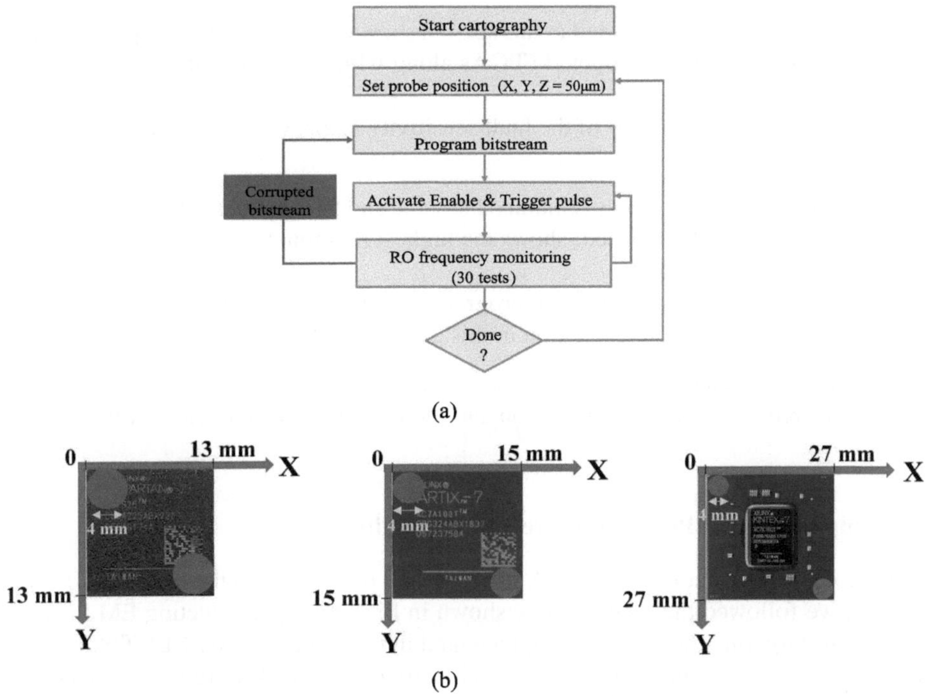

Fig. 3. (a) RO faults evaluation flow (b) FPGA Package Scan

Based on these observed effects, a specific methodology, depicted in Fig. 3(a), was adopted to inject and observe a single pulse into the RO. The goal is to detect the occurrence of harmonics while scanning over the FPGA package with the 4 mm CW or CCW probe. The probe tip is kept 50 μm on top of the package and displaced by steps of 1 mm (due to the probe's size and resolution) from the top left to bottom right corner as depicted in Fig. 3(b). The detailed steps are:

- 1st step: Set the initial EM pulse parameters for the test (amplitude = 450 V/PW = 100 ns). The choice of these values is motivated by the results reported in [4].

- 2nd step: Place the probe at the initial coordinate [X = 0, Y = 0] above the package.
- 3rd step: Program the FPGA with the bitstream.
- 4th step: Enable the RO and trigger the single EM pulse injection.
- 5th step: Monitor the output RO frequency after injection then disable the RO to detect the occurrence of harmonic induced frequencies and bitstream corruptions.
- 6th step: Repeat 30 times the steps 4 and 5 to assess the reproducibility of faults for the same (X, Y) coordinate.
- 7th step: Move the probe to the next position and restart the procedure at step 3 with a displacement step of 1mm until the last coordinate to obtain a fault sensitivity map of the whole FPGA package.

4 Experimental Results and Discussion

The experimental results reported in this section show the effect of the EM pulse polarity and timing on the different targeted FPGAs along with the impact of the RO layout on faults.

To improve the readability of the fault sensitivity maps, we assigned a specific color for each effect:

- White: No faults (Frequency remained the same and the bitstream was not corrupted).
- Gradient from Yellow to Red: shows the highest harmonic error that was monitored within 30 conducted tests.
- Black: represents mutes where reprogramming the bitstream was mandatory; the probability of bitstream corruption in this case is 100%.

It should be noted that the numbers in these maps refer to the ratio between the monitored frequency after EM injection and the fundamental frequency of the targeted RO.

4.1 Impact of the FPGA Structure and Packaging

To explore the influence of the FPGA structure and packaging on the fault sensitivity of the RO, we followed the methodology shown in Fig. 3(a) by conducting EM injection campaigns targeting the same RO implemented in the three FPGAs; 1 LUT/Slice and a vertical routing with short connections, as illustrated in Fig. 4, were used. It should be noted that even if the same P&R of the RO was adopted, its frequency slightly varied between them because of the difference in their internal structure and the output pin connection. The RO was originally running at 1250 kHz in Spartan7, at 1075 kHz in Artix7-100T, and at 1417 kHz in Kintex7.

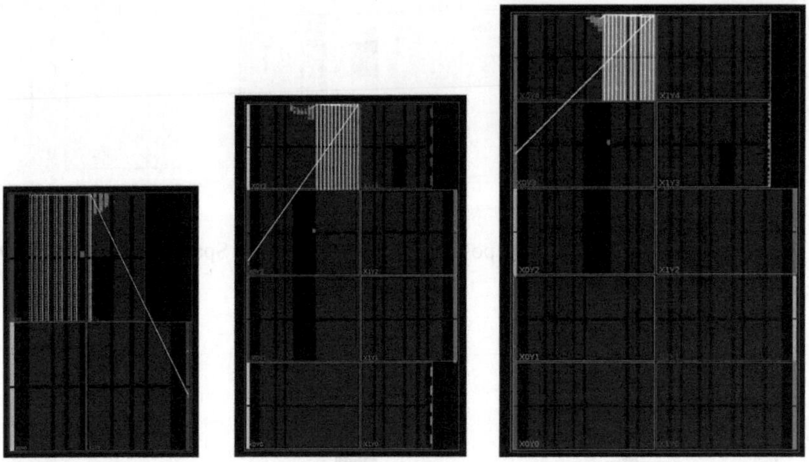

(a) (b) (c)

Fig. 4. FPGA floorplan from Vivado showing the implemented RO in (a) Spartan7 (b) Artix7-100T (c) Kintex7

Figure 5 represents the fault sensitivity maps of the three FPGAs with the positive polarity and shows that changing the FPGA family and packaging, even within the same process technology, can effectively influence the intensity and the location of the induced faults. The maximum impact was achieved in Artix7-100T with a harmonic error of 43, twice larger than the impact on Kintex7. Additionally, Spartan7 was the most sensitive to bitstream corruptions, as opposed to Kintex7 with no recorded vulnerability to this type of faults. This shows how Flip-Chip packaging, usually dedicated to highperformance FPGA, can reduce the fault sensitivity compared to wire-bond packaging. On another hand, if we focus on this later technology used for Spartan7 and Artix7100T, by comparing Fig. 5(a) and Fig. 5(b) we notice some similarities in the location of faults especially in the bottom center coordinates. However, only third harmonic errors were induced for Spartan7, likely because it includes less programmable logic, hence a lower coupling between the probe and its PDN.

4.2 Impact of the Pulse Polarity

Similar tests were conducted to investigate the effect of changing the pulse polarity and the results are depicted in Fig. 6, showing the new fault locations in the three FPGAs. Upon an initial examination of the three cartographies, one may observe a similar trend compared to the positive polarity with Artix7-100T being the most vulnerable to harmonics and Spartan7 being the least. However, comparing Fig. 5 and Fig. 6 highlights that the negative polarity reveals complementary fault locations in the FPGA package. This indicates a different susceptibility of the power and the ground network within FPGAs to the polarity of EMFI, which underlines the importance of this parameter when assessing the robustness of a design against this attack.

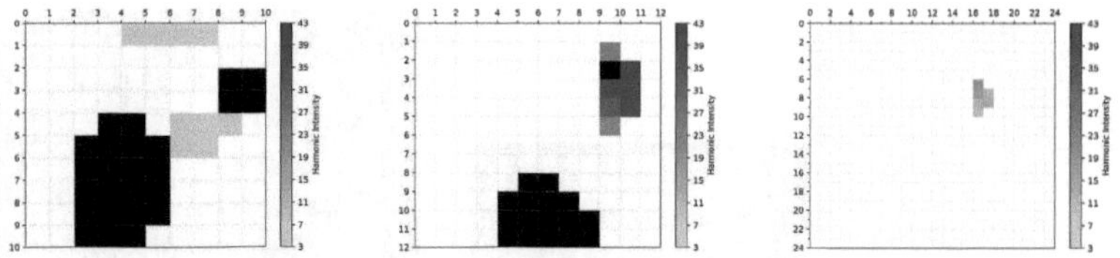

(a) (b) (c)

Fig. 5. Fault sensitivity maps with a positive pulse polarity (a) Spartan7 (b) Artix7-100T (c) Kintex7

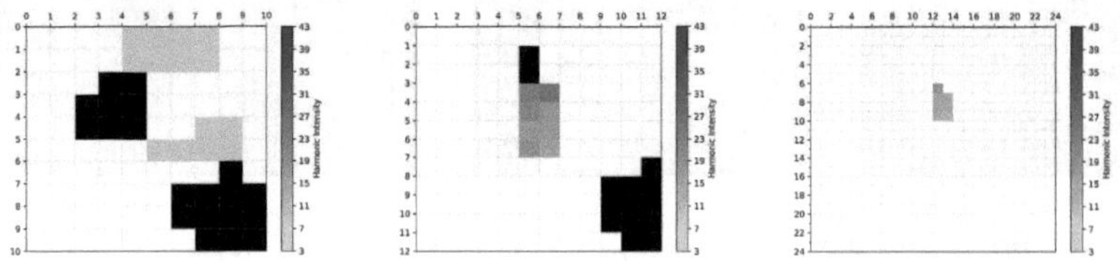

(a) (b) (c)

Fig. 6. Fault sensitivity maps with a negative pulse polarity (a) Spartan7 (b) Artix7-100T (c) Kintex7

4.3 Impact of the RO Layout

To further investigate the effect of changing the RO layout within the die, we performed new experiments while changing the placement constraints of the LUTs to enable different shapes of the RO. The intended goal is to obtain further insights into the impact that density and connections have on the ring sensitivity. Figure 7(a) to (c) show the three obtained RO shapes (horizontal, vertical and square) achieved through the use of 1LUT/Slice. For the sake of conciseness, although tests were conducted on all FPGAs using positive and negative pulse polarities, we will here present only the results related to the Artix7-100T FPGA with negative polarity and then compare and discuss the other cases. Table 2 lists the frequency of the RO depending on its layout. As shown in this table, changing the layout results in a difference of less than 1% between the output frequencies: this is mainly due to the different use of horizontal and vertical connections.

The results are represented in Fig. 8, showing how the fault sensitivity varies with the layout strategy. The most vulnerable layout was the square one with more sensitive locations and a harmonic error of 29. This indicates a better coupling between the probe and the FPGA when the RO is more compact within a single clock region, with few horizontal connections between the slices. This is likely due to the optimal density of inverters within the EM pulse. Similar tests on Spartan7 and Kintex7 enabled us to draw the same conclusion for both pulse polarities.

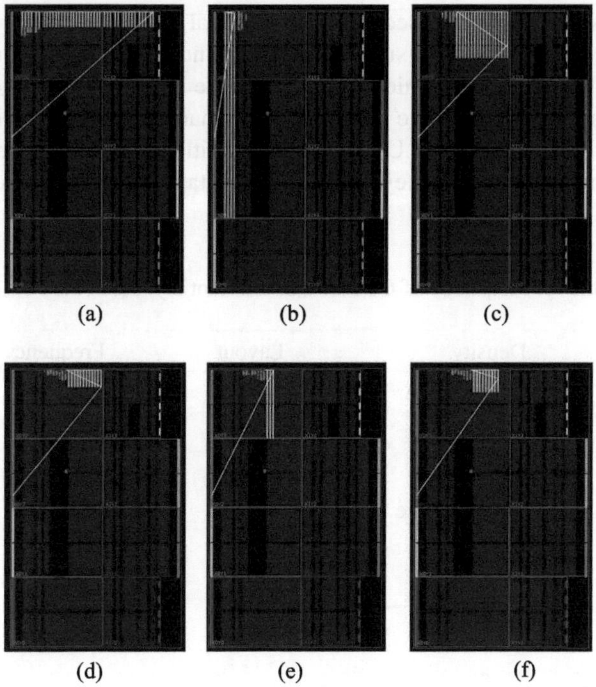

Fig. 7. Different layouts of the RO implemented in Artix7-100T FPGA using (above) 1LUT/Slice (a) Horizontal (b) Vertical (c) Square and (below) 4 LUTs/Slice (d) Horizontal (e) Vertical (f) Square

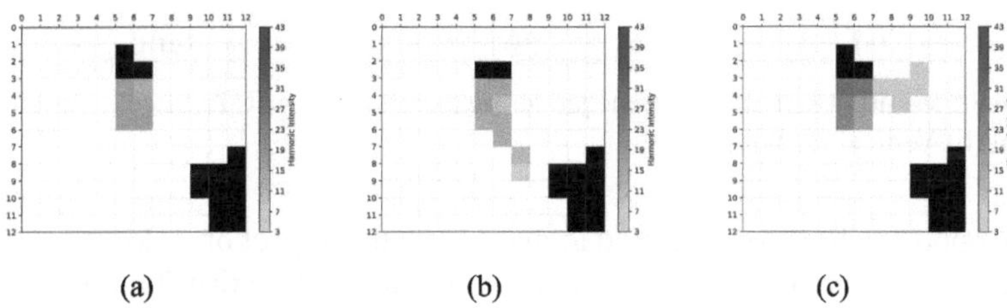

Fig. 8. Fault sensitivity maps with a negative polarity using 1 LUT/Slice configuration (a) Horizontal (b) Vertical (c) Square

4.4 Impact of the RO Density

After showing that choices in the RO distribution within the chip lead to consistent differences in the experimental results between the three FPGAs, we aimed to highlight the impact of the RO density on the observed faults. To this end, we implemented similar configurations but using 4LUTs/Slice instead of only one as illustrated in Fig. 7(d) to (f). Their corresponding frequencies are detailed in Table 2.

The results reported in Fig. 9 show how minimizing the use of Slices (from 1200 down to 300) had a noticeable impact on the harmonics intensity compared to the results in Fig. 8, especially for the square layout where the harmonic sensitivity was completely suppressed. This was mainly caused by the low spatial resolution of the 4mm probe that cannot couple with elements of a small size, which indicates the likely need for a more advanced setup to induce harmonic errors. The same result was obtained for the other FPGAs, which suggests that if we seek a minimal harmonic response of the RO, then adopting a square layout using 4 LUTs/Slice along with horizontal routing as reported in [5] remains the best option. This key finding is important for the robustness of RO-based PUFs and TRNGs against EMFI.

Table 2. Frequency of the RO with different layouts in the FPGAs

FPGA	Density	Layout	Frequency (KHz)
Artix7-100T	1 LUT/Slice	(a)	1086
		(b)	1076
		(c)	1078
	4 LUTs/Slice	(d)	1550
		(e)	1540
		(f)	1546

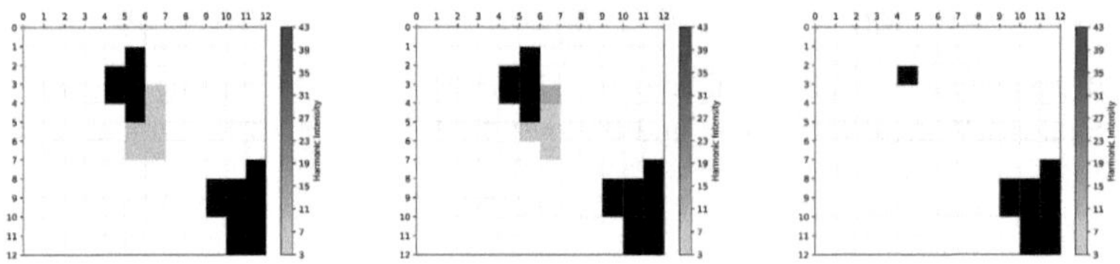

(a) (b) (c)

Fig. 9. Fault sensitivity maps with negative polarity using 4LUTs/Slice configuration (a) Horizontal (b) Vertical (c) Square

In the opposite direction, we tried to investigate the impact of making the RO layout less compact compared to the previous configurations while distributing the inverters all around the chip using 1LUT/Slice as depicted in Fig. 10. To explore the effect of reducing the number of delay elements on the harmonic errors, we implemented four RO implementations using 1200, 600, 228 and 54 inverters as shown in Fig. 10(a) to 10(d). Table 3 illustrates the RO frequency and the number of Programmable Interconnect Points (PIPs) for each configuration. The obtained fault maps are shown in Fig. 11 and they all demonstrate a higher number of impacted locations compared to previous results depicted in Fig. 8 and Fig. 9 where the RO was placed and routed within a specific region in the die. Furthermore, we can clearly observe that even when we reduce the number of inverters from 1200 down to 54 (factor of 22) which increases the frequency from 850 kHz to 11.7 MHz, we were still able to induce third and fifth harmonic errors on several locations. This indicates the importance of an optimal utilization of the PIPs in FPGAs for an effective EMFI detection with minimal overhead as they represent a critical block in the definition of the placement and routing constraints.

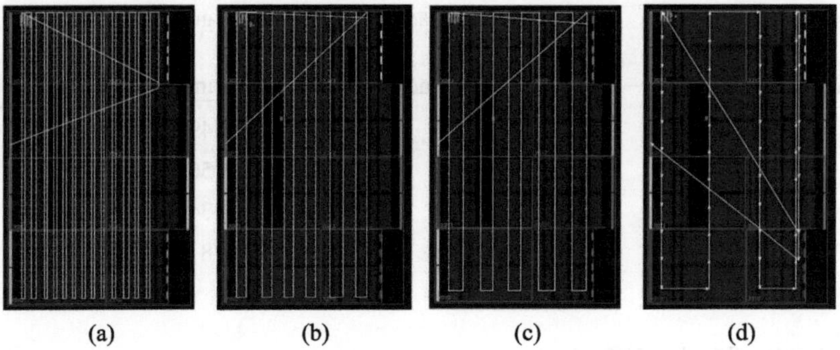

Fig. 10. RO implementation using 1LUT/Slice in Artix7-100T (a) N = 1200 (b) N = 600 (c) N = 228 (d) N = 54

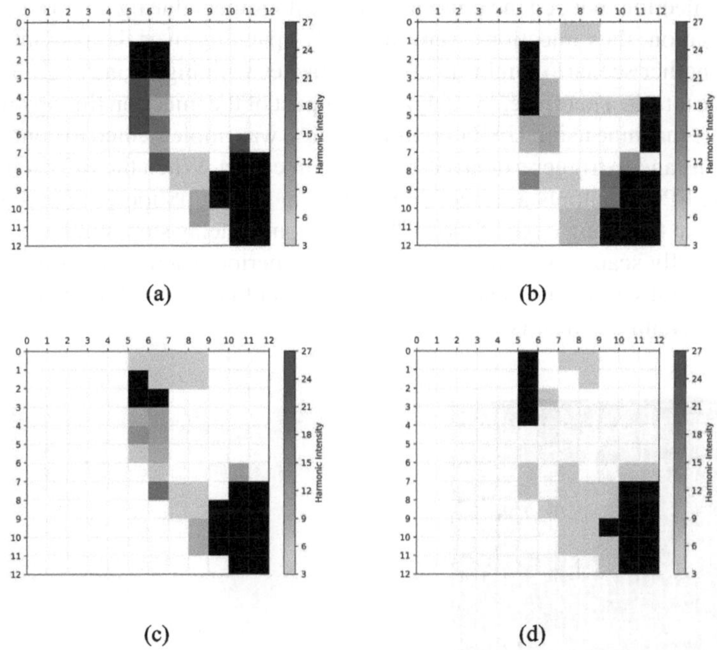

Fig. 11. Fault sensitivity maps with negative polarity (a) N = 1200 inverters (b) N = 600 inverters (c) N = 228 inverters (d) N = 54 inverters

Table 3. RO characteristics across different configurations

Number of inverters	RO Frequency	Number of PIPs
1200	850 kHz	5549
600	1779 kHz	3150
228	4065 kHz	1334
54	11.7 MHz	478

4.5 Injection Timing Effect

In the previous tests shown above, the attack scenario was based on the assumption that the attacker has low controllability over the timing of the attack: as a consequence, each performed injection induced the pulse at a different moment during the low or high level of the oscillation, thus injections were randomly spanning over the oscillation period. However, another scenario might involve an attacker with high controllability over the timing of the attack. Therefore, to analyze the impact of the injection timing on harmonic errors, a state machine using UART communication was implemented to control the start of oscillations and to trigger a delayed EM pulse injection. When the RO oscillations are enabled, the FPGA outputs a trigger signal forcing the ChipShouter to precisely inject an EM pulse at the rising edge of the 10th oscillation. A delay step of 20ns is configured to systematically scan across the entire oscillation period; such granularity is based on our experimental setup, nonetheless it is much smaller than an oscillation period in order to produce meaningful results.

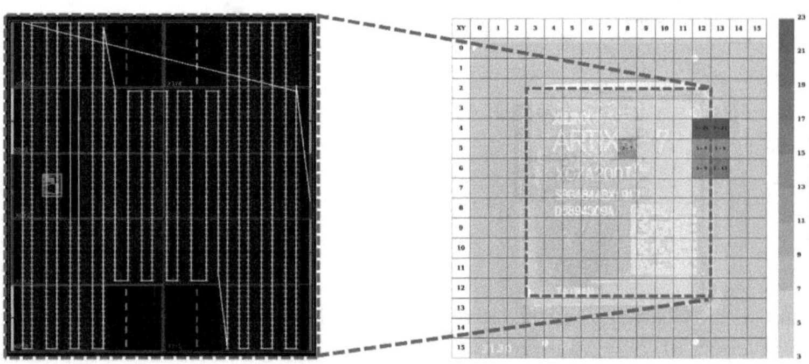

(a) (b)

Fig. 12. (a) Floorplan of a RO implementation in Artix7-200T using N = 1200 inverters placed and routed throughout the whole die (Frequency = 921 KHz) (b) Fault sensitivity map using random EMFI with positive polarity (500 V, 100 ns)

For the following tests, we chose to target an Artix7-200T FPGA embedded in a Nexys-Video board. Figure 12(a) shows the RO implementation with 1200 inverters placed and routed throughout the whole die leading to an oscillation period of 1086 ns.

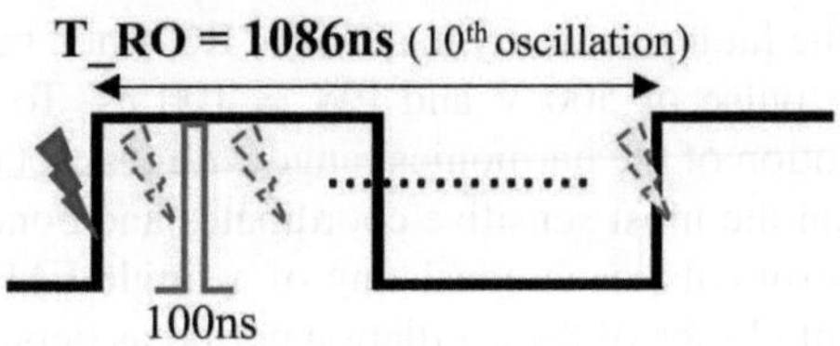

Fig. 13. Single EM pulse injection (PW = 100 ns) performed at different timings during the 10th oscillation period with a 20 ns delay step configuration

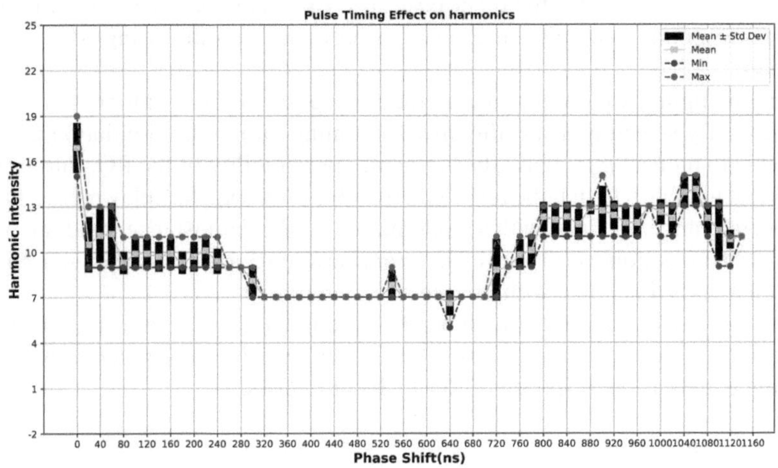

(a)

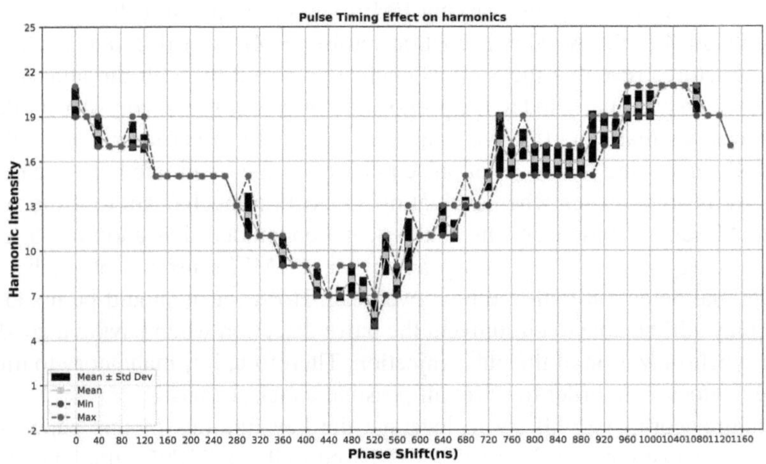

(b)

Fig. 14. EM injection timing effect on harmonic errors (a) X12Y4 (b) X13Y4

Figure 12(b) depicts the fault sensitivity map of the RO when targeted by random injections using a positive pulse of 500 V and PW = 100 ns. To enable a more detailed analysis over the evolution of the harmonics range with respect to the different injection timings, we focused on the most sensitive coordinates and conducted a campaign consisting of several experiments, each consisting of a single EM injection, with steps of 20 ns to affect different phases of the oscillation period as depicted in Fig. 13. For each phase shift, the test was repeated 10 times to assess the fault reproducibility. It should be noted that although tests were conducted on all sensitive coordinates, only the harmonic errors variation at the X12Y4 and X13Y4 coordinates are presented in Fig. 14 as similar conclusions were drawn for the other positions. As a reminder, the initial timing delay of 0 ns corresponds to a pulse injection synchronized with the rising edge of the 10th oscillation.

From the figure, we observe a periodic fluctuation of the harmonic errors for both coordinates. By selecting a specific injection timing during the oscillation period, one can be able to reduce or increase the harmonic susceptibility of the RO. Furthermore, it is important to highlight that the revealed errors for each specific delay represent subsets of the overall range obtained with a randomized timing. For instance, random injections on the X12Y4 position led to harmonic errors between 5 and 21 as shown in Fig. 12(b) compared to a (5–19) range with precise injection timing.

Therefore, we can deduce that tuning the injection timing parameter can be very efficient in controlling the outcome of an EMFI attack, which can be potentially leveraged, for example, to bias the response of RO-PUFs in FPGAs.

5 Conclusion

In this paper, we discussed the varying EMFI susceptibility of a RO while using various layouts in the FPGA. The evaluation on four FPGAs of different packaging and internal structures revealed the various challenges faced by both the attacker and the designer, which eventually led to the proposition of guidelines to consider for designing countermeasures that can effectively mitigate the EMFI threat in critical applications. By carefully analyzing the effect of pulse polarity on the harmonic response of the RO, we showed its significance when evaluating a detection mechanism to achieve an ideal behavior. Moreover, based on our analysis, we concluded that adopting a low compactness strategy when implementing the design of EMFI sensors can be advantageous for an optimal detection with minimal overhead. However, it should be noted that the attacker may still be able to circumvent the pulse detection when having a good control over the synchronization of the pulse injection. Therefore, it is mandatory to finely tune RO-based detectors in order to cover all possible attack scenarios.

As future work, we will try to leverage the key findings of this paper to assess and protect against the EMFI threat on RO-based PUFs or TRNGs implementations in FPGAs.

Acknowledgments. This work is partially supported by the "France 2030" government investment plan managed by the French National Research Agency (ANR-22-PECY0004) in the frame of ARSENE project, by the Cybersecurity Institute of Grenoble Alpes (ANR-15-IDEX-02) and by the Chips JU European Project: 101112282—Resilient Trust.

Conflicts of Interests. The authors have no competing interests to declare that are relevant to the content of this article.

References

1. Barenghi, A., Breveglieri, L., Koren, I., Naccache, D.: Fault injection attacks on cryptographic devices: theory, practice, and countermeasures. Proc. IEEE **100**(11). https://doi.org/10.1109/JPROC.2012.2188769
2. O'Flynn, C.: PicoEMP: a low-cost EMFI platform compared to BBI and voltage fault injection using TDC & external VCC measurements. In: 2023 Workshop on Fault Detection and Tolerance in Cryptography (FDTC), pp. 60–71 (2023). https://doi.org/10.1109/FDTC60478.2023.00015
3. Quisquater, J.-J., Samyde, D.: Eddy current for magnetic analysis with active sensor. In: Proceedings of the Smart Card Programming and Security (E-smart), pp. 185–194 (2002)
4. El Amraoui, S., Douadi, A., Leveugle, R., Maistri, P.: Harmonic response of ring oscillators under single ElectroMagnetic pulsed fault injection. In: 2024 25th Latin American Test Symposium (LATS), pp. 1–6 (2024). https://doi.org/10.1109/LATS62223.2024.10534602
5. El Amraoui, S., Leveugle, R., Maistri, P.: Choose your path: control of ring oscillators EMFI susceptibility through FPGA P&R constraints. In: 2024 27th International Symposium on Design & Diagnostics of Electronic Circuits & Systems (DDECS), pp. 118–123. IEEE, April 2024. https://doi.org/10.1109/DDECS60919.2024.10508906
6. Marrucco, F., Ahmed, M., Bouali, B., Mady, A.: EMplifier: hybrid electromagnetic probe for side channel and fault injection analysis. In: Proceedings of the 10th International Conference on Information Systems Security and Privacy, SCITEPRESS - Science and Technology Publications, March 2024, pp. 815–822 (2024). https://doi.org/10.5220/0012431800003648
7. Ghodrati, M., Yuce, B., Gujar, S., Deshpande, C., Nazhandali, L., Schaumont, P.: Inducing local timing fault through EM injection. In: 2018 55th ACM/ESDA/IEEE Design Automation Conference (DAC), pp. 1–6. IEEE Press. https://doi.org/10.1109/DAC.2018.8465836
8. Dehbaoui, A., Dutertre, J.-M., Robisson, B., Tria, A.: Electromagnetic transient faults injection on a hardware and a software implementations of AES. In: 2012 Workshop on Fault Diagnosis and Tolerance in Cryptography, pp. 7–15. IEEE, September 2012. https://doi.org/10.1109/FDTC.2012.15
9. Dumont, M., Lisart, M., Maurine, P.: Modeling and simulating electromagnetic fault injection. IEEE Trans. Comput. Aided Des. Integr. Circuits Syst. **40**(4), 680–693 (2021). https://doi.org/10.1109/TCAD.2020.3003287
10. Nabhan, R., Dutertre, J.-M., Rigaud, J.-B., Danger, J.-L., Sauvage, L., Sauvage, L.A.: A tale of two models: discussing the timing and sampling EM fault injection models. In: FDTC, September 2023. https://doi.org/10.1109/FDTC60478.2023.00010
11. Hasegawa, R., Monta, K., Wadatsumi, T., Miki, T., Nagata, M.: On-chip evaluation of voltage drops and fault occurrence induced by Si backside EM injection. In: Wacquez, R., Homma, N. (eds.) COSADE 2024. LNCS, vol. 14595, pp. 22–37. Springer, Cham (2024). https://doi.org/10.1007/978-3-031-57543-3_2
12. El-Baze, D., Rigaud, J.-B., Maurine, P.: A fully-digital EM pulse detector. In: Design, Automation & Test in Europe Conference & Exhibition (DATE), Dresden, Germany, pp. 439–444, March 2016
13. Gujar, S.S., Nazhandali, L.: Detecting electromagnetic injection attack on FPGAs using in-situ timing sensors. J. Hardw. Syst. Secur. **4**(3), 196–207 (2020). https://doi.org/10.1007/s41635-020-00096-9

14. Chen, Y.P., et al.: Single-event transient induced harmonic errors in digitally controlled ring oscillators. IEEE Trans. Nucl. Sci. **61**(6), 3163–3170 (2014). https://doi.org/10.1109/TNS.2014.2364813
15. Paquette, M., Marquis, B., Bainbridge, R., Chapman, J.: Visualizing electromagnetic fault injection with timing sensors. In: Proceedings of the 2021 IEEE International Conference on Physical Assurance and Inspection on Electronics, PAINE 2021 (2021). https://doi.org/10.1109/PAINE54418.2021.9707696
16. Amraoui, S.E., Leveugle, R., Maistri, P.: Capture the pulse: impact of FPGA resource utilization on EM fault injection attacks detection. In: 2024 IFIP/IEEE 32nd International Conference VLSI SoC, 2024, pp. 1–6 (2024). https://doi.org/10.1109/VLSI-SoC62099.2024.10767826
17. Bayon, P., et al.: Contactless electromagnetic active attack on ring oscillator based true random number generator. In: Schindler, W., Huss, S.A. (eds.) COSADE 2012. LNCS, vol. 7275, pp. 151–166. Springer, Heidelberg (2012). https://doi.org/10.1007/978-3-642-29912-4_12
18. Poucheret, F., Tobich, K., Lisarty, M., Chusseauz, L., Robissonx, B., Maurine, P.: Local and direct EM injection of power into CMOS integrated circuits. In: 2011 Workshop on Fault Diagnosis and Tolerance in Cryptography, Nara, Japan, pp. 100–104 (2011). https://doi.org/10.1109/FDTC.2011.18
19. Zhang, Z., Yang, S., Su, T.: The behavior of frequency locking of ring oscillators with RF interference on the supply. Microelectron. J. **116**, 105247 (2021). https://doi.org/10.1016/j.mejo.2021.105247
20. Mureddu, U., Bochard, N., Bossuet, L., Fischer, V.: Experimental study of locking phenomena on oscillating rings implemented in logic devices. IEEE Trans. Circuits Syst. I Regul. Pap. **66**(7), 2560–2571 (2019). https://doi.org/10.1109/TCSI.2019.2900017
21. Osuka, S., et al.: EM information security threats against RO-based TRNGs: the frequency injection attack based on IEMI and EM information leakage. IEEE Trans. Electromagn. Compat. **61**(4), 1122–1128 (2019). https://doi.org/10.1109/TEMC.2018.2844027

An Open-Source Containarized Toolchain for Behavioral FSM Logic Locking

Esrat Khan[1(✉)], Shahzad Muzaffar[2], Lamees M. Al Qassem[1], and Ibrahim M. Elfadel[1]

[1] Center for Secure Cyber-Physical Systems, College of Computing and Mathematical Sciences, Khalifa University, Abu Dhabi, United Arab Emirates
{100062833,lamees.alqassem,ibrahim.elfadel}@ku.ac.ae
[2] IMEC, Eindhoven, The Netherlands

Abstract. This chapter presents the Open-source Secure Hardware Design and Analysis (OSHDA) framework, specifically developed for the logic locking of finite-state machines (FSMs) at the behavioral abstraction level. OSHDA employs the State Permutation Logic Locking (SPeLL) algorithm, a recent algorithm designed to obfuscate FSM transition graphs. This method circumvents traditional dummy state insertion, minimizing vulnerability to reverse engineering threats. Beyond incorporating the SPeLL algorithm, OSHDA offers a comprehensive logic synthesis pipeline, capable of quantifying the gate-level hardware overhead associated with SPeLL for both FPGA and ASIC implementations. Notably, OSHDA facilitates automated analysis of the balance between security strength and incurred hardware costs. The chapter also examines the resilience of SPeLL by evaluating its resistance against state-of-the-art deobfuscation attacks, highlighting critical research gaps that require attention for effective behavioral level logic-locking deobfuscation. Moreover, OSHDA provides a flexible scripting environment to extend analytical capabilities, integrate additional deobfuscation strategies, and interface seamlessly with physical design tools. To further enhance accessibility and deployment, OSHDA is implemented as a hardware security microservice encapsulated within a Docker framework.

Keywords: Hardware Security · Behavioral Logic Locking · Finite-State Machines · Obfuscation · Deobfuscation

1 Introduction

With the rise of third-party involvement in IC design for faster and cost-effective production [8], hardware security has become critical. Outsourcing stages of chip development expose designs to threats like IP piracy, counterfeiting, reverse engineering, and hardware Trojans [2, 10]. Logic locking has emerged as a key defense, introducing obfuscation to protect circuit integrity. Historically, it has evolved through ongoing battles between locking and deobfuscation techniques, mainly at the gate level [6, 11].

Published by Springer Nature Switzerland AG 2026
E. -I. Vatajelu (Ed.): VLSI-SoC 2024, IFIP AICT 744, pp. 127–142, 2026.
https://doi.org/10.1007/978-3-032-09575-6_8

Logic locking could be either key-based or keyless [15]. In key-based logic locking, the correct operation of the circuit is guaranteed solely upon providing the secret key value, thereby validating its intended functionality [13]. Typically, the key value is securely loaded from tamper-proof memory (TPM) into the circuit upon powering it up. In keyless logic locking, the confidential data can consist of an implicit sequence of input patterns originating from primary inputs (PIs) that direct the circuit's finite-state machine (FSM) to transition through its intended design states.

Most of the research has focused on logic-locking at the gate level for combinational and sequential circuits. However, behavioral logic locking has emerged as a prominent research domain in recent years [12]. In the current EDA landscape, the absence of a full toolchain capable of obfuscating and deobfuscating logic designs at the behavioral level presents a significant challenge to the advancement of research in this important area of hardware security. This gap is mainly due to a legacy of existing open-source tools the community has been using to implement logic-locking algorithms for gate-level netlists. In our own experience with existing tools, we have encountered a bewildering heterogeneity in HDL file formats, parser capabilities, gate libraries, output file formats, and, of course, implemented algorithms for obfuscation and deobfuscation.

It is against this backdrop that we have developed Opensource Secure Hardware Design and Analysis (OSHDA), which is our attempt at building an opensource, behavioral logic locking toolchain from the ground up. The philosophy of OSHDA is *behavioral HDL in, secured behavioral HDL out* and is meant to ensure that the HDL syntax remains unrestricted both before and after obfuscation. The core of OSHDA is the transition graph obfuscation algorithm, which, unlike existing approaches, does not introduce any fake states or fake transitions to secure behavioral netlists. It should be noted that the selection of state encodings and permutations is executed with strict adherence to a uniform probability distribution, which endows the secured behavioral netlists with a higher degree of resilience against frequency cryptanalysis attacks. OSHDA offers a flexible scripting subsystem that enhances ease of use by allowing users to integrate custom scripts in their preferred languages, such as C or Python. This capability supports specific design and analysis requirements. Using OSHDA, users can effectively engage in logic design using HDL, encrypt behavioral netlists, perform logic synthesis, perform simulations and tests, facilitate gate-level mapping, and perform analysis and optimization processes for both application-specific integrated circuits (ASIC) and field-programmable gate arrays (FPGA). This design flow consists of four main steps: (1) entry of HDL files and logic synthesis; (2) generation of the encrypted file utilizing behavioral logic locking; (3) hardware security testing and evaluation at the logic level; and (4) simulation of the secure digital logic design. The OSHDA tool is packaged and deployed using containerization technology. Over recent years, microservices have gained significant popularity, particularly within cloud computing, due to their scalability and flexibility advantages [1]. Containerization involves bundling the CAD tool and its dependencies into a standardized unit called a container, which is easily deployed and runs consistently across different computing environments. This OSHDA container deployment is designed to offer hardware security as a microservice in distributed design environments.

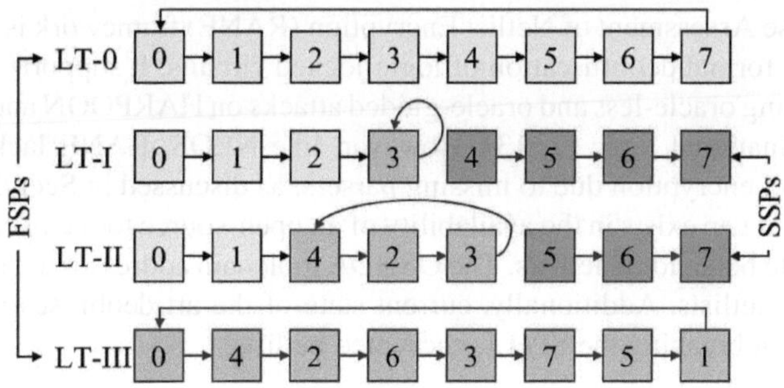

Fig. 1. LT-0, LT-I, LT-II, and LT-III FSM lock types.

This chapter integrates and expands upon our previous contributions to OSHDA, a containerized CAD tool developed for the design and security analysis of behavioral FSM logic locking, initially presented in [9].

The rest of the chapter is structured as follows. Section 2 reviews existing research on behavioral logic locking of FSM, state-of-the-art logic locking attacks, and deobfuscation tools. Section 3 presents the OSHDA toolchain design and its architecture in detail. Test cases of the behavioral logic locking and security analysis are presented in Sect. 4 and Sect. 5, respectively. Section 6 explores existing research gaps in the deobfuscation of behavioral logic locking and outlines potential avenues for future advancements in the field of SAT-based attacks on behavioral logic locking. Finally, Sect. 7 provides the concluding remarks of this chapter.

2 Background

2.1 Logic Locking

The SPeLL algorithm integrates logic locking at the behavioral level, reducing hardware needs and complicating reverse engineering by obscuring state transitions. The transition obfuscation algorithm assumes attackers have access to the hardware and know the encryption method but not the design details. Correct state transitions require the correct key. Incorrect keys trigger different Lock Types (LT-I, LT-II, and LT-III) and incorrect transitions, as shown in Fig. 1. LT-0 represents the correct transitions [9].

2.2 Overview of NEOS and RANE

The Netlist Encryption and Obfuscation Suite (NEOS) is a C++-based tool for obfuscating and deobfuscating gate-level netlists [3]. It parses Bench-format files with standard logic gates and uses SAT-based polymorphic algorithms via the Glucose solver. NEOS also supports sequential deobfuscation using modelchecking and bounded modelchecking (BMC) [7]. NEOS lacks behavioral-level logic-locking encryption, a capability unique to OSHDA for sequential circuits written in Verilog. Deobfuscating the SPeLL algorithm with NEOS has encountered several challenges mainly due to parser limitations. In fact, NEOS is designed for gate-level netlists in Bench format. The limitations of NEOS are further detailed in Sect. 5.

The Reverse Assessment of Netlist Encryption (RANE) framework is another open-source tool for formal deobfuscation of logic-locked circuits. It supports various attack models, including oracle-less and oracle-guided attacks on HARPOON and both sequential and combinational logic [2, 13]. However, like NEOS, RANE lacks support for behavioral-level encryption due to missing parsers, as discussed in Sect. 5.

A significant gap exists in the availability of an open-source tool that can both secure and deobfuscate behavioral netlists. The OSHDA toolchain addresses the need for securing behavioral netlists. Additionally, current state-of-the-art deobfuscation algorithms are ineffective in breaking the SPeLL encrypted netlists.

3 OSHDA Design and Architecture

The containerized OSHDA toolchain offers an adaptable platform for hardware design and analysis. As shown in Fig. 2, it supports syntax validation, simulation, gate-level translation, and synthesis for FPGA or ASIC targets. It also auto-generates testbenches and circuit diagrams for encrypted designs. The flow converts Verilog input into an optimized, secure version using gate primitives and Flip-Flops. ASIC synthesis outputs Verilog with selected logic gates and AOI/OAI structures, while FPGA synthesis produces architecture-specific designs with LUTs, DFFs, and SLRs. OSHDA also reports obfuscation features and statistics.

3.1 Interface Overview

The *Process Settings* tab in Fig. 3 provides several customization options:

1. Checked: Optimize logic during gate-level translation.
2. Options for cleaning up the active design directory.
3. Select if the design and/or testbench should be verified.
4. Select synthesis target.
5. If FPGA, specify the vendor.
6. If ASIC, select whether to use LUTs only or gate logic.
7. If LUTs are chosen, specify the maximum number of LUT inputs (limiting LUT size).
8. If gates are chosen, indicate which gates to include in synthesis—note that flip-flops and inverters are automatically added during synthesis as necessary.

9. Select whether to generate translated and/or synthesized circuit diagrams, including the symbols to be used for drawing the circuits.

The *New Design/Script* tab in Fig. 4 provides the following options:

1. Create a design using the schematic editor.
2. Create a design using the default Verilog template.
3. If the default template is unchecked, specify the number of states, inputs, and outputs of the design.
4. Decide if you want to apply a script to the new design.
5. Enter the new design name.

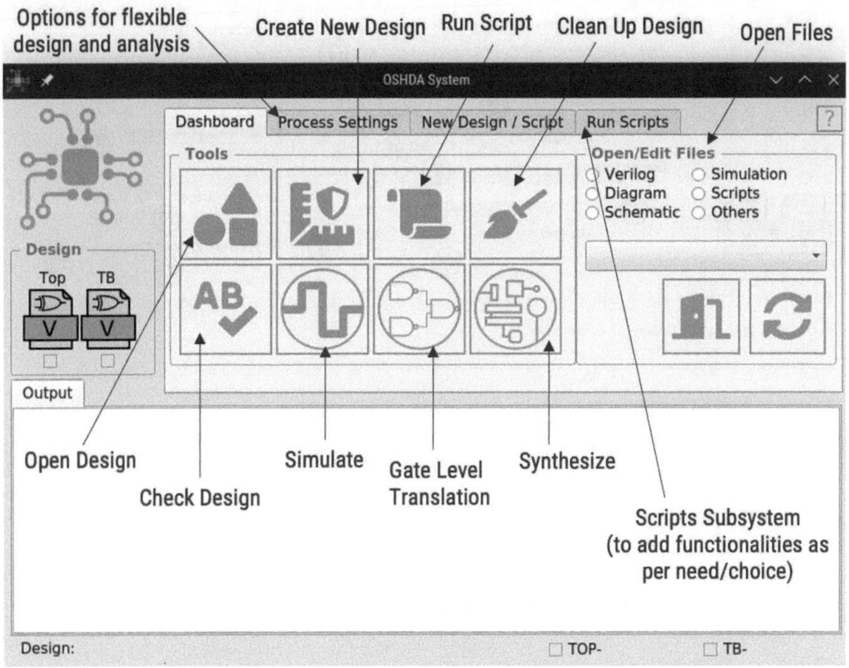

Fig. 2. OSHDA user interface (UI).

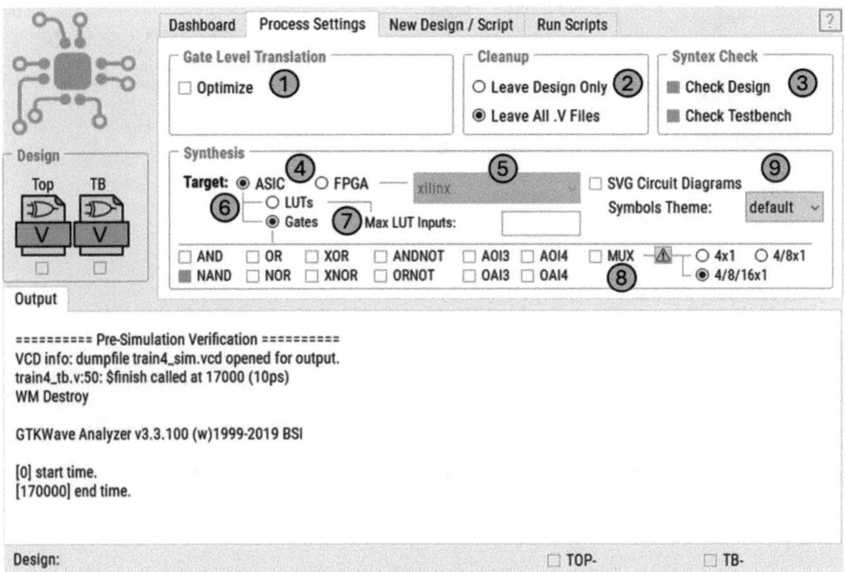

Fig. 3. Process settings.

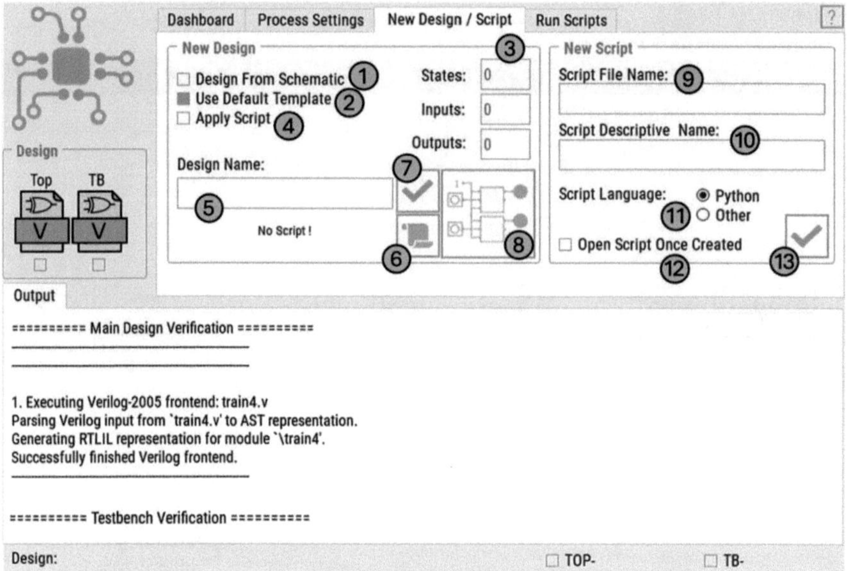

Fig. 4. New design or new script.

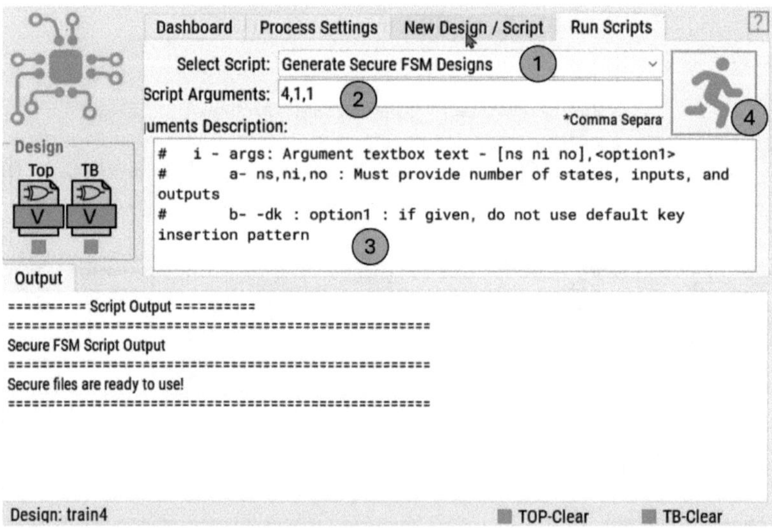

Fig. 5. Run scripts and generate secure designs.

6. If "Apply Script" is checked, select a script to apply.
7. Create the new design based on the selected options.
8. If the schematic option is chosen, create the design and launch the schematic editor.

9. Enter the new script name, which is also the script file name.
10. Provide a descriptive name for your script, typically summarizing the script's purpose in five words or fewer.
11. Specify the scripting language (Python or another language).
12. Decide whether to open the new script in a text editor after creation.
13. Create and integrate the new script into the system.

The *Run Scripts* tab in Fig. 5 provides these functionalities:

1. Select the desired script.
2. Enter arguments for the script, separated by commas.

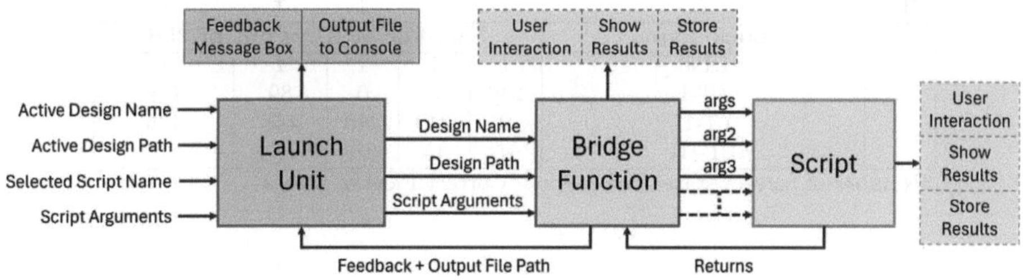

Fig. 6. Architecture of scripts subsystem.

3. View a description of the selected script's arguments.
4. Execute the selected script.

3.2 Scripts Subsystem

The OSHDA scripts subsystem supports extensibility by integrating scripts for design handling, output, logging, and system operations. As shown in Fig. 6, it includes three main components: the Launch Unit, the Bridge Function, and the script itself. The Launch Unit triggers the script with input/output arguments, which are processed by the Bridge Function to provide feedback and output paths. Each script has a Bridge Function to standardize interactions and pass arguments: args (script inputs), arg2 (design path), and arg3 (output file path), all of which can be customized. OSHDA also provides templates for Python and launchers for other languages like C.

Table 1. Encryption when $n_k = n_{states}$.

8 States + 8-bit Key + Level 2						
Key-Bits-Insertion Pattern ⟶		Bit 0	Bit 1	Bit 2	ZigZag	Triangular
	Correct States[a]	Number of Keys out of 256				
	-	128	128	128	128	128
	0	64	64	64	64	64
	1	32	32	32	32	32
	2	16	16	16	16	16
	3	8	8	8	8	8
	4	4	4	4	4	4
	5	2	2	2	2	2
	6	1	1	1	1	1
CFS[b]	7	1	1	1	1	1
	Lock Type	Number of Keys out of 256				
	LT-0	1	1	1	1	1
	LT-I	240	0	0	80	119
	LT-II	0	240	240	168	135
	LT-III	15	15	15	7	1

[a]Number of correct states before lock [b]Correct Flow of States

3.3 Key Size vs. Number of States - Encryption Levels

In the context of finite-state machine (FSM) logic locking, the relationship between the key size (n_k) and the number of FSM states (n_{states}) significantly influences the security level and effectiveness of the locking mechanism. The encryption strategy can be categorized into three distinct levels based on this relationship:

- Level 1 ($n_k < n_{states}$): In this scenario, the number of bits in the encryption key K is smaller than the total number of states in the FSM. Consequently, some key bits are necessarily reused multiple times across different states. While feasible, this approach is not recommended due to reduced cryptographic strength and potential vulnerabilities arising from the repeated usage of key bits.
- Level 2 ($n_k = n_{states}$): At this encryption level, the number of key bits (n_k) is equal to the number of FSM states, specifically using an 8-bit key to protect an 8-state FSM. Table 1 compares five different key-bit insertion patterns—Bit 0, Bit 1, Bit 2, ZigZag, and Triangular—and evaluates how many of the 256 possible keys allow correct traversal of the FSM states before a transition obfuscation occurs in the rows labeled 0 through 7. The *CFS* row identifies the one key that enables full and correct traversal of all states. Most incorrect keys lead to SPeLL activation, and their distribution across different lock types—LT-0, LT-I, LT-II, and LT-III—is also shown. Patterns like ZigZag and Triangular display a more even spread across lock types, suggesting they enhance obfuscation and reduce predictability compared to static patterns like Bit 0, Bit 1, and Bit 2. While this level of encryption provides balanced security by assigning a unique key bit to each FSM state, it still limits the number of possible permutations and key diversity to 2^n for n states.

Table 2. Encryption when $n_k > n_{states}$.

8 States + 16-bit Key + Level 3

Correct States[a]	**Key-Bits-Insertion Pattern**							
	Bit 0	Bit 1	Bit 2	ZigZag	Triangular	Bit 0 & 2	Bit 1 & 2	Bit 0 & 1
-	32768	32768	32768	32768	32768	49152	49152	49152
0	16384	16384	16384	16384	16384	12288	12288	12288
1	8192	8192	8192	8192	8192	3072	3072	3072
2	4096	4096	4096	4096	4096	768	768	768
3	2048	2048	2048	2048	2048	192	192	192
4	1024	1024	1024	1024	1024	48	48	48
5	512	512	512	512	512	12	12	12
6	256	256	256	256	256	3	3	3
7 (**CFS**[b])	256	256	256	256	256	1	1	1
Lock Type	**Number of Keys out of 65,536**							
LT-0	256	256	256	256	256	1	1	1
LT-I	61440	0	0	20480	30464	33856	0	38080
LT-II	0	61440	61440	43008	34560	31104	64960	26880
LT-III	3840	3840	3840	1792	256	575	575	575

[a]Number of correct states before lock [b]Correct Flow of States

- Level 3 ($n_k > n_{states}$): This level involves scenarios where the key size exceeds the number of FSM states. Here, the encryption process utilizes a subset of the key bits to directly secure the FSM states, while the remaining bits are leveraged to secure additional logic elements either within or outside the FSM boundary. This enhances overall security by introducing complexity beyond the basic FSM state transitions as outlined in Table 2.

The OSHDA toolchain employs the LT-III lock type, shown in Table 1 and Table 2, in its logic locking approach to protect FSMs from side-channel attacks by using complex state permutations. This method effectively counters both power and frequency analysis-based attacks by complicating the analysis of power consumption patterns for attackers. Unlike other methods that increase FSM states for security, the obfuscation mode in OSHDA introduces deliberate errors in state transitions, making it difficult for attackers to distinguish between protected and unprotected FSMs. Additionally, it safeguards against register overwrite attacks, ensuring that protective mechanisms of the obfuscation mode remain active throughout the entire operation of the FSM, rendering attempts to tamper with registers ineffective.

3.4 Lightweight Encryption and Decryption Process

The lightweight encryption and decryption method specifically designed for securing finite-state machines (FSM) through state permutations is identified as LT-III permutations. The encryption process aims to generate factorial ($n!$) permutations for an FSM consisting of n states, significantly enlarging the search space and complexity for potential attackers. The corresponding lightweight decryption process ensures that each of the $n!$ possible permutations occurs exactly once, establishing uniqueness in state permutations. This uniqueness effectively mitigates frequency-analysis attacks by eliminating repetitive patterns. The provided example in Table 3 clarifies key parameters: n_s refers to the number of states, n_b indicates encoding bits per state, and n_{bk} represents the number of key bits used. The LT-0 + LT-III column denotes permutations involving all FSM states, including the correct path (LT-0), while LT-I + LT-II describes the subset permutations associated with incorrect transitions, often involving loops or fixed states. In essence, this method secures FSM transitions by exponentially increasing the permutation possibilities, thereby greatly enhancing hardware security.

Table 3. $n!$ LT-III permutations for n-states FSM.

n_s	n_b	n_{bk}	**LT-0 + LT-III**	**LT-I + LT-II**
2	1	2	2	2
3	2	8	6	25
4	2	8	24	232
5	3	24	120	16777096
6	3	24	720	16776496
7	3	24	5040	16772176
8	3	24	40320	16736896
9	4	64	362880	$1.844674407370919 \times 10^{19}$
10	4	64	3628800	$1.8446744073705923 \times 10^{19}$
11	4	64	39916800	$1.8446744073666934 \times 10^{19}$
12	4	64	479001600	$1.8446744073235055 \times 10^{19}$
13	4	64	6227020800	$1.8446744076482532 \times 10^{19}$
14	4	64	87178291200	$1.8446744073563216 \times 10^{19}$
15	4	64	1307674368000	$1.8446742766035184 \times 10^{19}$
16	4	64	20922789888000	$1.8446723150919664 \times 10^{19}$

3.5 Hardware Optimization and Reducing Hardware Resources

The SPeLL locking technique is a strategy used to secure FSMs against reverse engineering and unauthorized modifications. To illustrate this concept, an example FSM with four states and a 2-bit output is used, where transitions occur without conditional logic. Three security modes are introduced: *Mode 1* (*M1*), *Mode 2* (*M2*), and *Mode 3* (*M3*). In *Mode 1*, both the current and next state logic are key-dependent, providing the highest level of security. *Mode 2* introduces key dependency only in the current state logic, while *Mode 3* affects only the next state logic. Each mode offers a trade-off between hardware overhead and security strength.

The comparison between *M1*, *M2*, and *M3* is based on their Full State Table Key-Insertion Pattern (FKIP). Simulations are used to analyze the effect of key insertions on state flow patterns. These simulations, particularly for FSMs with eight or more states, are computationally intensive in terms of time, memory, and processing requirements. Therefore, mathematical formulations are introduced to determine the number of unique permutations for secure FSMs under different security modes.

In the FKIP analysis, key parameters include the number of FSM states (n_s), number of bits required (n_b), and total possible states using n_b bits (n_{ps}). The number of visited states ($r = n_{vs}$) is also considered. In Partial Key-Insertion Pattern (PKIP), only specific portions of the state logic are altered. A new index C representing the MSB to LSB column is introduced to control key placement within the state parameter table. These models enable designers to quantify the number of secure configurations available under each mode.

Hardware resource optimization is addressed across four stages. Instead of inserting key bits directly into the behavioral code, which increases logic complexity, a two-step synthesis process is proposed. An unsecured FSM is synthesized first, followed by insertion of secure MUX-based logic in the synthesized Verilog file, which is then re-synthesized. This approach significantly reduces gate count. For *Mode 3*, the next-state logic is rerouted through MUXes based on key-insertion patterns. For *Mode 1*, the process starts with an *M2* FSM, undergoes optimized gate-level translation, and then applies *M3*-equivalent logic, yielding a secure *M1* FSM with fewer gates. The trade-off between security and hardware resources is analyzed in the OSHDA toolchain. Factors that influence this trade-off include the number of FSM states, the number of state transitions, inputs, outputs, key size, and the interdependence between current and next states. The mode of locking and key-insertion strategy also significantly impact the hardware footprint.

To systematically represent the transformations applied to FSMs, a notation is introduced. The original design is represented as δ, and various synthesis and security operations are denoted by letters. For example,

$$\delta_{2To3F} = E_{M1}(S_F(E_{M3}(S_{To}(E_{M2}(\delta))))) \quad (1)$$

where S_F stands for synthesize for FPGA, E_{M3} stands for apply *M3* security, E_{M2} stands for apply *M2* security, E_{M1} stands for *M1* security, and S_{To} stands for gate-level translation with optimization. Additionally, $2T_o3F$ stands for applying *M2* encryption to the original netlist, *M3* encryption to the netlist of gate-level translation with optimization, and executing the synthesis for FPGA in order to get the final netlist with the *M1* security embedded. This notation helps track the synthesis flow and optimize resource usage. The synthesis strategy for FPGAs, such as the direct mapping of NAND gates to Look-Up Tables (LUTs), results in excessive resource usage. Optimized MUX insertion mapped directly to LUTs is analyzed to be more efficient. Examples include resource estimates for MUXes in FSMs with varying states—from 2 Logic Blocks (LBs) for 4-state FSMs to 840 LBs for 218-state FSMs.

3.6 OSHDA Docker Image

This section presents a cloud-based OSHDA microservice architecture using Docker and docker-compose, as shown in Fig. 7. Versioned Docker images enable easy rollback and parallel testing without performance loss. The system runs natively across platforms with a single command. New tools can be added as separate containers and connected via gRPC [5], offering low-latency, high-throughput integration. This transition to a lighter-weight virtualization solution (i.e., microservice) helps in better meeting the QoS requirements, lowers costs, enhances availability, reduces virtualization overhead, and increases resource utilization.

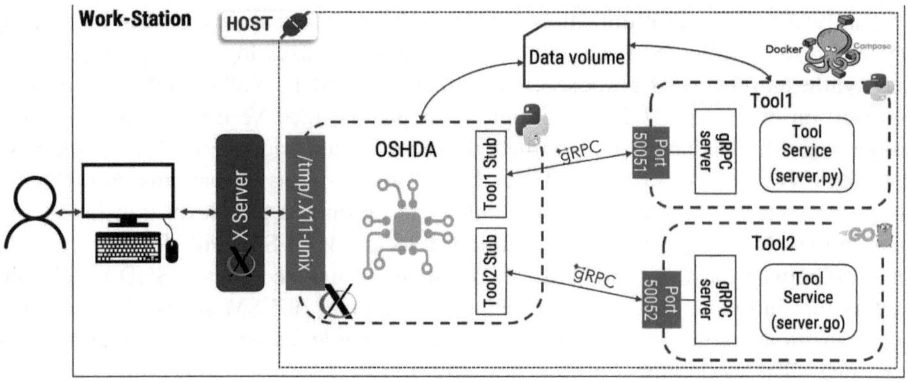

Fig. 7. Microservice OSHDA.

4 Use Cases

4.1 FKIP and PKIP

Table 4 compares Full Key Insertion Pattern (FKIP) and Partial Key Insertion Pattern (PKIP), highlighting their trade-offs. FKIP offers higher security by encrypting all state bits, resulting in an exponential increase in Full-set State Permutations (FSPs) and resource usage. In contrast, PKIP selectively encrypts bits, reducing FSPs and hardware overhead. FSM obfuscation is achieved by replacing fixed state bits with encrypted ones. A non-identity permutation is chosen before key assignment to obscure transitions, with the key derived from permuted state encodings to ensure correct transitions only occur with the valid key.

4.2 LGSynth91 Benchmark Circuits

Unlike prior work [3, 13] that applies FSM obfuscation at the gate level using ISCAS89 benchmarks, OSHDA implements security at the behavioral level. ISCAS89 lacks RTL state information and functional documentation, making a direct comparison with OSHDA infeasible. Similarly, register pattern comparisons with [4] are not applicable. Therefore, Table 5 reports synthesis results using LGSynth91 circuits.

5 Security Analysis

Figure 8 shows that obfuscation mode Full-set State Permutations (FSPs) grow rapidly with the number of FSM states. Remarkably, even the minimum number of FSPs shows a significant increase with the number of states when compared with the unique number of register patterns in [4], under the assumption that all the D Flip-Flops in the netlist are state registers. Minimum FSPs occur when specific inputs minimize the states in the FSM transition graph. Identifying these inputs reduces the FSPs for analysis. Despite this reduction, OSHDA's logic locking remains difficult to deobfuscate.

Table 4. Hardware resources required for FSP in counter FSMs

Counter Size	S-I-O-T		Original Design	FKIP	PKIP				
					3	2	1	0	No. of States in FSM
4	4-0-2-4	FSP	-	24	-	-	4		24
		Logic Blocks	1	6	-	-	5		6
8	8-0-3-8	FSP	-	40320	-	16			576
		Logic Blocks	2	18	-	9			16
16	16-0-4-16	FSP	-	$> 10^{13}$	256				$> 10^5$
		Logic Blocks	2	104	22				45

Table 5. Synthesis results of LGSynth91 benchmark circuits

Circuit Name	S-I-O-T	Original Design (Logic Blocks)	Locked Design (FKIP)		Locked Design (PKIP)	
			(Logic Blocks)	%↑	(Logic Blocks)	%↑
train4	4-2-1-14	6	10	66	134	2133
dk15	4-3-5-32	10	19	90	17	70
beecount	7-3-4-28	35	47	34	57	63
dk14	7-3-5-56	23	38	65	63	174
dk17	8-2-3-32	14	35	150	60	328
ex6	8-5-8-34	36	64	77	85	136
cse	16-7-7-91	71	163	129	145	104
kirkman	16-12-6-370	87	160	84	100	15
sand	32-11-9-184	215	332	54	242	12
s298	218-3-6-1096	1098	2592	136	1270	15

Table 6. Comparative Analysis of OSHDA Toolchain with State-of-the-Art NEOS and RANE Tools

Limitations	NEOS [14]	RANE [13]	OSHDA
File Format Support	Bench format	Bench format and Verilog (gate level modelling)	Supports Verilog (gate level, structural, and behavioural modelling)
Circuit Complexity Support	Gate level netlists	Gate level netlists	Behavioral and Gate level netlists
SAT Solver Dependency	Glucose SAT solver	Reverse Assessment of Netlist Encryption attack (SAT based attack)	State-of-the-art SAT attack tools fail to parse behavioral netlists

(continued)

Table 6. (*continued*)

Limitations	NEOS [14]	RANE [13]	OSHDA
User Documentation and Support	Unavailable	Unavailable	Comprehensive documentation and user guide available
Advanced Security Scheme Support	Cannot parse Obfuscated Behavioral Netlists	Cannot parse Obfuscated Behavioral Netlists	Parsers available for Obfuscated Behavioral Netlists
Oracle Information Dependency	Oracle guided and oracle less approaches	Oracle guided approach only	Not Dependent
Containerization Support	No support	No support	Hardware security microservice

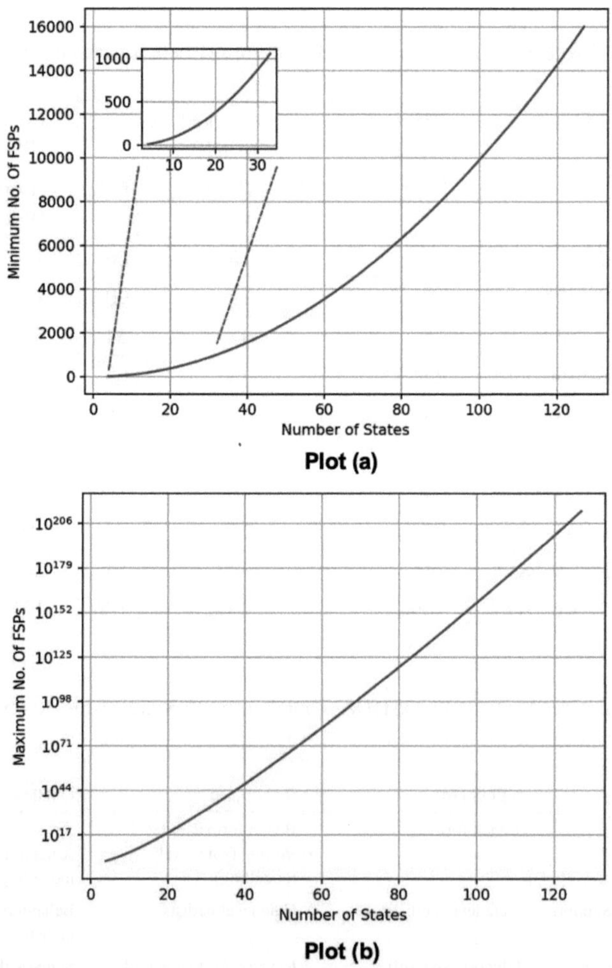

Fig. 8. Number of Unique FSPs/Register Patterns (a) Minimum (b) Maximum.

5.1 Limitations of NEOS and RANE for Attacking and Deobfuscating the OSHDA Encryption Mode

Table 6 provides a feature-based comparison between NEOS, RANE, and OSHDA. NEOS supports only the Bench HDL, which is less widely adopted than Verilog, VHDL, or SystemVerilog, thereby limiting its analysis range. It is tailored for simpler gate-level netlists, overlooking the complexity of advanced circuit components. Its exclusive reliance on the Glucose SAT solver may also reduce deobfuscation effectiveness in scenarios where alternative solvers would be better suited. Moreover, both NEOS and RANE lack comprehensive documentation and community support, which hampers user engagement and tool utility. They also do not support advanced security schemes like the SPeLL algorithm, reducing their ability to counter sophisticated obfuscation techniques. RANE further depends on accurate oracle information for deobfuscation, which adds another layer of complexity, as such data can be challenging to procure. Lastly, the absence of containerization support in both tools affects consistent execution and hinders the sharing and reproducibility of research across different computational environments.

6 Discussion and Future Work

Prior research on CAD tools for logic locking mainly used ISCAS89 benchmarks, which are unsuitable for validating OSHDA obfuscation due to their gate-level netlists and lack of state count information. The LGSynth91 benchmarks in Kiss2 format offer comprehensive FSM data, and OSHDA converts this to behavioral Verilog. The behavioral-level encryption within OSHDA is resilient against SAT attacks, unlike traditional gate-level methods. Future work includes developing a deobfuscation feature that targets behavioral-level encryption in sequential circuits. Such a feature should have comprehensive HDL parsers.

7 Conclusions

This paper introduces OSHDA, a containerized tool suite for behavioral logic locking. It supports custom scripts in any programming language for sequential logic circuit design and analysis and includes SPeLL for logic obfuscation. OSHDA handles Verilog design, synthesis, encryption, simulation, testing, gate-level mapping, ASIC/FPGA analysis, and design optimization. Built from scratch, it emphasizes logic-locking FSMs at the behavioral level.

Acknowledgments. This research is conducted at Khalifa University with the financial support of the Technology Innovation Institute (TII), Abu Dhabi, UAE, under contract TII/CRP/2036/2020.

References

1. Berardi, D., Giallorenzo, S., Mauro, J., Melis, A., Montesi, F., Prandini, M.: Microservice security: a systematic literature review. PeerJ Comput. Sci. **8** (2022). https://doi.org/10.7717/PEERJ-CS.779

2. Chakraborty, R.S., Bhunia, S.: HARPOON: an obfuscation-based SoC design methodology for hardware protection. IEEE Trans. Comput. Aided Des. Integr. Circuits Syst. **28**(10), 1493–1502 (2009). https://doi.org/10.1109/TCAD.2009.2028166
3. Datta, R., Zhao, G., Basu, K., Shamsi, K.: A security analysis of circuit clock obfuscation. Cryptography **6**(3) (2022)
4. Dofe, J., Yu, Q.: Novel dynamic state-deflection method for gate-level design obfuscation. IEEE Trans. Comput. Aided Des. Integr. Circuits Syst. **37**(2), 273–285 (2018). https://doi.org/10.1109/TCAD.2017.2697960
5. gRPC: grpc. https://grpc.io/. Accessed 14 Sept 2023
6. Hu, W., Chang, C.H., Sengupta, A., Bhunia, S., Kastner, R., Li, H.: An overview of hardware security and trust: Threats, countermeasures, and design tools. IEEE Trans. Comput. Aided Des. Integr. Circuits Syst. **40**(6), 1010–1038 (2021). https://doi.org/10.1109/TCAD.2020.3047976
7. Jin, Y., Pan, D.: Quantitative metric and automated toolset for obfuscated logic security evaluation. Technical report, Air Force Research Laboratory Sensors Directorate, Wright-Patterson Air Force Base, Oh 45433-7320, Air Force Materiel Command United States Air Force, September 2020
8. Juretus, K., Savidis, I.: Synthesis of hidden state transitions for sequential logic locking. IEEE Trans. Comput. Aided Des. Integr. Circuits Syst. **40**(1), 11–23 (2021). https://doi.org/10.1109/TCAD.2020.2994259
9. Khan, E., Muzaffar, S., Al Qassem, L.M., Elfadel, I.M.: OSHDA: a containerized cad tool for the design and analysis of behavioral fsm logic locking. In: 2024 IFIP/IEEE 32nd International Conference on Very Large Scale Integration (VLSI-SoC), pp. 1– 6 (2024). https://doi.org/10.1109/VLSI-SoC62099.2024.10767810
10. Limaye, N., Kalligeros, E., Karousos, N., Karybali, I.G., Sinanoglu, O.: Thwarting all logic locking attacks: dishonest oracle with truly random logic locking. IEEE Trans. Comput. Aided Des. Integr. Circuits Syst. **40**(9), 1740–1753 (2021). https://doi.org/10.1109/TCAD.2020.3029133
11. Mankali, L., Patnaik, S., Limaye, N., Knechtel, J., Sinanoglu, O.: VIGILANT: vulnerability detection tool against fault-injection attacks for locking techniques. IEEE Trans. Comput. Aided Des. Integr. Circuits Syst., 1 (2023). https://doi.org/10.1109/TCAD.2023.3259300
12. Pilato, C., Collini, L., Cassano, L., Sciuto, D., Garg, S., Karri, R.: Optimizing the use of behavioral locking for high-level synthesis. IEEE Trans. Comput. Aided Des. Integr. Circuits Syst. **42**(2), 462–472 (2023)
13. Roshanisefat, S., Mardani Kamali, H., Homayoun, H., Sasan, A.: RANE: an opensource formal de-obfuscation attack for reverse engineering of logic encrypted circuits. In: Proceedings of the 2021 on Great Lakes Symposium on VLSI, GLSVLSI 2021, New York, NY, USA, pp. 221–228. Association for Computing Machinery (2021)
14. Shamsi, K., Jin, Y.: Cad for assurance. https://cadforassurance.org/tools/evaluation-of-obfuscation/neos/
15. Zuzak, M., Mondal, A., Srivastava, A.: Evaluating the security of logic-locked probabilistic circuits. IEEE Trans. Comput. Aided Des. Integr. Circuits Syst. **41**(7), 2004–2009 (2022)

Author Index

Published by Springer Nature Switzerland AG 2026
E. -I. Vatajelu (Ed.): VLSI-SoC 2024, IFIP AICT 744, p. 143, 2026.
https://doi.org/10.1007/978-3-032-09575-6

MIX
Papier aus verantwortungsvollen Quellen
Paper from responsible sources
FSC® C105338

If you have any concerns about our products,
you can contact us on
ProductSafety@springernature.com

In case Publisher is established outside the EU,
the EU authorized representative is:
Springer Nature Customer Service Center GmbH
Europaplatz 3, 69115 Heidelberg, Germany

Printed by Libri Plureos GmbH
in Hamburg, Germany